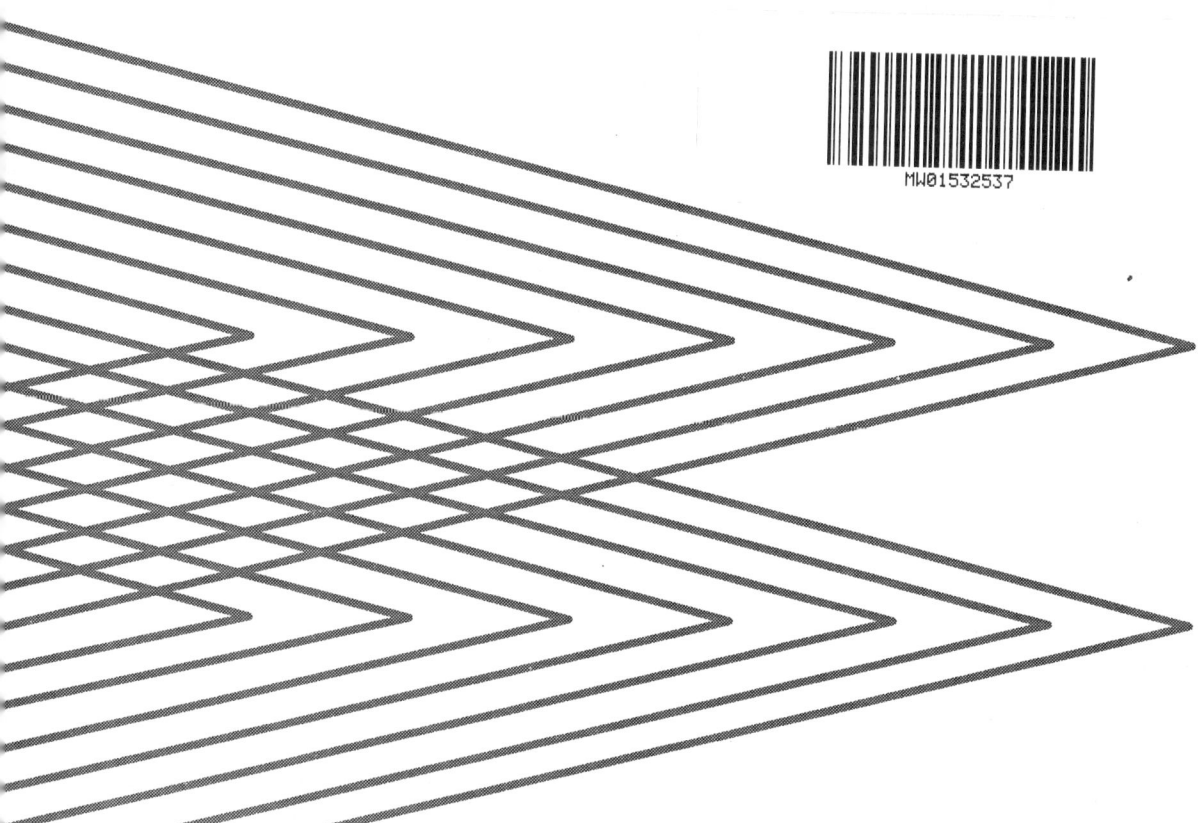

A Professional's Guide to

COLLEGE PLANNING

Raymond D. Loewe, CLU, ChFC

NATIONAL UNDERWRITER®
The Last Word For Over 100 Years

The National Underwriter Co. • 505 Gest Street • Cincinnati, Ohio 45203-1716

This publication is designed to provide accurate and authoritative information in regard to the subject matter covered. It is sold with the understanding that the publisher is not engaged in rendering legal, accounting or other professional service. If legal advice or other expert assistance is required, the services of a competent professional should be sought. — **From a Declaration of Principles jointly adopted by a Committee of the American Bar Association and a Committee of Publishers and Associations.**

ISBN: 0-87218-198-7

Printed in U. S. A.

About the Author

Raymond D. Loewe, CLU, ChFC, is a nationally known authority in college financial planning. Through his company, College Money, he has helped over 40,000 families solve their college funding problem.

Mr. Loewe has shared his experiences about college funding at the national convention of the International Association of Financial Planners (IAFP) and the national retreat of The Institute of Certified Financial Planners. He has appeared on a segment of *The CBS Evening News With Dan Rather,* and ABC's *Good Morning America.* Mr. Loewe has also provided information for *USA Today, Fortune, Medical Economics* and *Money Magazine.*

Practicing in the insurance and financial planning business, Mr. Loewe is currently an independent professional. He began his career in the early 1970s as an agent with Penn Mutual Life Insurance and ran a district office for the New England Life Insurance Company during the 1980s.

Mr. Loewe holds an MBA from the Wharton School of Business and is a member of IAFP.

Preface

Whether you need to help an existing client with college planning or you desire to build a full-time college planning practice, this book is designed to help you. It will position your college planning activities in the right market segments including the upper middle income professional, the business executive and the business owner.

Almost every financial professional runs into a client that has a college financing problem. If you underestimate the importance of solving this problem, your client is likely to seek help from another financial professional. You run the risk of losing the client just before he reaches the lucrative retirement and estate planning years.

College planning can also be an effective money making business. It provides you with the opportunity to meet new prospects in the 40-45-year old age group. You can establish a quality relationship with them by helping them solve a major problem that no one else wants to take on. This invaluable assistance will earn you the right to continue the relationship which will grow stronger as you help your new clients plan and solve their retirement and estate planning problems.

Many financial professionals have tried to enter the college planning business through asset repositioning instead of client building. Most have left frustrated because they attacked the market the wrong way which they thought was to focus on helping clients secure more financial aid. In reality, most people who qualify for financial aid tend to be lower income prospects. And any professional who is building a practice will tell you he wants the high income prospect—that is where the future lies!

Sometimes asset repositioning is the correct approach. Upper income families with two or three small children attending college at the same time can qualify for financial aid and the information in this book will certainly help you help those clients obtain more financial aid. The true market, however, is the family who is not going to receive any financial aid—the upper middle and upper income family earning $75,000 to $250,000. These families have considerable retirement savings and they are worried those savings will be depleted by paying for college. They need you to show them how to pay the college bill so they can still retire as they had planned. In return, they will pay you for your time and give you all of their insurance and investment business.

We have incorporated our strategies for you to help those families in crisis who don't know *what* to do. It will also help those families who don't know *how* to do it.

Some of the strategies involve the use of computer software programs which we have designed to provide us with critical planning data. The illustrations used in this book were produced using those programs. That software, *College Money*, is a registered trademark of Educational Planning Systems, Inc. During the college planning analysis we also provide our clients with our workbook entitled, *A Practical Guide to Paying for College*. If you would like further information about our programs you can reach us at:

Educational Planning Systems, Inc.
112B Centre Boulevard
Marlton, NJ 08053
Telephone: (609) 596-4702

Table of Contents

1

A Nine Step Process to Pay for College

Paying for college is a huge problem. Costs for four years at many private colleges already exceed $100,000. College inflation has exceeded the general increase in the cost of living almost every year in recent memory and there is no indication that it will slow down. Parents often need to treat the college problem like buying another house, it's that big. Most disheartening is the fact that this problem occurs at a time when most parents ought to be saving for their own retirement.

Most parents reach a crisis level when their student becomes a junior or senior in high school and they suddenly realize they have not saved enough money and don't know what to do. Even those parents that plan ahead, and there aren't many, don't know how to set up savings plans that take advantage of tax and financial aid options.

Step 1: Learn the Basics

As a professional, you need tools to help your clients develop good college plans. You need good answers to questions like:

◆ How much is college actually going to cost? Not just tuition, room and board, but fees, books, travel expenses, laundry money and all those other miscellaneous costs not listed in the guidebooks.

◆ What are the four types of financial aid and how do you help your clients plan differently to obtain each type?

◆ How does financial aid work? Which of my clients are true candidates for aid and which ones are just kidding themselves? Can planning ahead help my clients qualify for aid?

◆ How can students find the best college within an acceptable price range? Does college selection have an effect on the ability to qualify for financial aid? Are colleges with the lowest list price really the cheapest? To how many colleges should a student apply? Out of over three thousand colleges, how can a student effectively find the right ones?

◆ Is it possible to negotiate a college financial aid package? What is the best way to do it?

◆ How do I help my clients when they don't receive enough financial aid? How can I help them finance the balance of their college costs so they can have a chance to someday retire?

The net cost of college, what your clients have to pay, is the list price less any financial aid they receive. Your clients need to know as soon as possible whether or not they can plan on financial aid to reduce their college cost. Fortunately, eligibility for need-based financial aid is predictable. A financial aid test will tell you realistically if your clients can expect to receive financial aid and for how much they will be eligible.

If your clients are eligible for need-based financial aid, you will need to help them plan to maximize it. If they won't receive any need-based financial aid, you will need to help them plan differently.

Learning the basics starts with mastering a series of concepts. These concepts provide the basics for the strategies laid out in the remaining steps.

Step 2: Help Your Clients Complete a Trial Financial Aid Test

Completing a financial aid test is probably the single most important diagnostic tool in the college planning process. (A sample Trial Financial Aid Test can be found in Appendix 3.) It will tell you realistically whether or not your clients can expect to receive need-based financial aid and, if so, how much. Many parents hang on too long hoping for financial aid when, realistically, they won't qualify. Your clients need to know early about their financial aid eligibility because it will affect their planning in each of the remaining steps.

There are other benefits to a financial aid test. It will help clients avoid mistakes that many parents make in filling out their financial aid forms (Step 6). It will help them determine if they are getting a good financial aid package (Step 7). Most important, it will help them make better college selection decisions (Step 4).

Step 3: Help Your Clients Construct a College Budget Based Upon the Adequacy of Their Retirement Plans

This number will most likely be different than what colleges feel your clients can afford to pay. A good guide to help your clients make the right decision is to evaluate their retirement resources. If they have a good plan, they can extend themselves on behalf of their children. If their plan isn't so good, they don't want to be saddled with college loans at a time when they should be saving for their own retirement. Remember, college is a retirement problem and linking your clients' ability to retire to what they are paying out for college is critical.

Often an answer to the college cash flow problem is for parents to cost share with their student. Coach your clients to inform their students that there isn't a blank check for college. Students may need to take on student loans. In this way, if the student cooperates by working to earn that extra scholarship or by helping to choose a lower cost college, they will benefit along with your client by having less debt.

Step 4: Teach Your Clients and Their Students How to Select the Proper Colleges

Whether a student is exceptional academically, athletically, or is just a well-rounded student, there is a school somewhere that fits. This school either is priced right or has financial aid dollars that can help make it more affordable. Different colleges use different kinds of financial aid to attract the students they want. The problem is to find the right college. Both parents and students need to do their homework. There are many good college information books available with detailed data on a college's background and financial aid. Since there are over three thousand accredited colleges from which to choose, college selection is the key to receiving a good financial aid package.

Step 5: Plan the Financial Aid Strategy During High School

The earlier you plan the better. Colleges track income and assets for financial aid purposes from the tax return the year before the actual financial aid package is disbursed.

If your clients' financial aid test (Step 2) indicates they will qualify for need-based financial aid, you must take immediate steps to help them preserve their financial aid eligibility. These steps include:

♦ Refraining from putting money into an account bearing the student's name.

♦ Carefully timing when to liquidate financial investments and take capital gains.

♦ Planning if and when a spouse should go back to work.

♦ Monitoring how much income your client's student reports and how he or she saves that income.

If Step 2 indicates your client won't qualify for need-based aid, you will need to help formulate a different plan for the client.

Step 6: Fill Out Financial Aid Forms Correctly

In January and February of the student's senior year, parents begin the process of completing financial aid forms. Filling out the financial aid form correctly will qualify a student for all of the aid to which he or she is entitled. Filling out the form the wrong way will mean delays, aggravation and loss of aid. Mistakes that parents often make include:

- Not filing all the required forms.

- Missing deadlines.

- Over valuing the home (college forms only).

- Including retirement account values that are not required.

- Giving more information than required.

Step 7: Compare and Evaluate Every Financial Aid Award

Don't assume that a financial aid award is correct or that an initial award is the best that a college will offer. You need to do your homework. The Trial Financial Aid Form (TFAF), (Step 2) can help you determine the amount of the aid award your client should expect from a college. Using the college reference books referred to in Step 4, you can determine an expected mix of gift aid vs. self-help aid for most colleges.

Colleges make mistakes and by knowing what to expect, you can head off problems. Sometimes parents can improve their financial aid packages by asking the right questions. It is also permissible to send one college another financial aid offer to ask them to explain the difference. Colleges have certain flexibility when it comes to interpreting financial aid rules. If you do a good job coaching your clients to match their student with a college, he or she has a much better chance at receiving a good financial aid package.

Step 8: Integrate Any College Borrowing Plan Into the Retirement Plan

It's April of the student's senior year. Your clients have just received their financial aid award. They now know exactly what financial aid they will receive and what portion of college they need to pay. Now, you as a professional need to help them develop a plan to pay their portion. How much of their savings and investment should they liquidate? How big of an emergency reserve fund should they keep? Most parents will have to borrow to meet their college cash flow needs. Should they use their home equity? Should they use a PLUS (Parent Loan for Undergraduate Students) loan? Should they borrow on a 401K plan?

It is critical that any college debts be amortized prior to retirement. It is important that retirement assets are managed for effective growth. The planning your clients do now will have a critical effect on their retirement later. Both the college and retirement problems need to be addressed as a whole rather than individually. Taking on college loans for one student in the family means the rest of the family will be in a more precarious financial position. When stretching family resources to pay for college, don't let the premature death or disability of a breadwinner cause a catastrophe. This is the time to review your clients' life and disability insurance to cover college loans and other needs.

Step 9: Save, Save, Save...But Do It the Right Way

It may seem strange that this is the last step. Understanding what families go through if they haven't saved enough will help you as a professional develop a stronger commitment to helping your clients save for college. Most parents can't save enough to pay for all college expenses. Yet, they don't have to save it all. Every dollar they save now is a dollar that won't have to be borrowed later which will minimize the potential for a retirement problem after college is over. Just saving, however, isn't enough. A good college savings plan will build on seven key features that make the plan tax efficient, financial aid efficient and investment efficient. Those key points are:

♦   Avoid the "kiddie tax."

♦   Control taxation of savings growth.

♦   Control taxation during the withdrawal phase.

♦   Provide flexibility to deal with future financial aid eligibility.

♦   Allow multiple investment options that consider:

◊   Staying ahead of college inflation rates.

◊   Diversifying investment risk.

◊   Making changes at a reasonable cost both as markets change and as client needs change, particularly as the client gets close to the withdrawal phase.

♦   Consider self-completion in the event of the death or disability of all breadwinners.

♦   Consider a "pay-yourself-first" option that allows automatic, systematic plan deposits.

Setting up savings plans the *right way* can preserve your clients' financial aid eligibility. Saving *enough* money for college preserves all of your clients' options, including the ability to handle that special college opportunity for a special student even if it means ignoring financial aid.

The Nine Step Process

1. Learn the Basics

2. Help Your Clients Complete a Trial Financial Aid Test

3. Help Your Clients Construct a College Budget Based Upon the Adequacy of Their Retirement Plans

4. Teach Your Clients and Their Students How to Select the Proper Colleges

5. Plan the Financial Aid Strategy During High School

6. Fill Out Financial Aid Forms Correctly

7. Compare and Evaluate Every Financial Aid Award

8. Integrate Any College Borrowing Plan Into the Retirement Plan

9. Save, Save, Save…But Do It the Right Way

2

Learning the Basics

The first step of the nine step process to achieve a successful college plan begins with learning the basics. For over twenty years, we have been working with parents and professionals and have identified concepts that you, as a financial professional, need to understand in order to develop a successful college plan. Please do not confuse the concepts we are going to discuss with the nine steps—they are different. Understanding these nine concepts will allow you to weave effective strategies to provide for:

♦ a great financial aid package,

♦ a better college selection process,

♦ a more complete college savings plan,

♦ a responsible college borrowing plan, and

♦ an all-around better college planning approach for your clients.

After you've mastered these concepts, we'll show you how to apply them throughout the remaining eight steps of the nine step process that each of your clients need to complete for a successful college plan.

Concept 1: Parents who have not saved for college do not have a college problem—they have a cash flow problem and a retirement problem.

When we make this statement in front of parent groups, we can usually look into the audience and see astonished faces. Almost everyone thinks of the college problem as just a college problem, and as such, they limit their flexibility to solve the problem. When you think of college in its real component pieces—a cash flow problem and a retirement problem—the time horizon lengthens thus giving the professional more time and more tools to solve the problem.

It's not hard to convince your clients that college is actually a retirement problem. Just ask your clients the following questions:

♦ How old will you be when your youngest child graduates from college?

♦ After you've wiped out all of your savings, borrowed on your house and borrowed on your retirement plans, how are you going to provide for your own retirement?

Thinking of college as a retirement problem will scare your clients into taking some action. This process alone can be a positive response but it also gives them options that a longer planning time horizon can provide.

The second part of the problem, that college is a cash flow problem, is much easier for clients to grasp. All you need to do is show your clients the cost of college today and then watch them visualize the cash flowing out of the family coffers.

We mentioned that viewing college as a retirement problem lengthens the planning time horizon. Here are two examples of what we mean. You will also find more examples dispersed among the remaining chapters.

Imagine your clients with a senior in high school. Suddenly they find the student has performed on an above average basis and that the student has scored very well on the college application tests, such as the SAT or ACT. This means the student has the ability to get into some super quality colleges all, by the way, with high price tags. Your clients are very proud parents but they haven't saved enough money so, naturally, they get scared. They see their family savings rapidly diminishing and the tremendous pressure that is put on cash flow.

So they say to the student, "I'm sorry, but you can't go to these great schools that you are qualified to enroll in. You need to go to a cheaper college, one that we can afford."

By looking at college as a retirement problem, however, the financial professional can extend the college financing period beyond the college years. This will allow the clients to make the decision to permit the student to apply to and attend a top-notch school if that is what's best for the student.

The danger, however, is that your clients must thoroughly realize that during the years when they are paying off the college loans, they are not going to be able to put cash as anticipated into their retirement plans. This trade-off, however, does give your clients the option to be "proud parents" and make it work.

Let's take another example.

When we think of devising a savings plan just for college, we need to think in terms of short-term investments that provide lower yields as the college years approach. The reason for this is that we must convert the college savings into cash flow to pay the college bills. We can't afford the market risk of potentially higher yielding investments so we are forced into lower yields by the time horizon.

When we look at college as a retirement planning problem, we can take a different viewpoint. If we save for retirement instead of college, we can invest in higher yielding instruments because we have a longer time horizon. Perhaps we can even get tax deductions or tax-deferred yields by putting our money into retirement plans as opposed to college plans.

Here is the key: If we have substantial retirement balances, we can afford to borrow for college because we won't need to worry about retirement after the college years are finished. Often this strategy gives us better results in structuring college savings plans. We'll discuss this concept in considerably more detail when we get to Step 9, "Saving for College the Right Way."

Concept 1

> Parents Who Have Not Saved For College
> Do Not Have a College Problem
>
> ► A Cash Flow Problem
>
> ► A Retirement Problem

Every financial professional needs constant reminding of the link between college planning and retirement planning when designing college plans for their clients. Every dollar spent on college is a dollar that won't be available for the client's retirement. Every dollar borrowed for college is a dollar that must be repaid, probably out of moneys that would have otherwise gone toward retirement. Clients are having children later in life and they are going to college closer to the time many clients retire. Clients are living longer and will need more retirement money. Treating college as a retirement problem helps the client select that more expensive college if a more expensive college is the college of choice. Remember, *college is definitely a retirement problem!*

Concept 2: College is expensive.

The educational community tends to classify colleges into three categories: state colleges, private colleges and Ivy League-type schools. But the parents we represent when we're helping them develop a college plan look at these classifications differently. They think in terms of expensive colleges, very expensive colleges and absolutely ridiculously priced colleges!

What is the real cost of college? You will see many articles explain tuition but tuition alone isn't the cost of college. We need to take tuition, room, board, books, fees, laundry money and transportation back and forth into account. And when we're done adding all of those expenses, and throwing in the miscellaneous things that colleges add, most parents tell us to add another $2,000 to $3,000 for "pizza money." "Pizza money" is the sum of all those $50 and $75 checks that parents periodically send to their children throughout the year. All of these items add up to a significant amount of money.

If you want to latch on to specific college costs, there are many books that categorize the colleges. Refer to Appendix 1 and you will see books by Peterson's Guides, Barron's Educational Series and many others that will provide you with specific details. For our purposes, we will use typical college costs from three categories to calculate reasonable cost projections for the client.

♦ State colleges, for in-state residents, run in the $10,000 to $12,000 neighborhood per year by the time all the costs are included. State colleges for out-of-state residents approximate the cost of private schools.

♦ Private schools range between $17,000 and $28,000.

♦ Numerous clients choose prestige colleges for their children. Many of these prestige schools or Ivy League-type schools cost in the $30,000 to $33,000 price range per year.

Concept 2

College Is Expensive

Typical College Costs
1996-1997

COLLEGE TYPE	COLLEGE COST
IVY LEAGUE	$30,000 to $33,000
* PRIVATE	$17,000 to $28,000
STATE (RESIDENT)	$10,000 to $12,000
Information Source: College Money Survey	Our college cost figures include from $2,500 to $3,000 over and above Tuition, Fees, Room & Board, etc. We do this to give parents a more realistic idea of how much college will cost them.

* For Private colleges a two-tier approach might be more appropriate:
  Low end $17,000
  High end $28,000

These are the real costs parents face today so sending a child to college represents a great deal of money. Multiply these yearly costs by four years, or in some cases five years, for most college programs. Multiply the results again by the number of students in the family and the total becomes a very large expense, larger than most families pay for their homes. College is probably the largest expense families will pay for anything.

Concept 3: College inflation is rising faster than regular inflation and there is no end in sight.

Concept 3 illustrates the cost of college during the last 17 years.

The dashed line indicates college inflation and the solid line indicates the Consumer Price Index (CPI). We see that over this period of time, with the exception of a few years, college inflation has been running substantially greater than regular inflation. (If you would like more infomation about this area, Appendix 6 outlines the history of college inflation during the last 40 years.) As shown in Concept 3, although college cost inflation seems to be decreasing, the gap between college costs and the CPI is still significant and there are indications that it may be widening.

Obviously, college inflation is an important concept to understand if we're going to project values to encourage our clients to save. Many parents ask us when college costs will drop below normal inflation. Their feeling is that college inflation can't continue to rise; our observations show the opposite is true. Although many institutions have been trying to hold the line on costs, we see spot rises of large proportions. One state college raised its tuition by 14% for 1997-1998. We expect to see many state institutions raise tuition levels by double-digits as taxpayers push for lower taxes. We believe college costs will continue to rise faster than inflation for the foreseeable future for several reasons.

♦ First, and perhaps the biggest reason, is that a college education is worth it. As long as college is worth it, parents will drive up the prices at the better schools so their children can attend these prestigious institutions.

♦ Second, college is labor intensive. It hasn't been as easy to apply technological advances to the college classroom as it has been to other industries in the United States.

♦ Finally, everything Uncle Sam is doing is inflationary to the college process. One mechanism Uncle Sam has created is a loan to help parents pay college costs called the Parent Loan For Undergraduate Students (PLUS). This loan provides parents with the ability to borrow 100% of the cost of college less any other financial aid they might receive. When colleges see this unlimited amount of money floating on the horizon, they have very little incentive to reduce costs. They show the proud, emotional parent, whose student has just been accepted, how easy it is to make the college dream come true by just paying a few more dollars each month.

Concept 3

Regular Inflation vs. College Inflation

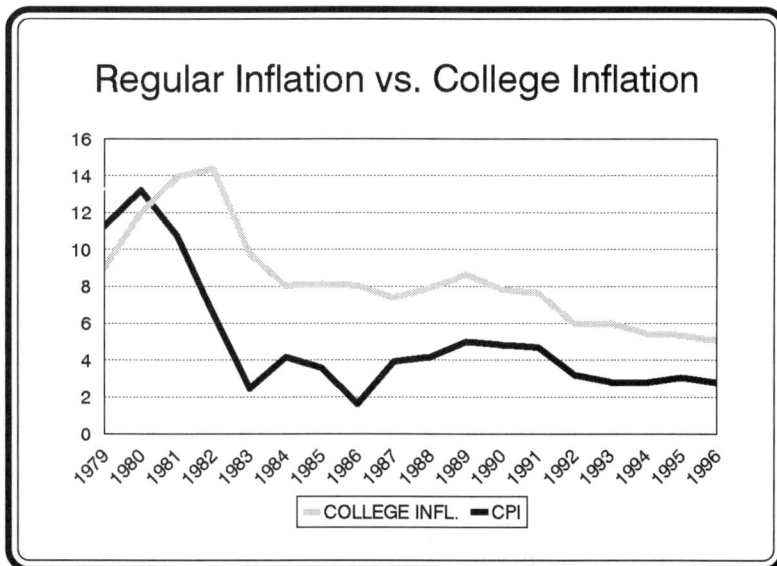

College is an emotional issue. Students work hard to get accepted to the best colleges and the parents are proud of their children. College is, perhaps, the last great gift that parents can give to their children before they leave home. Often, parents are under tremendous pressure to ante up some extra dollars to pay college bills. Understanding college inflation is an important factor in helping your clients plan better.

Concept 4: College is worth it.

College helps students learn what they need to know and trains them how to adapt to changes. Most important, students develop a network of contacts that can be extremely lucrative throughout the rest of their lives. Many parents feel that a price tag can't be put on the value of a college education. In addition, college graduates tend to have more confidence in life than their counterparts. College gives students a range of experiences that teaches them how to communicate better throughout their lifetime and how to enjoy many of the arts and sciences to which non-college graduates may not be exposed. College is also worth it in increased lifetime earnings. A recent Department of Labor study gave us the following numbers.

◆ Students not earning a high school diploma are likely to average about $608,000 over their lifetime.

◆ With a high school diploma, the amount of earning capacity jumps to $820,000; some college ups the ante to $992,000.

◆ A bachelor's degree increases earnings to $1,400,000.

◆ Professional degrees show earnings as high as $3,000,000 over a lifetime.

Concept 4

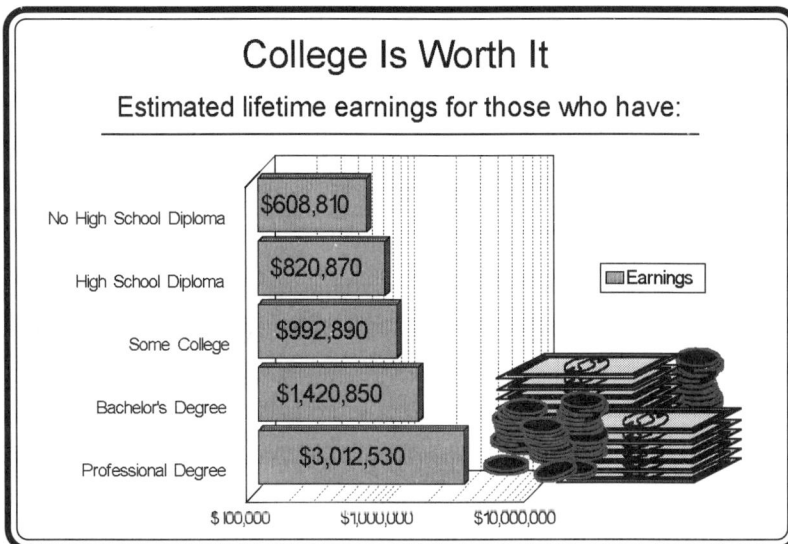

College Is Worth It

Estimated lifetime earnings for those who have:

	Earnings
No High School Diploma	$608,810
High School Diploma	$820,870
Some College	$992,890
Bachelor's Degree	$1,420,850
Professional Degree	$3,012,530

$100,000　　$1,000,000　　$10,000,000

Those numbers are averages. Obviously, some people do better than others. Yet, those figures graphically portray the increased economic benefit of a college education. One of our clients recently calculated his return on his college investment for his student to be over 14% and then complained that he did all of the investing while his student benefited from all of the return. Although this rate of return number is extremely difficult to calculate accurately, college is worth it. As we enter the information age, many experts believe that the ability to get ahead in this environment will require that extra edge that a college education can provide.

Concept 5: There are only four ways to pay for college.

Having studied the college planning process for over 20 years, we've come to the conclusion that there are only four ways to pay for college.

1. Pay for college out of savings.

    Unfortunately, most parents don't save enough for college. Out of some 40,000 parents that we've worked with over the years, fewer than 10 saved enough to pay the college bills. Not long ago we prepared a study for one of the major magazines. We were asked to poll business executives to find out what they had saved for college. Although it was an unscientific survey, we found that the typical business executive, earning between $100,000 and $200,000 a year, had enough money saved for *one year* of college expenses. We're not talking about one year per student but one year for the entire family.

    When we started in the college planning business, our objective was to teach parents of sixth graders how to save money for college without hurting their ability to obtain financial aid. When we sat down with them, one-on-one, most of them became excited about our ideas and committed to the program. We were amazed at the amount of monthly savings they pledged to the college process, often $500 or more per month. We walked away with substantial checks which were invested in mutual funds and other vehicles. Unfortunately, the average college savings plan stayed on the books less than six months. As soon as those extra special expenses came up—braces for the kids, tires for the car, maybe a vacation—it was the college savings plan that was affected. Most parents said the reason the plan was terminated was that college seemed so far away but the expenses had to be taken care of immediately.

Just because parents don't save for college is no excuse. We will find out that saving for college is important and that saving for college doesn't have to hurt a client's ability to obtain financial aid if it's done correctly. We'll talk more about savings plans in Step 9 of our process.

2. The pay-as-you-go plan.

    Pay-as-you-go is a plan in which your clients attempt to increase their earnings by enough money during the college years to be able to pay the taxes on the increased earnings and have enough remaining to pay the college bill. Most clients can't do this effectively. To pay a $30,000 tuition bill at an Ivy League school might require additional earnings of as much as $45,000 in order to pay $15,000 in taxes and have enough leftover to pay that $30,000 college bill.

    As we examine financial aid we will discover that if the client is lucky enough to qualify for financial aid, the pay-as-you-go system can be a trap. We will learn that financial aid is based on the income of your clients prior to the year they receive financial aid. For example, if they raise their income to pay for the first year of college because they don't receive enough financial aid, that additional income will lower the financial aid the following year. This means the clients must work harder the second year which means they will obtain even less financial aid the third year and so on and so on. Pay-as-you-go is a system that appears to work well on paper but often doesn't do the job.

3. Pay for college by borrowing.

    We're going to talk about borrowing options in Step 8 of our program but this is where the retirement problem especially rears its ugly head. We find that parents borrow far too much for college because they are not prepared to handle the costs and the emotional issues of college which cause them to bite off more then they should.

4. Let someone else pay for it.

   This is my favorite and most parents' favorite way of paying for college. Unless there are wealthy grandparents in the picture, letting someone else pay for college involves trying to qualify for this thing called financial aid.

Concept 5

There Are Only Four Ways To Pay For College

▶ Save

▶ Pay-As-You-Go

▶ Borrow

▶ Let Someone Else Pay

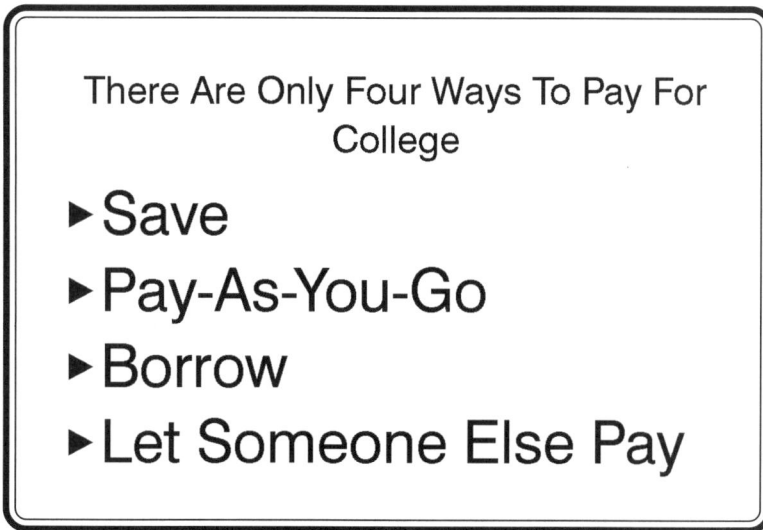

Concept 6: There are four types of financial aid.

Each type of financial aid is entirely different. We need to understand all four types in order to help our clients plan better for college.

1. Need-based financial aid.

   This is the most prevalent type of financial aid in the system. Need-based financial aid means simply that our clients cannot afford to pay the college bill according to their Expected Family Contribution (a number the colleges and the government calculate for the family). In this situation, if the college wants that student to attend their college, the college must develop a financial aid package that makes up the difference between the cost of college and what the parents can afford to pay. We'll explore need-based financial aid in-depth a little later on.

2. Merit-based financial aid.

Merit-based financial aid has been available for years. Typically, merit-based aid comes in two forms: i) athletic scholarships given to students based on their ability to perform in sports on behalf of the college; and ii) academic scholarships and grants given to academically talented students. Most merit-based aid takes the form of scholarships and grants whereas need-based aid might take on loans and jobs as well as scholarships and grants.

3. Negotiated financial aid.

In recent years we have found that some colleges were having a hard time attracting the students they wanted. If you understand how to negotiate a financial aid package, you can assist your clients in obtaining additional valuable dollars for college. This will also preserve more of your clients' money for their own retirement. We will discuss how to negotiate for college bills in Step 7 of our nine step process.

4. Discounted tuition on a selective basis.

In order to understand this concept we need to look at some major changes that took place in the financial aid process. Reauthorization of educational funding by the government reoccurs every five years but when Congress passed the Education Reauthorization Act of 1992, some significant events took place.

Congress and the colleges had banded together to determine a set of systematic formulas for both federal financial aid and college financial aid. Prior to 1992, the one financial aid form was simply called the Financial Aid Form. For years, Congress had been receiving a substantial number of complaints from parents because the financial aid formulas included the value of the home as an asset available to pay for college. In 1992, Congress decided to remove the value of the home as an asset when calculating a person's ability to pay for college. The private colleges disagreed. It was their feeling that if the value of the home was taken out of the financial aid formula, everyone would be eligible for more financial aid. Having limited resources, the colleges believed it would be more difficult to allocate their funds under the new circumstances.

Since 1992, we've had two different financial aid formulas: i) the federal methodology for government financial aid (determined by the Free Application for Federal Student Aid or FAFSA); and ii) the institutional methodology for college financial aid. The big difference that we need to understand is that prior to 1992, colleges and the federal government allocated their financial aid the same way. There was a firm, fixed set of rules. Since 1992, the government allocates their financial aid on a set of firm, fixed rules, but the colleges have the freedom to determine what they want.

The second event to have an impact since 1992 was a court case that we will call the MIT Court Case because MIT was the organization that fought the battle. Prior to 1992, a group of northeastern colleges compared notes on every student applying for financial aid, the financial aid packages being almost identical. Uncle Sam challenged this system of comparing notes by contending that it was price fixing and, therefore, illegal. MIT fought the battle and lost in the first round. When the MIT financial aid director came out of the courtroom he made the following statement, "It's a shame that we lost this court case because now we're going to have to competitively bid on a blind basis for those students that we really want. This means that we may not have enough financial aid to meet the needs of those students at the bottom of our selection list." What he was really saying is that financial aid is now negotiable if your clients' student has something to offer to the college.

There is a third piece of information we need to throw into our equation to better understand this type of financial aid. We need to think like a college president might think. College presidents have always been concerned about enrollment because tuition is a significant part of a college's operating budget. When there are empty seats in the classroom, the college has less money with which to operate the following year. Empty seats also translate into less alumni annual giving and that lessens the chance the college will hit a home run and have an alumnus donate a substantial amount of money to the college. Therefore, filling those seats is extremely important.

In recent years, colleges have awakened and realized that an empty seat in a classroom doesn't cost much to fill. The professor at the front of the room is still being paid, the heat and light bill is still being paid and the building is still being maintained. They suddenly realized that giving away that seat at a discount could mean money for the college and not cost them anything. For example, let's say a college normally charges $12,000 in tuition to fill a seat in a classroom but they decide to give that seat away for $6,000, a substantial discount. We certainly have a happy student and parents because they receive a significant discount off their college bill and the college profits from $6,000 that it didn't have before to contribute towards its expenses. The end result is that it is good business to discount empty seats.

Colleges, however, won't give away that seat for free. They are going to extract a price and the price is that they are going to acquire a student who will improve their statistical averages by filling that seat. If average SAT scores at a college are 1100, the college might give that empty seat at a discount to someone with 1150 college boards, or to a good athlete, or to a well-rounded student they think will be successful and might be loyal to the school in the future.

When we think about the Education Reauthorization Act of 1992, the MIT Court Case and how college presidents think, we can see a pattern evolve as to why colleges are willing to selectively discount seats. If you walked down the aisle of an airplane and asked everyone what they paid for their seat, you would find that most people on the plane paid different prices. The same is true with colleges; most students pay different prices for their seat in that classroom. Understanding this form of financial aid will give us tremendous leverage as we help our clients reduce their college bill.

Concept 6

Four Types of Financial Aid

▶ **Need-Based**
▶ **Merit-Based**
▶ **Negotiated**
▶ **Selectively Discounted Tuition**

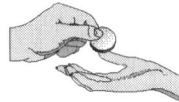

Concept 7: Knowing your Expected Family Contribution (EFC) is a key to financing college.

EFC, Expected Family Contribution, is a need-based financial aid concept. Need-based financial aid is one of the four types of financial aid currently in use by colleges. Although the other three types of financial aid, merit-based aid, negotiated aid and selectively discounted tuition, are becoming more important, need-based financial aid is the traditional form of aid offered by most schools and is still the most widely used. We've found it to be the best starting point in discussing financial aid with clients. If clients qualify, it is the most predictable and easiest to obtain.

The EFC is a concept developed by the government and the colleges as a way to dole out financial aid dollars. It is a measurement of what parents can technically afford to pay for college.

The easiest way to explain the EFC concept is to use what we call our "black box approach." For years, engineers and scientists have used black boxes to explain concepts because, since no one can see into a black box, they don't have to explain all of the details going on in the system. Chapter 3 opens up the black box and looks in detail at the financial aid formulas. For now, in our black box, there is a computer and two mystical formulas: i) the federal methodology for granting federal financial aid; and ii) the institutional methodology for awarding college financial aid. Although there are differences between the two formulas, both formulas are similar in concept.

Figure 2.1

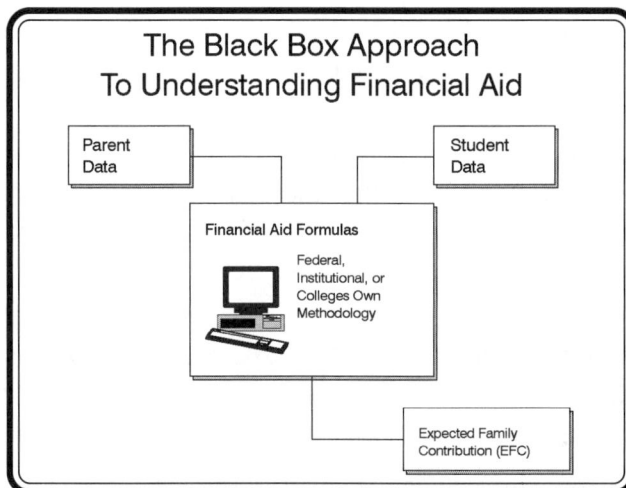

The Black Box Approach
To Understanding Financial Aid

Parent Data

Student Data

Financial Aid Formulas

Federal, Institutional, or Colleges Own Methodology

Expected Family Contribution (EFC)

When our clients decide they want to secure financial aid, they must fill out a form called a Financial Aid Form. Actually, there are two types of financial aid forms: i) the Free Application for Federal Student Aid (FAFSA) which is used to access the federal methodology; and ii) the Profile Form which is used to access the institutional methodology. Basically, both forms ask the same kind of questions but the Profile Form requires more detail. Both forms want to know about parental income and assets and both want to know about student income and assets. This data is then sent to a processing bureau where it is run through a computer system with the formulas. Out of the black box pops a number called the Expected Family Contribution or EFC. This number calculates what the colleges and the government determine your clients can afford to pay for college each year for their family. This number, once it is calculated, is sent directly to the specific college or university to which the student has applied. The financial aid officer at that college or university compares your client's EFC with their cost. If the EFC for the client is greater than the cost of college, then your client theoretically can pay the entire college bill and, therefore, is not eligible for financial aid. On the other hand, if your client's EFC is less than the cost of college, your client theoretically cannot afford to send the student to that college. It then becomes the job of the college to put together a financial aid package in order to meet the needs of the student and help him or her pay for college.

This concept is extremely important, so let's look at several examples.

♦ Suppose your client fills out a Financial Aid Form and it is determined his EFC is $10,000. Further, assume that the best college for this student is a state college costing $10,000. Is this student eligible for financial aid? The answer is no. Since the family can afford $10,000, at least according to the formulas, and the cost of college is $10,000, there is no financial need and, therefore, no eligibility for need-based financial aid.

♦ Now let's assume the right college is a private college costing $22,000 and the EFC is still $10,000. This time there is a $12,000 need, the difference between the cost of college and the EFC. Your client is eligible for financial aid and should qualify for a $12,000 financial aid package.

♦ Suppose the student wants to attend an Ivy League college costing $33,000? With a $10,000 EFC, the student should be eligible for $23,000 of need-based financial aid.

You can also look at these examples in a slightly different way. In each case, how much is your client required to pay? The answer is $10,000. The lesson to be learned is that if you can tell your client his Expected Family Contribution, that number will represent his college cost. If the system works correctly, the remainder of the college cash flow will be taken care of by the financial aid system.

Note that the last statement has an "if" clause in it because often the system doesn't work correctly. There are two problems with the need-based financial aid system we need to explore.

1. The first is called the College Financial Aid gap.

    Unfortunately, not every college has the funds to meet every student's financial need. If your client qualifies for need-based financial aid, it's important that the student finds colleges with enough money to help. If your client's student attends a college that does not have enough money, a College Financial Aid gap occurs and your client must come up with more than his Expected Family Contribution to pay the college bill.

2. The second problem is referred to as the Parent Financial Aid gap.

    Many clients are surprised by the magnitude of the EFC because it is almost always substantially higher than they believe they can afford. Parents tend to think of paying college bills out of savings, investments and cash flow. Colleges add the parents' ability to borrow to the EFC equation.

Most parents don't find out what their EFC is until late in the game, when it's too late to plan. They need to know early where they stand so they can attain a planning edge. As a professional, you can do this by insisting that every client takes the financial aid test we explain in Step 2, Chapter 3.

Concept 7

Knowing Your Expected Family Contribution (EFC) is a Key to Financing College

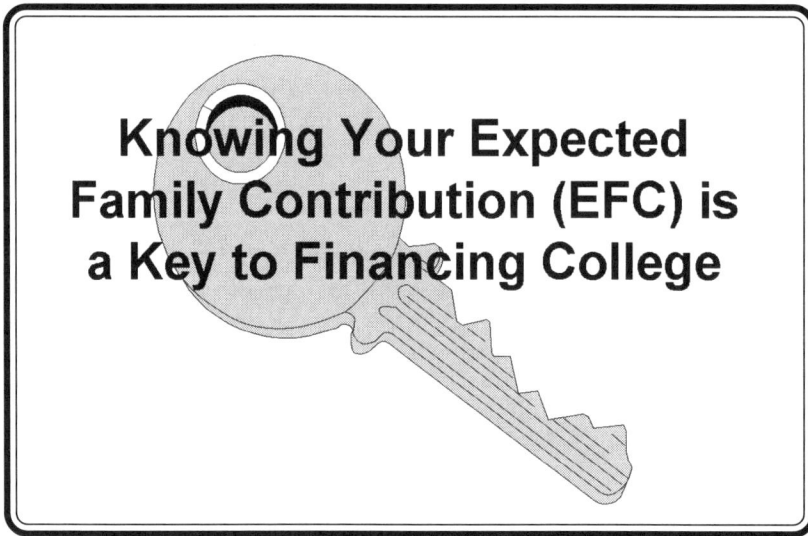

The EFC gives us a tremendous amount of useful information that we can translate into college planning strategies for our clients.

♦ It tells us whether or not the client will realistically qualify for need-based financial aid. Many clients hold on too long, hoping for need-based aid when they should be planning a different strategy, perhaps opting for merit-based aid or selectively discounted tuition. Later chapters will illustrate how this strategy change drastically affects the planning process.

♦ If the client is eligible for need-based financial aid, knowing the EFC tells us our target. That number is the amount your client needs to acquire which can be much lower than those awful list prices discussed earlier. Theoretically, the remainder of the college bill will be paid by the financial aid system.

♦ Knowing the EFC can help us negotiate a better financial aid package because it gives us a frame of reference. How can you know if a financial aid package is any good unless you know what it's supposed to be? This knowledge alone can give our clients tremendous leverage.

In the course of your planning remember, your client needs to know his EFC and he needs to know it as early as possible in the planning process.

Concept 8: Financial aid formulas are income driven not asset driven.

This is a major misconception of most professionals and clients. Many people think that if they have too many assets they won't qualify for financial aid. While this may be true, it is your clients' income that most often prevents them from obtaining financial aid. This is one of the reasons why it is so important that your clients save money for college. Many clients don't save because they think it is going to preclude them from securing financial aid. Then one day they wake up, apply for financial aid, and find out that because their income has grown over the last several years, they are not going to qualify for financial aid. On top of that, they don't have any money in the bank to help them pay for college. This creates a disaster.

The chart for Concept 8 shows the relative weights in the financial aid formulas for the various kinds of incomes and assets. Next is a summary of the four rules of thumb that apply to financial aid. These four rules will serve as a guide as to when and how to set up savings plans and when and how to help your clients plan better to obtain more financial aid.

Concept 8

> ### Financial Aid Formulas Are Income Driven -- Not Asset Driven
>
> ► 50% Student Income
>
> ► 47% Parent Income
>
> ► 35% Student Assets
>
> ► 6% Parental Assets

1. The fifty percent rule applies to the student's income.

The formulas don't simply take fifty percent of a student's income and subtract it from the financial aid package. There are deductibles which we will explore in the next chapter but, generally, here is what happens.

Suppose your client's student comes home one afternoon and says, "Mom and Dad, I know college is going to cost a lot of money and I'd like to help. So I've just landed an extra job to help pay for college. The new job will pay me an extra $2,000 per year over and above what I was going to make before."

Well, the student may think that is wonderful and the parents may think it is wonderful and the financial aid people will think it is wonderful. The financial aid people see that this student has the ability to pay more for college. Simply put, the financial aid formulas will take fifty percent of the student's net after-tax income and lower their financial aid package by that amount.

2. The forty-seven percent rule applies to the parent's income.

Again, there are deductibles as well as a graded percentage that are applied against the parent's income based upon the amount of that income. However, most parents that you will be counseling will find themselves in the forty-seven percent bracket. Here's what happens.

Mom receives a pay raise of $2,000 net after taxes. Everyone thinks this is wonderful because it will help pay for college. Colleges, though, see higher income. They take forty-seven percent of the $2,000, or $940, and reduce the financial aid package by that amount.

3. The thirty-five percent rule applies to assets listed in the student's name.

There are no deductibles here. Colleges simply look at the amount of money shown under a student's name and determine that a student ought to spend his or her own money on his or her college education.

Suppose your client has diligently saved $10,000 and put that amount into an account in the student's name. The financial aid people will say the student can apply thirty-five percent, or $3,500, of that money towards the first year of college, thirty-five percent of the balance towards the second year of college, thirty-five percent of the remainder towards the third year of college and so on.

4.   The six percent rule applies to the assets in a parent's name.

The same $10,000 under a parent's name will cost the student $600, six percent, in financial aid the first year and six percent of the balance in succeeding years. In addition, there is a substantial deductible that allows your clients to show some savings in their own name and not have it count at all.

These rules work both ways. As incomes and assets increase, financial aid decreases. As incomes and assets decrease, financial aid increases. As a financial professional, you can already see a pattern developing as to how you can help the parents of college bound students. The main point is that assets don't hurt as much as the income. If assets are structured the correct way, they hurt very little. Therefore, there is very little reason why parents should not save money for college. They just need to do it the right way.

Concept 9: Knowing the financial aid strength of each college is critical to a successful plan.

All colleges are not created equal when it comes to the amount of money they have available to put into the financial aid system. Some colleges are rich and some are poor. Often it is cheaper for a student to attend a higher cost college that has the ability to provide a good financial aid package than it is to attend a lower cost college that does not have that ability.

How do you find which colleges have money and which ones don't? There are a number of sources listed in Appendix 1, but one of my favorites is Peterson's *College Money Handbook.* This book classifies most of the four-year accredited colleges and explains their financial aid history. This information is valuable to parents and students in helping them make better choices. Keep in mind that no one should pick a college based solely on how much money a college might give us. Obviously, the priority is to get the best education value for the dollar. If a student doesn't receive a quality education, it doesn't matter if the college is cheap; it's a waste of four years of precious time.

Concept 9

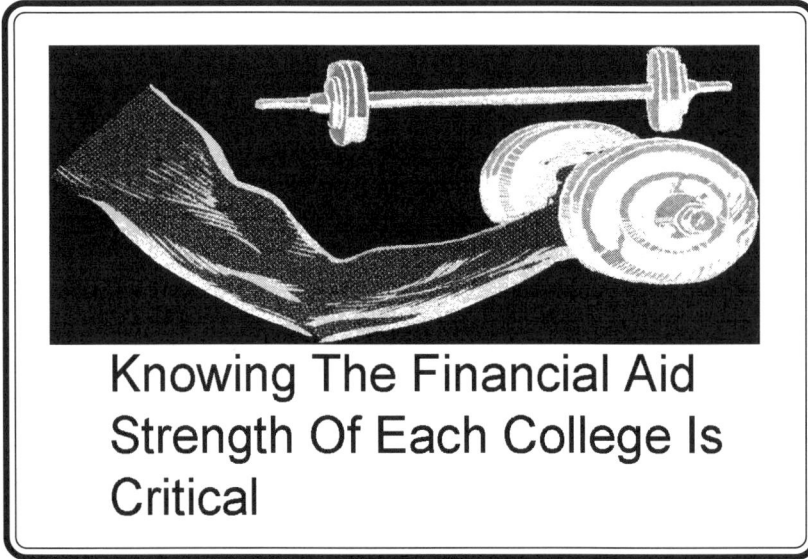

Knowing The Financial Aid Strength Of Each College Is Critical

There are over 3,000 accredited colleges in this country. There are probably 25 to 30 colleges that will fit each student by meeting his social needs and providing a quality education. Some of these colleges have need-based money if the student qualifies for it and others don't. Therefore, sifting through the applicable colleges and applying the information about the financial aid strength of each college can pay big dividends to your clients. It will also help them keep more money for their own retirement funds.

Next is an example of the kind of information we can compile from Peterson's *College Money Handbook 1997.*

Look at Figure 2.2 which is a chart for the University of Pennsylvania, an Ivy League school and quite expensive. In 1996, it cost $27,398 to attend that school— and that's not counting "pizza money." The book points out that forty-nine percent of the freshmen applied for financial aid and ninety-three percent of those freshmen were judged to be in need of the money. This means that those parents and students went through our black box approach (Concept 7) and found that their Expected Family Contribution was less than the University of Pennsylvania's cost.

Figure 2.2

University of Pennsylvania (1996)	
Comprehensive Cost	**$27,398**
% Freshmen Applying for Aid	49%
% Judged to Have a Need	93%
% Actually Receiving Aid	100%
Average Amount of Aid Awarded	**$19,559**
% Self-Help (Loans & Jobs)	34%
% Gift Aid	66%
% of Need Met	**100%**

Source: Peterson's *College Money Handbook 1997*

The next number shown in the chart is extremely important because it illustrates that 100% of those students who qualified for financial aid money obtained it. The average amount of aid received by students at Penn was a whopping $19,559. Peterson's *College Money Handbook 1997* also depicts how that financial aid was broken down. In this case, 34% of the money secured by Penn students was in the form of loans and jobs—free cash flow to the parents but not really free money to the students. The students either have to work or pay it back. However, 66% of the financial aid dispensed was free money and is indicated on the chart as Gift Aid. This is money that never has to be paid back.

The last number, and probably the most important on the chart, indicates that the University of Pennsylvania was able to meet 100% of the need. This demonstrates that if you know your Expected Family Contribution and can find that amount of money, the remaining dollars will be taken care of by the financial aid system. As a result, there will be no college financial aid gap.

Let's examine a different kind of school, Rutgers University, as displayed in Figure 2.3. Rutgers is a wonderful school. It's one of the top 45 schools in terms of difficulty for entrance among all the schools in the country. The expense or total cost of $10,167 is quite reasonable for a quality education. However, when it comes to financial aid on a need-based basis, Rutgers simply doesn't do as well.

Figure 2.3

Rutgers University (1996)	
Comprehensive Cost (In State)	**$10,167**
% Freshmen Applying for Aid	62%
% Judged to Have a Need	83%
% Actually Receiving Aid	99%
Average Amount of Aid Awarded	**$7,450**
% Self-Help (Loans & Jobs)	60%
% Gift Aid	40%
% of Need Met	**83%**

Source: Peterson's *College Money Handbook 1997*

Sixty-two percent of the freshmen applied for financial aid and 83% of those freshmen were judged to be in need of that aid. Again, that's our black box. But here's the major difference. Only 99% of those students who actually qualified for financial aid succeed in attaining it; some didn't secure any money at all. Most likely this was because they applied late or never followed up on their financial aid forms. Since Rutgers doesn't have as much money as some other schools, they run out.

The average financial aid award was $7,450 which, percentage wise, is a good chunk of money. Yet there is another distinction. Sixty percent of the financial aid package was in the form of loans and jobs, free cash flow to the parents but, again, not truely free money. Gift Aid amounted to only 40% which is the free money.

Finally, looking again at the most important number on the chart, Rutgers was able to meet only 83% of the need. This indicates that if your clients need $5,000 in a financial aid package they will probably get closer to $4,000 which will result in a college financial aid gap.

When you look through a book such as Peterson's *College Money Handbook 1997* you will find many schools that meet 90% to 100% of the financial need. There are also many schools that meet 30%, 40% and 50% of a student's financial need.

When it comes to looking for financial aid, the financial aid strength of the college is critical to the process. We'll also see in later chapters that the information from this concept can be used to help predict a financial aid package in advance. One final note: if your client's student does not qualify for need-based financial aid, there are three other types of financial aid the student can pursue. All is not lost simply because a school doesn't have need-based financial aid funds.

3

Help Your Clients Complete a Financial Aid Test

Completing a trial financial aid test is probably the single most important diagnostic tool in the college planning process. It quickly tells us whether or not our clients have a chance to obtain need-based financial aid. If they are going to qualify for need-based financial aid, we need to help them plan to maximize it. If, on the other hand, they are never going to realistically qualify for need-based financial aid, we must get them to forget about it quickly and move on to other areas of planning. Remember, there are four types of financial aid; need-based aid is only one type. It is, however, the largest single source of financial aid money.

What Is a Financial Aid Test?

A financial aid test is a practice run for filling out the real financial aid forms and ascertaining the result. Two of the biggest benefits of this practice are:

1. It gives the parents practice in an otherwise intimidating process. After they've gone through a trial financial aid test, filling out the real forms will be easier. Parents will understand the data they are required to submit and they will know how the answers they give will affect their ability to receive need-based financial aid.

2. It gives the professional and the client the EFC (Expected Family Contribution) results early, letting them choose to either plan to maximize need-based financial aid, or choose a different method of attack on the college problem.

Several Ways to Complete a Financial Aid Test

1. Manual calculations.

    We have included a Financial Aid Worksheet in Appendix 2. This worksheet will enable you to approximate the EFC for your clients.

2. Software.

    There are several software vendors offering EFC programs. If you will be running numerous EFC calculations for your clients, you'll probably want your own software.

3. The Internet.

    Tap into the Internet and use the web page software. There are sites on the World Wide Web that give you or your client the ability to calculate the EFC online. See Appendix 1 for a partial list of sites.

4. A professional service.

    There are a number of firms which will process data for you or your client. They will send you a printout and offer expert counsel to help you and your client make decisions. The service approach is especially helpful if you engage in college planning on an occasional basis.

Whichever method you choose, it is necessary to understand the importance of inputting good numbers into the calculations. It is easy to play games with numbers and make the resulting EFC go up or down. However, the government and the colleges may not accept your data as being valid. Just like preparing tax returns, there is a right and a wrong way to fill out a financial aid test. It is very easy, therefore, to give your client false and misleading information.

You must have a general understanding about how financial aid works. The financial aid system is based on two formulas called the Federal Methodology and the Institutional Methodology. The section that follows gives a complete description of the Federal Methodology and discusses the ways in which it varies from the Institutional Methodology. The Federal Methodology is reasonably straightforward and its rules for input data that describes your client's circumstances are predictable.

The Institutional Methodology is not as easy to use. Colleges have their own questions and their own sense of what should and should not be included. If you don't understand the way colleges think, find someone who knows. Let that individual lead your client through this planning phase or use a professional service to calculate the EFC. Your results will certainly be more accurate and your planning will be more effective.

Key Factors Affecting Financial Aid

Before we actually examine the Federal Methodology formula, there are several definitions we need to understand.

1. Family income, for financial aid purposes, is the income from the year before the financial aid is needed.

    For example, if a student was planning to apply for financial aid for September, 1998, 1997 would be the critical income year for financial aid purposes. By using the prior year's income, the financial aid administrators are able to document income by asking for tax returns. This is not always fair to families. If, for example, the parents' income is lower the following year, parents may not have adequate funds to meet an Expected Family Contribution calculated on the previous year's higher parental income. Generally, exceptions cannot be handled at the financial aid form level. Parents can, however, deal with these problems later by talking with a college financial aid officer.

2. Assets for financial aid purposes are valued as of the date the form is completed.

    Sometimes financial aid administrators will question why assets are low when interest income from the previous year indicates that the asset values were higher in the previous year. They will ask for documentation and explanations of why the assets decreased. Occasionally they will ask for copies of bank statements as of the day the form is filed. Choosing the date that the form is dated can be an important factor in the planning process.

3.   The cost of college is a critical factor.

Remember that it is the relationship between college costs and the Expected Family Contribution that determines the student's financial aid eligibility. If a student is attending a $10,000 college and the EFC is $12,000, the student does not qualify for financial aid. If, on the other hand, the student attends a $15,000 college, the student does qualify.

4.   The number of family members in college during the same year significantly affects financial aid.

Please note the emphasis on family members, not children. Many colleges count parents if they are attending college on a full-time basis and, sometimes, on a part-time basis. As you will see in the following paragraphs, the Federal Methodology gets the parents to pay as much as possible in any year that any student is in college. Therefore, in the years when two or more students are in college at the same time, the parents are not expected to pay much more. The parents' contribution in those years is divided among the students in college. The Expected Family Contribution may be different for each student because each student's resources are different, but the parents don't pay more.

5.   Financial aid is recalculated annually.

As family income and assets change during the college years, so will financial aid.

The Financial Aid Formula is Really Two Formulas, Not One

There are two sets of calculations that make up the Expected Family Contribution. The purpose here is not to generate the formulas so you can calculate the EFC, but rather to give you an understanding of the formulas so you can plan effectively. Remember, computer software and several service companies as described earlier are available to help you produce the calculations, but only an understanding of the process can help you plan effectively.

Figure 3.1

Parent Expected Contribution	+	Student Expected Contribution	=	Family Expected Contribution

Both parents and students are expected to contribute their fair share. As we explained above, often the expected contribution is different for two students of the same family. The students' differing incomes and assets cause this; the parents' contribution is the same for each student.

Calculating the Parent Expected Contribution

Chart 1 is a schematic diagram of the steps required to calculate the Parent Expected Contribution (PEC).

Chart 1

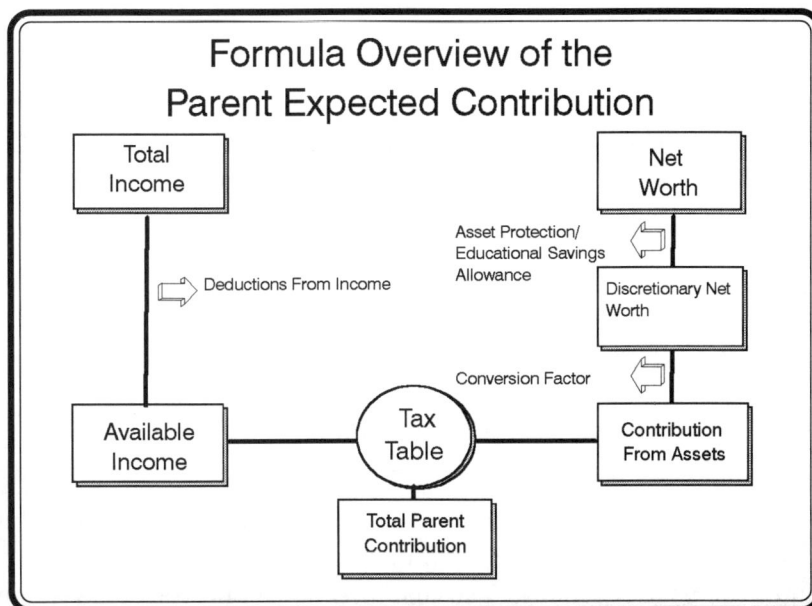

This chart can give us a feel for how the formulas work. Each block represents the result of a series of calculations that are tied to the trial financial aid worksheets regardless of whether software or hand calculations are used. We'll get specific in the next few paragraphs about what is included in each calculation.

In general, the parent's portion of the financial aid calculation starts with the parent's income. Although the formula expects a parent to list the total of his income, some items can be deducted from that income. Subtracting the deductions from the parent's income gives us a number called Available Income. Let's set this number aside for a few minutes and switch over to assets.

The asset side of the formula starts with a list of the parent's assets. As we will see, however, it doesn't necessarily consider a parent's debts. The formula does deduct an amount of money which is called the Asset Protection/Educational Savings Allowance before calculating a new number called Discretionary Net Worth.

The formulas force parents to use a percentage of their Discretionary Net Worth on college and, as a result, arrive at a number called Contribution From Assets.

Finally, the formula adds the Contribution From Assets and the Available Income and applies that number to a tax table which is based upon a sliding scale, the higher the number, the higher the percentage. The net result is the Total Parent Contribution. That contribution is divided among the number of students in college during that financial aid period.

The Specifics of the Formula

1. Step 1: Determine the Parent's Total Income.

    Parent income is a dominant factor in determining financial aid. Financial aid forms ask for a complete list of income and, at the college level, tax returns are usually requested so that income can be verified. All income is included. Next is a partial list of income sources on which information is required.

Chart 2

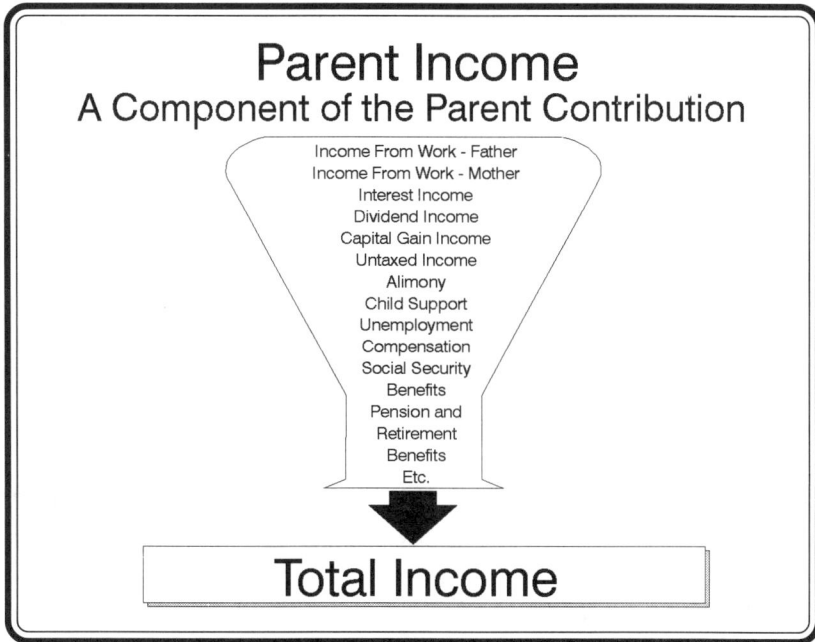

Parent Income
A Component of the Parent Contribution

Income From Work - Father
Income From Work - Mother
Interest Income
Dividend Income
Capital Gain Income
Untaxed Income
Alimony
Child Support
Unemployment
Compensation
Social Security
Benefits
Pension and
Retirement
Benefits
Etc.

Total Income

In most cases, all of this data shows up on a tax return and, therefore, it is important to be accurate. Sometimes parents can plan in advance to control future income and thus control, at least to some extent, financial aid.

1. Step 2: Determine the Allowable Offsets Against the Parent's Income.

    The formulas allow a parent to offset some family expenses.

    ◊   First, the parent can exclude the federal income tax paid the previous year.

    ◊   Second, the formulas internally calculate the FICA [Federal Insurance Contribution Act] taxes (Social Security) and exclude them.

    ◊   Third, there is an allowance for state and local taxes, including real estate and sales taxes. However, there is no place to list these taxes; they are estimated as a percentage of the total income. This percentage varies from state to state and to some extent by income class within a state. Percentages usually shortchange high and middle income parents.

◊ Fourth, the formulas calculate an Employment Allowance. This allowance permits a family with two working parents to deduct 35 percent of the smaller of the two earnings. This allowance is capped, however, at $2,700. It acts very much as the child care credit does for income tax purposes.

◊ Last, the formulas calculate an Income Protection Allowance. This allowance provides minimum support for the family in order to provide food and clothing. For the 1997-1998 school year, this allowance amounts to $18,070 for a family of four with one student in college. As you can see from this number, the formulas are skewed in favor of low income families.

Prior to the 1992-1993 formula, private school tuition and medical expenses were allowable offsets. For 1992-1993 and later, they have been removed from the federal formula. Colleges, through the Institutional Methodology, have the discretion to make allowances for excessive medical expenses and private school tuition. The Profile Form, which provides the data for the Institutional Methodology, may have questions concerning medical expenses and private school tuition.

Chart 3

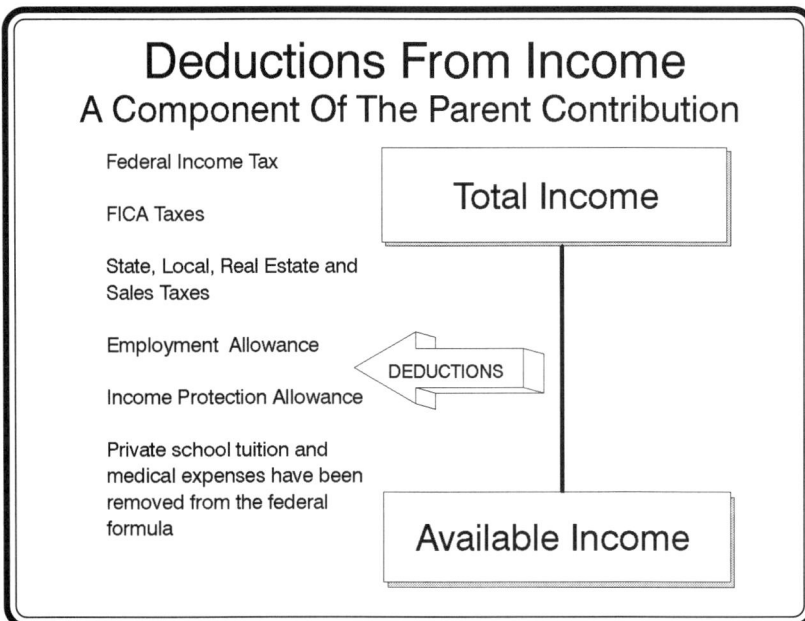

Deductions From Income
A Component Of The Parent Contribution

Federal Income Tax

FICA Taxes

State, Local, Real Estate and Sales Taxes

Employment Allowance

Income Protection Allowance

Private school tuition and medical expenses have been removed from the federal formula

DEDUCTIONS

Total Income

Available Income

Step 3: Calculate Available Income.

The Available Income is the difference between the Total Income in Step 1 and the Allowable Offsets in Step 2. Once this number is calculated it will be set aside and returned to in a later step.

Step 4: Compile a List of the Parent's Assets and Liabilities and Calculate the Net Worth.

In determining a parent's net worth, the financial aid forms have questions concerning the parent's cash accounts, home equity, investments and business ownership.

Chart 4

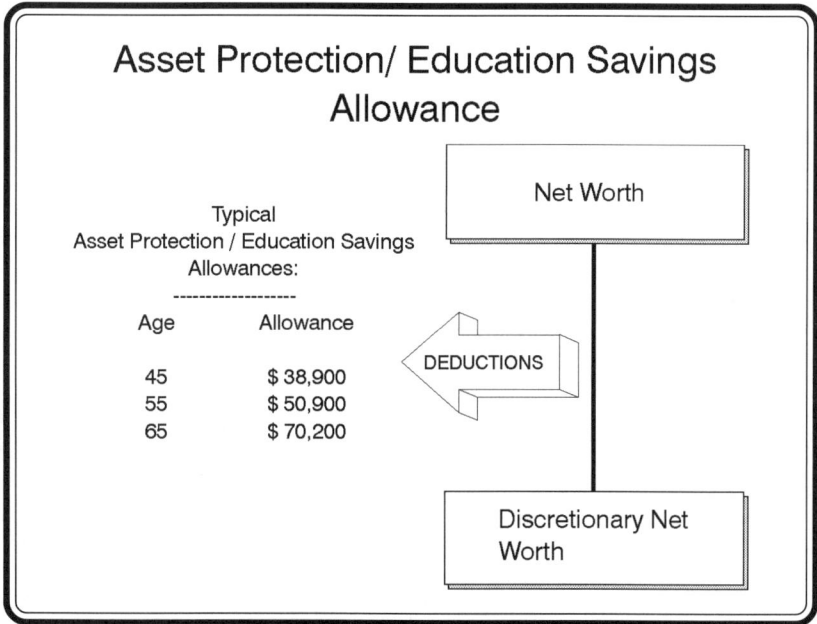

Asset Protection/ Education Savings Allowance

Typical
Asset Protection / Education Savings
Allowances:

Age	Allowance
45	$ 38,900
55	$ 50,900
65	$ 70,200

Net Worth

DEDUCTIONS

Discretionary Net Worth

◊ Cash is defined as checking accounts, savings accounts, money market accounts, certificates of deposit, etc. It is important to note there is no place to record your debts such as Visa, MasterCard, other charge cards or auto loan. The system simply does not care.

◊ Home equity and farm equity was removed from the Federal Methodology in 1992-1993. Most colleges will still consider home equity when allocating their own funds.

◊ The financial aid form seeks information regarding the value of investments including stocks, bonds, mutual funds, real estate and so on. Parents can offset these values with any investment debt. Please note that retirement accounts, such as pension plans, IRAs, 401(k) and tax sheltered annuities (403(b) plans), do not need to be listed for federal financial aid. Some colleges, however, will ask for these values and may include them.

◊ Finally, if the parent owns a business, the value of that business must be listed minus any business debts. Both methodologies discount business values when calculating the EFC.

The sum of these values equals the Parent Net Worth.

Chart 5

Parents' Assets
A Component of the Parent Contribution

Asset Category	Inclusions	Reductions
Cash	Checking Accounts Savings Accounts Certificates of Deposit Money Market Accounts	Cannot Offset: Installment Loans Credit Card Balances
Home Equity	No Longer Included	No Longer Included
Investments	Market value of: Stocks, Bonds, Mutual Funds, Real Estate	Any Loans Tied to the Investment Do Not Include Retirement Funds
Business Value	All Real Assets	Any Business Loans

Step 5: Identify the Asset Protection Allowance/Educational Savings Allowance and Calculate the Parent's Discretionary Net Worth.

Once a list of the parent's net worth has been compiled, it must be determined how much of those assets can be preserved for the client's retirement by examining the Asset Protection Allowance/Educational Savings Allowance Table.

This formula is based upon age. As we become older more of our assets can be protected for our own personal use. Before we get too excited, however, it must be mentioned that the numbers are not large. It is important because the formulas are slanted toward low income families so they can grasp for every straw available to help them. The following Asset Protection Allowance figures are typical.

◊ If the parent is in his mid-forties, the system is going to allow him to protect approximately $40,000.

◊ If the parent is in his mid-sixties, the system is going to allow him to protect approximately $72,000 range.

When the Asset Protection Allowance is subtracted from the parent's Net Worth, the remainder is called the Parent's Discretionary Net Worth.

Step 6: Determine the Asset Conversion Percentage and Calculate the Parent's Income Supplement.

Both the Federal Methodology and most college formulas indicate that parents ought to use a portion of their net worth to finance their children's education. The formula expects them to take 12 percent of their Discretionary Net Worth each year as an income supplement.

Chart 6

Conversion Rate
A Component of the Parent Contribution

12%

Discretionary Net Worth

Income Supplement

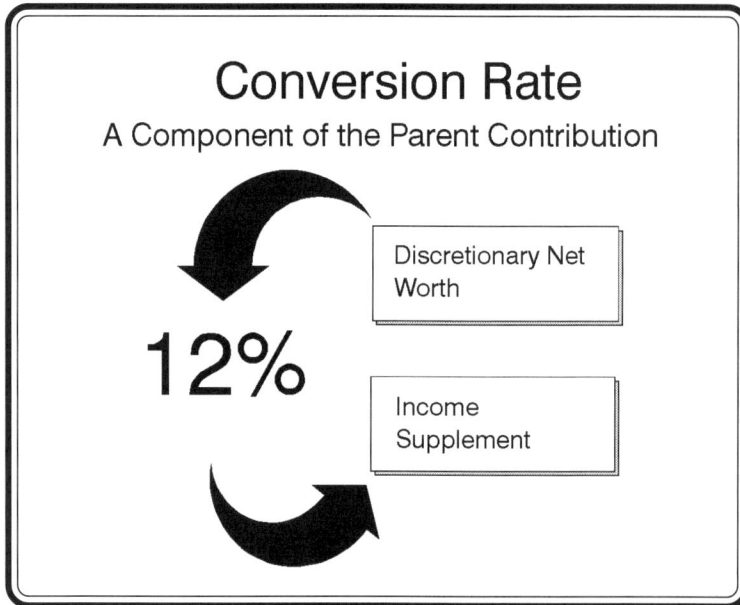

Step 7: Determine the Adjusted Available Income by Adding the Available Income to the Income Supplement.

The Income Supplement calculated in Step 6 is added to the Available Income that was calculated in Step 3. The sum of those two numbers is called the Adjusted Available Income.

Step 8: Determine the Adjusted Available Income Taxation Rate and Calculate the Total Parent Contribution.

At this point, a tax is applied to the formulas. The taxation rate starts at 22 percent when the sum of the Adjusted Available Income and the Income Supplement is small. The percentage grows as this Adjusted Available Income number grows, much like our income tax tables. When the Adjusted Available Income exceeds $21,200, however, parents find themselves in a 47 percent tax bracket. In other words, they are expected to use 47 percent of their Adjusted Available Income toward college. This number, then, becomes the Total Parent Contribution.

Chart 7

Tax Rates
A Component of the Parent Contribution

Adjusted Available Income **+** Income Supplement

TAX RATES 22%-47%

Total Parent Contribution

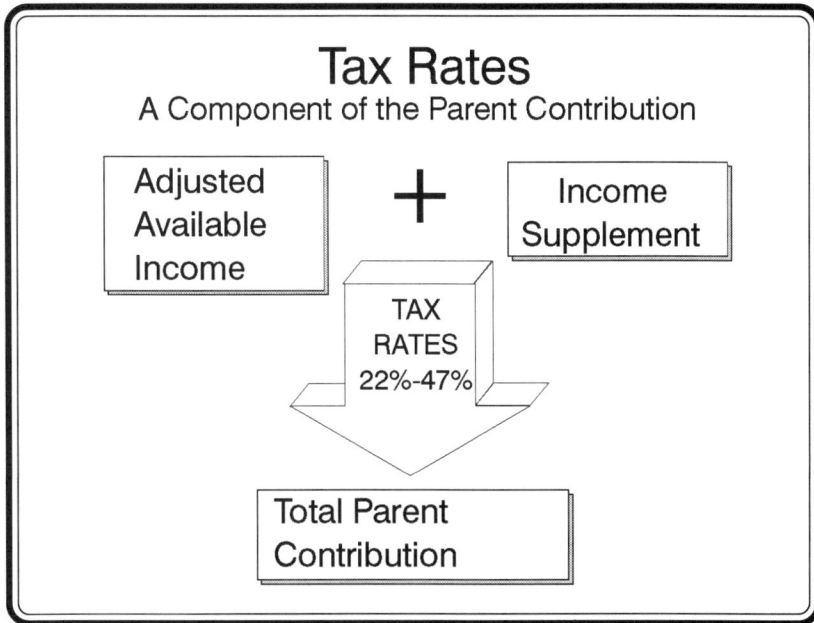

Step 9: Calculate the Parent's Contribution Per Student

The parent's total contribution is divided by the number of family members in college during that year, and that becomes the parent contribution per student.

Determining the Student Contribution

Chart 8 depicts the schematic formula which will help us understand the steps necessary to establish the Student Expected Contribution (SEC). Fortunately, the student's contribution is easier to calculate than the parent's.

Step 1: Compile the Student's Total Income.

Basically, the system looks at the student's income and tabulates it for the prior year. Just as with the parent income process, all of the income the student receives is counted.

Chart 8

Formula Overview of the
Student Expected Contribution

| Total Income |
| Net Worth |

Income Tax
FICA Tax

35%

SPENDING RATE

| Available Income |

50% Tax Rate On Income Over $1,750

| Income Supplement |

| Student Contribution |

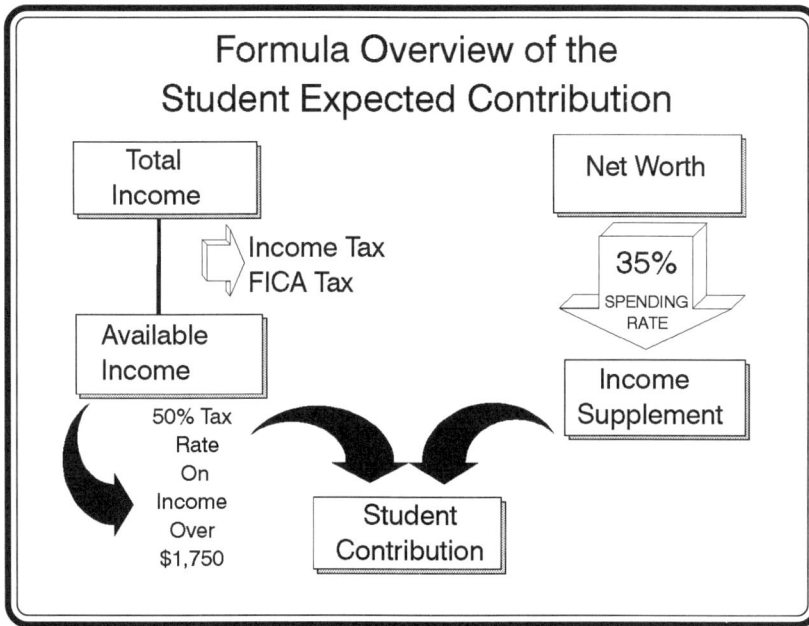

Step 2: List the Allowable Offsets Against the Student's Income.

From the above income, the student is allowed to subtract certain expenses. In this case, however, those expenses are the income taxes and any Social Security taxes the student paid.

Step 3: Calculate Available Income.

The system permits the student to earn up to $1,750 each year without it having an effect on financial aid. If the student earns more, however, financial aid will be reduced by 50 cents for each dollar earned. It doesn't matter whether the income is earned or unearned. Offsets for federal tax, state tax and FICA are allowed.

The Institutional Methodology does not have a $1,750 deductible. It counts student earnings from dollar one and applies the 50 percent tax rate after deductions for income and Social Security taxes. If a student doesn't work, the Institutional Methodology plugs in a $900 minimum contribution from income for freshmen and $1,100 for upper classmen.

Step 4: Compile a List of the Student's Assets and Calculate the Net Worth.

Now flip over to the asset side of the student situation. In this case, assets are considered anything listed under the student's Social Security number. All of the assets are tabulated just as they were on the parent side of the contribution.

Step 5: Calculate the Student's Income Supplement.

This time the system expects the student to use 35 percent of his money for the first year of college, 35 percent of what's remaining for the second year, and so on. At the end of college, basically all of the student's money has been spent on his own education. This becomes the Student's Income Supplement.

Step 6: Calculate the Student's Expected Contribution.

The Income Supplement is added to the Available Income that was calculated before; the sum of these two numbers becomes the Student Expected Contribution toward this year of college. The Student Expected Contribution is then added to the Parent Expected Contribution and that total becomes the Expected Family Contribution.

How to Complete a Financial Aid Test

Previously we mentioned there are four ways to complete a financial aid test: manual calculations, purchasing a software program, using the Internet to tap into the many available web sites, and employing a professional service. In our office we use proprietary software we have developed and which we update annually.

Have the Clients Fill Out the Form

A copy of our Trial Financial Aid Form is illustrated as Chart 9. Please note the simplicity of this form; actual financial aid forms are overwhelming and intimidating. We want to make it easy for our clients to take the first step of the process by providing us with the information we need to help them. Even with our simple form, clients often become confused. Usually the first time they fill out the form they get it wrong.

The beginning of this chapter defined how important it is to obtain accurate data. We ask the clients to write us notes and to express their situation as best they can. We spend considerable time reviewing the data with the client to make sure we both understand the input data.

If we are seeing a potential client we prefer to have completed trial Financial Aid Forms prior to the first meeting. That gives us several advantages:

1. It saves time. It enables a staff assistant to run an analysis of the data prior to the meeting so we're prepared, thus saving valuable meeting time to spend with the client.

2. We can screen data in advance to make sure a new prospect qualifies as a client. Look carefully at the fact finder and you will see how valuable the data is for qualifying purposes. For non-qualified prospects, we use a telephone appointment in order to save valuable time while still helping the prospect.

Chart 9

Trial Financial Aid Form

SECTION 1 - PARENT DATA:	PARENT #1	PARENT #2
LAST NAME, FIRST NAME		
HOME ADDRESS		
CITY, STATE, ZIP		
HOME TELEPHONE		
BUSINESS TELEPHONE		
COMPANY, OCCUPATION & TITLE		
DATE OF BIRTH		

SECTION 2 - FAMILY FINANCIAL DATA:		VALUE
1	Age of Older Parent	
2	Number of Parents in Family	
3	Number of Dependent Children in the Family	
4	Father's Wages	
5	Mother's Wages	
6	Other Taxable Income	
7	Nontaxable Income	
8	Adjustments to Income	
9	Federal Income Tax Paid	
10a	Market Value of Family Residence*	
10b	Mortgage Balance of Family Residence*	
11a	Market Value of Other Real Estate	
11b	Mortgage Balance of Other Real Estate	
12a	Business Net Value (Your %)	
12b	Farm Net Value (Your %) *	
13	Parent Cash (Checking, Saving, Money Market, etc.)	
14a	Parent Investments (Qualified Retirement Plans)*	
14b	Other Parent Investments (Exclusive of Retirement Plans)	
15	Debts Other than Mortgages *	

* These values are not included for federal financial aid. Some colleges, however, ask for these values in order to make decisions in allocating their own private financial aid funds.

Help Your Clients Complete a Financial Aid Test

SECTION 3 - STUDENT DATA

	A	B	C	D	E	F	G	H	I	J
	STUDENT FIRST NAME	DATE OF BIRTH	HIGH SCHOOL GRAD- UATION YEAR	UNDERGRAD. SCHOOL PLANS	GRADUATE SCHOOL PLANS	CURRENT SCHOOL COSTS	STUDENT SAVINGS AND INVEST- MENTS	INCOME LAST YEAR FROM WORK	INCOME LAST YEAR FROM SAVINGS & INVEST- MENTS	INCOME TAXES PAID LAST YEAR
SAMPLE		4/7/80	1990	4 YRS-HIGH	2 YRS-MED	NONE	$7,500	$1,500	$500	$150
1										
2										
3										
4										
5										
6										
7										
8										

SECTION 4 - DESIGN DATA

1. Do any of your children have special skills or qualifications that may impact college funding, such as athletic skills, high SAT scores or grades, leadership skills, etc.?

2. Please list any special scholarships or grants for which your student has or will apply.

3. Are there any obligations to provide college funds to children from previous marriages?

4. Will any student receive funds for college as part of a divorce or separation agreement from a previous marriage?

5. How much of your present monthly income could you currently use to pay or save for college?

6. How much of parent cash and investments are allocated for college use?

7. Do any of your students have any trust funds or other college resources not included above?

Processing the Data Through Our Software Is Easy

Chart 10 is a sample of the output produced by our trial financial aid software. (In analyzing the input data, the software reorganizes some sections of Chart 9 to produce a slightly modified data form that is shown as Chart 10.) Please remember there are other ways to complete a trial financial aid test. Appendix 1 lists several web sites where trial financial aid software is available for purchase. Appendix 2 also gives you a do-it-yourself worksheet so you can work with clients on a pen and paper basis.

Simplicity is everything because you want your clients to focus on the important matters, not the details. As you look at Chart 10 you will notice that two-thirds of the page recaps the input data. If the input data is not correct, then the output data won't be correct either. The remaining section of the chart shows the two critical numbers: the Family Expected Contribution Summary using both the Federal Methodology and the Institutional Methodology. Based upon the input numbers the clients provided, these figures represent an estimated financial aid picture for the clients if they had submitted an actual financial aid form to the various processing bureaus.

Now we need to compare these numbers to the typical costs of the colleges that our clients are going to review. If those college costs are higher than the expected contribution, then our clients are likely to qualify for need-based financial aid. If the costs are lower than the expected contribution, then they will not qualify for need-based financial aid.

Different colleges use different formulas but almost every college in the country requires the FAFSA form. Completing this form gives the clients a calculation based upon the Federal Methodology. For most state colleges and some private schools that is all that is required. The Federal Methodology is the king. Other colleges that require more extensive diagnostics request the Profile Form issued by the College Scholarship Service which yields results under the Institutional Methodology. Since we are in the early stages of the planning process, we may not know exactly where the clients' student will choose to go to college. We can get some idea by running them through both of these formulas.

Chart 10

Trial Financial Aid Form Analysis (Ver. 98a)

Prepared for:	Mr. & Mrs. Sample
And Student:	Jane

Prepared by:	Raymond D. Loewe, CLU, ChFC	609-596-4702
	College Money	
	112-B Centre Boulevard	
	Marlton, NJ 08053	

INPUT DATA VERIFICATION SUMMARY AS OF:	26-Aug-97
1	Age of older parent	59
2	Number of parents in family	2
3	No. of dependent children in the family	1
4	Number of children in college now	1
5	Father's wages	$48,000
6	Mother's wages	$12,000
7	Other taxable income	$2,600
8	Non taxable income	$0
9	Adjustments to income	$3,000
10	Federal income tax paid	$15,000
11	Net home equity (not used in calculation)	$200,000
12	Net equity of other real estate	$0
13	Business net value (your share)	$0
14	Parent cash	$130,000
15	Parent investments (non retirement)	$0
16	Student assets	$700
17	Student income	
	a From work	$100
	b From investments	$5
18	Student income tax paid	$0
	State code	NY

FAMILY EXPECTED CONTRIBUTION SUMMARY:	Federal	Institutional
Parent Contribution Per Student	$7,152	$15,053
Student Contribution	$245	$1,145
FAMILY CONTRIBUTION THIS STUDENT:	$7,397	$16,198

This analysis provides estimated financial aid data for planning purposes only. Actual financial aid awards are determined by each college at the time of admission.

(Calculations are based on the 1997-1998 Federal Methodology and the 1997-1998 Institutional Methodology using *College Money* software, copyright 1985-1997, All Rights Reserved. *College Money* is a registered trademark of Educational Planning Systems, Inc.)

Interpreting the Results—The College Planning Flow Charts

Once the clients know their Expected Family Contribution, they will fit into one of three categories for need-based financial aid. Depending upon which category they are in, they will need to plan differently.

1. Some financial aid all of the time;

2. Some financial aid some of the time; or

3. No financial aid at any time.

A candidate who will qualify for some need-based financial aid all of the time is someone whose Expected Family Contribution will be less than $10,000. The reason for choosing this figure is that there are very few colleges that cost less than $10,000 once all the costs are totaled. If a client is in this category, he will probably receive some financial aid at almost any school the student attends.

A candidate who does not qualify for any need-based financial aid at any time is one whose Expected Family Contribution is more than $33,000. Many families with a combination of high incomes and high assets will have Expected Family Contributions greater than this amount. Experience has shown that a family who has this level of EFC isn't likely to be able to use many strategies to lower their Expected Family Contribution. Since this family will pay the entire college bill, need-based financial aid factors become unimportant. Other types of financial aid and other financial planning options become more significant.

If your client is not a candidate to receive need-based financial aid all of the time, and is not a candidate to never receive financial aid at any time, then there is a middle category—a candidate who will receive some need-based financial aid some of the time. A student in this middle category can act like a financial aid candidate or an unlikely financial aid candidate depending upon certain decisions he makes.

For example, if we have clients with a $13,000 EFC and they decide to send their student to a $12,000 state university, then they are not financial aid candidates. On the other hand, for $1,000 more, paying their Expected Family Contribution, they could qualify for need-based financial aid at an expensive college should their student have the qualifications to be accepted. Under these circumstances, the family would complete their planning in the same manner as might a likely candidate. This is an extremely important point that many parents don't realize. Most parents fit into this middle category and by making choices they may have the opportunity to send their student to a more expensive college for just a little more money. Depending upon the qualifications, the needs of the student and the feelings of the family, this may be a significant planning opportunity.

Chart 11 shows what must be done in each of the three planning categories. Please note that this chapter simply gives an overview of the kind of planning that needs to be accomplished. More detail will be forthcoming in later chapters.

Chart 11

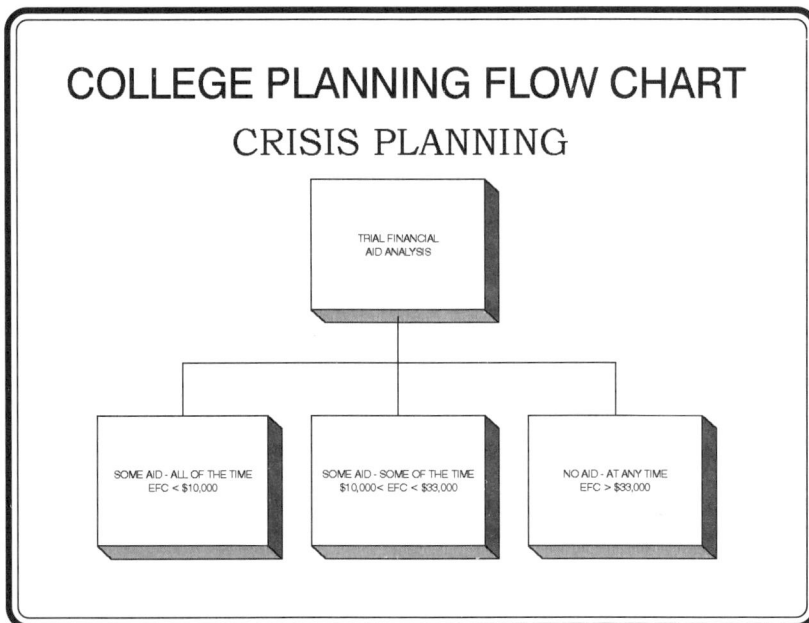

Planning for the Candidate Who Will Receive Some Aid All of the Time

The Probable Financial Aid Candidate

Chart 12

COLLEGE PLANNING FLOW CHART

SOME AID - ALL OF THE TIME

SOME AID
ALL OF THE TIME
EFC < $10,000

COLLEGE
SELECTION

FINANCIAL
AID
PLANNING

CASH FLOW
PLANNING

CAREFUL
FAFSA
COMPLETION

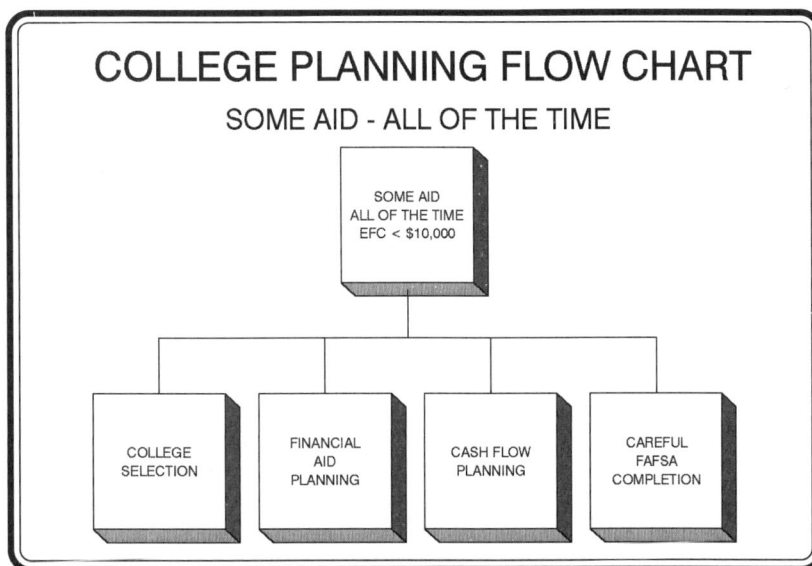

College Selection is first on the list of planning strategies for two reasons.

1. Since this family will probably receive all of the financial aid they need, as long as they pay their Expected Family Contribution, they can afford to look at more expensive colleges.

2. This family must make sure that the college they choose has the need-based money to give! If the college doesn't have enough money, then we have the College Financial Aid Gap to deal with as we discussed earlier.

The next item on the list of planning considerations is Financial Aid Planning. Financial Aid Planning tries to reduce the Expected Family Contribution as much as possible by using certain approved techniques. Obviously, if we can reduce the family's EFC from $6,500 to $5,000, then the family will pay out $1,500 less each year they have a student in college. This can do wonders for taking the financial pressure off the family both now and in the future. We will talk more about these techniques later in the book.

Once the Expected Family Contribution has been reduced to its lowest possible figure, the family must plan how they are going to come up with the balance. Cash Flow Planning for a candidate who will receive some financial aid all of the time is largely a borrowing problem. Should a non-working spouse return to work? Can the family save some money in the short period of time before college? Do they have to borrow on their home? Can they alter their lifestyle to save some more money? This is an area of planning that demands care because certain actions may have a circular effect on financial aid. The non-working spouse adds to cash flow, but that increases income thus increasing the Expected Family Contribution and reduces the amount of financial aid the following year.

Finally, since borrowing is probably going to figure in most plans, it's important to assure the client that monthly payments are reasonable, that debt is cleared prior to retirement and that there is adequate life and disability coverage to protect those loans. We don't want to lose some of the family's most valuable assets due to an unavoidable disaster.

The financial aid form is the family's chance to present itself in the best light to the financial aid system. Careful completion of the FAFSA (Free Application for Federal Student Aid) and the Profile Form is imperative!

Planning for the Candidate Who Will Never Receive Any Aid

The Unlikely Financial Aid Candidate

Chart 13

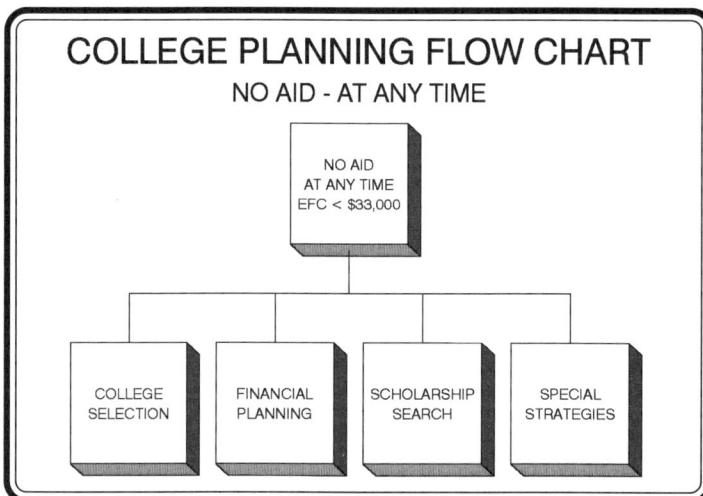

Now let's look at the opposite end of the financial aid spectrum. The family that is unlikely to receive need-based financial aid does many of the same things as the candidate who is likely to receive financial aid, but from an entirely different perspective.

College Selection will be critical to this family also. However, the family isn't looking for colleges with need-based financial aid money since they aren't going to obtain any need-based financial aid. What they are looking for are cost-effective colleges. Not only are they looking for low-cost schools but also for special programs such as co-op arrangements where the student works half of the year and goes to school the other half.

Another cost-saving option is an accelerated degree program. Since this family is footing the whole bill, college selection based upon value is extremely important. Keep in mind the other types of financial aid: merit-based aid, negotiated financial aid and discounted tuition; these options are a real consideration for this student.

Financial Planning is the next step for the candidate unlikely to receive financial aid. Not only do the parents have to find the dollars to pay the bills, but they must avoid creating a retirement problem. Many parents in this situation will borrow on their home and also use some of their retirement plan money to fund the college education. After the last child graduates, the parents are saddled with the loans, little or no money remaining in their retirement plan and only a few years left to recoup those moneys. Traditional financial planning, which integrates college planning with retirement planning and estate planning, is a logical step in the plan.

The third step in preparing for the college bills is what we call the non-need-based financial aid search or the Scholarship Search. There are numerous scholarships available that don't examine the family's ability to pay. Instead, they are based on unique characteristics and/or competitive strengths. Families using this category need to be aggressive in going after this money. This approach is not necessarily an appropriate strategy for a candidate likely to obtain aid or for someone who will possibly receive some aid. Often the financial aid officer will still expect the family to meet their Expected Family Contribution and use the non-need scholarship money to reduce the financial aid package they put together.

⚷ Non-need-based financial aid often involves contests, essays, etc. Prepare your clients to work if they want this money.

The fourth option for families who are unlikely to receive need-based financial aid is called Special Strategies. Special Strategies look for unique family circumstances that allow a family to move from the "Unlikely" aid category to the "Probable" aid category—at least for some years. One of these approaches is the ability to control incomes and assets as we discussed earlier. Other options are trusts, hiring your student or purchasing a campus residence for the student, all of which should be explored. In some situations involving divorce, whichever spouse applies for aid can make a difference.

Planning for the Candidate Who Will Receive Some Aid Some of the Time

The Possible Financial Aid Candidate

The last classification is for the family that may possibly receive financial aid. These families have choices to make and, depending upon their decisions, they may or may not receive need-based financial aid.

Suppose a family has an Expected Family Contribution of $15,000 so they opt to look at lower priced colleges. If they choose a $12,000 college, they won't qualify for any need-based financial aid. They will have to pay the whole college bill and, consequently, will have to do the things that an unlikely financial aid candidate must do.

If, on the other hand, the family chooses a more expensive college, they will qualify for financial aid. They must then do what the probable financial aid candidate is doing and try to lower the Expected Family Contribution as much as possible while searching for colleges with lots of need-based money.

Conclusions

Helping your clients complete a financial aid test gives them the critical information they need to help them plan. Without knowing their EFC, your clients might:

♦ Hold out for the wrong type of financial aid.

♦ Choose the wrong types of colleges.

♦ Choose the wrong planning strategy.

Helping your clients complete a financial aid test can help you:

♦ Build stronger relationships with your clients by positioning them to solve what might be the most expensive problem they face in life.

♦ Attract and screen new potential clients. The financial aid questionnaire gives you some great qualifying information.

Chapter 2 and Chapter 3 gave us the basic concepts we need to help our clients plan. The remaining chapters of this book will provide us with additional details and specific strategies to help our clients pay for college without ruining their retirement.

4

Help Your Clients Construct a College Budget Based Upon the Adequacy of Their Retirement Plans

If your clients have a good retirement plan, they can afford to make college commitments on behalf of their students. If their retirement plans aren't so good, they need to be concerned about taking on college loans and repaying them between the end of college and the start of retirement. That is normally the time period when people save substantially for their own retirement and repaying college loans reduces their ability to do that. Remember, college is a retirement problem and linking your clients' ability to retire with their college budget is critical.

If you are looking for a method to develop a precise college budget figure, you're not going to find it in this chapter. You can, however, help your clients comprehend the magnitude of the college budget by showing them the effectiveness of their own retirement plans and helping them understand the emotional pressures that college will put upon them.

In this chapter we will talk about retirement planning. The purpose is not to show you how to design a retirement plan for your clients; that's far beyond the scope of this book. Yet, we will show you how to communicate to your clients the strengths and weaknesses of their retirement plans so they can develop a college budget.

The College Process Involves Highly Emotional Decisions

From a parent's point of view, college is an emotional issue. Consider this scenario.

> Parents encourage their students to work hard for good grades. This approach usually starts when the students begin their freshman year of high school and continues through their senior year. The reason parents think this way is because they want their students to be accepted at a good college and they're afraid the kids might not make it. Before the parents know it, the beginning of the senior year rolls around and they suddenly realize that all of that encouragement has paid off. Their student has actually earned good grades. They have taken either the SAT or the ACT and they've achieved some good scores. Now they're looking at quality colleges and they are likely to be accepted at some of those schools. The college choices being considered are expensive and worth it.

Now here is the dilemma. Parents are under extreme pressure to pay, perhaps more than they should, because they are proud of their kids and they feel good about the situation. This is a positive expenditure of money, not a negative one. As a financial professional, you can ease this crisis by simply asking your clients to sit down and analyze the situation before college. In doing so, they can get a handle on what they can realistically afford to pay.

By the way, it is not enough to simply help your client develop a budget. We believe it is important for clients to discuss money matters with their students as soon as possible. In many families, however, this topic is not discussed. Children don't understand the value of a dollar and they don't understand that their parents are going to retire. Their concern seems simply to be able to get into the college of their choice and not be too worried with how mom and dad are going to pay the bill.

Clients Often Ignore Their Own Retirement for Their Children's Education

Believe it or not, clients sometimes don't want to spend their children's money for college even when they are having cash flow problems. Many parents are reluctant to let their children take on student loans.

We recently had a couple ask us to help them with their college plan. This client had one student in college and another in a private high school. They were experiencing significant cash flow problems even with a substantial income and substantial dollars in their students' accounts. For some reason, they were trying to hold onto the children's money so they could give them the cash as a graduation present. Even though this money was set aside for education, there was a barrier to spending it.

Another couple was also slow to let their students take on student loans. They didn't want to saddle their children with large loans as they started life after college. Even after posing the question, "Who's better off with college loans, your student with a long time to retirement, or you with retirement right around the corner?", they still showed reluctance. Until clients truly understand the retirement dilemma, they may hang on to these philosophies.

Both of these situations are typical of parent sacrifices for their children and both of them are wonderful, providing that parents can afford them. Most parents, however, are making these decisions without thinking through their own retirement plans. When we show parents how their own retirement plans stack up, they often change their tune about the children's money and student loans.

Building a Bridge From College Planning to the Retirement Problem

In Chapter 2 we presented Concept One which states that college is a retirement problem.

In Chapter 3 we talked about the Expected Family Contribution, the EFC, and how colleges use this number to measure what your clients can afford to pay for college prior to the college and the government doling out need-based financial aid. Most clients find the EFC number extremely high. Clients tend to think of the dollars as coming out of their current cash flow and savings. Colleges, on the other hand, think in terms of cash flow, savings and a parent's ability to borrow money. Therefore, the budget number that you help your client come up with is often far different and somewhat less than the EFC calculated by the college.

If you have communicated Concept 1 effectively, your client will understand that college is a retirement problem. This gives you as a professional the opportunity to present some retirement planning ideas immediately. If you haven't clearly communicated the concept to your client, then your client isn't going to focus on retirement because he is thinking about college as a college problem. It's critical to build this bridge between college and retirement before you actively approach your client to start work on this step of the college process. To do this you need to show parents where they stand.

♦ What they will need to live on when they start their retirement.

♦ How that amount will grow due to inflation and how it will become quite large as they approach their life expectancy.

♦ That their life expectancy may be longer than they think and how they don't want to grow old and be without money.

♦ Why they don't want to be dependent upon their children.

♦ How money given to young adults is usually squandered.

♦ That an inheritance could help their children retire or their grandchildren pay for college.

Understanding the College-Retirement Link Makes College Decision Making Easier

Once parents truly understand the college-retirement problem, it is easier for them to make the hard decisions and to balance spending between college and retirement. Here are some of the decisions that must be confronted.

1. College should not be covered with a blank check. Parents need to establish a college budget.

2. How much of a student's debt should the parents let a student incur?

3.   How much of and when should the student's assets be liquidated?

4.   What kind of student-parent cost sharing arrangement should be made?

5.   Which is the best way to communicate the plan to the student?

Other Reasons to Do Retirement Planning...Now!

Unfortunately, there are only four ways to acquire more retirement money.

1.   Save more.

2.   Have someone else save for you.

3.   Manage your retirement money better.

4.   Inherit lots of money.

Clients only have control over two of these four items: 1) Save more; and 3) Manage their retirement money better. How much your clients save during the college years will affect their retirement. Often clients cut back on saving due to college cash flow pressures.

How much other people save on your clients' behalf usually stems from employer contributions to a plan. Usually the clients don't control this. An exception is the employer's contribution to a 401(k) plan. If the client decreases his contribution to the plan during college, he may also be decreasing the employer's matching contribution. You owe it to your clients to make them focus on better money management. This is an area that can pay big rewards and won't affect the college cash flow situation. Most clients don't manage IRA, 401(k) or 403(b) money very well. A small increase in return or decrease in risk can increase retirement funds significantly. Focusing on the clients' money management problem can improve their retirement situation during the college years even if they are not saving more.

How We Demonstrate the College-Retirement Problem

When we sit down with clients to show them how their retirement plans stack up, we use a series of spreadsheets to illustrate their situation. Any retirement software program can be used as long as it does the following.

1. Shows annual cash needs from the date of retirement through life expectancy.

2. Demonstrates the sources of retirement dollars and shows any shortages.

3. Calculates the present value of the dollars required to fund the retirement.

4. Allows you to play a "what if" game by varying:

   ◊ Retirement dates;

   ◊ Savings amounts;

   ◊ Life expectancy; and

   ◊ The rate of return on investments—both pre and post retirement.

In this chapter, Charts 1 through 4 show a sample plan laid out for one of our clients. Chart 1 summarizes the input data the client gave us. Chart 2 takes the client's retirement income goal in today's dollars and produces an equivalent dollar figure for each year of retirement.

Chart 1

Data Input:	26-Aug-97
Last Name:	Sample
First Name (Older Spouse)	Ray
First Name (Younger Spouse)	Michelle
Birth Date: Ray	03/16/55
Birth Date: Michelle	12/26/56

Part I: How Much Money Do You Need to Fund Retirement

1	How Much Pretax Income in today's dollars will you require at retirement?	$50,000
2	At What age do you plan to retire?	65
3	Your age today: Ray	42
	Michelle	40
4	Inflation Rate	4.00%
5	Max Life Span	85
6	After tax return on investment - Postretirement	8.00%

Part II: Resources for Retirement

1	Company Retirement Benefit	Ray	@ age = 65	$0
		Michelle	@ age = 63	$0
2	Social Security	Ray	@ age = 65	$9,600
		Michelle	@ age = 63	$4,800
3	Planned Annual Savings	Nonqualified		$5,000
		Qualified		$0
4	Lump Sum Savings	Nonqualified		$0
		Qualified		$120,000
5	Preretirement After tax return	Nonqualified		9.00%
		Qualified		11.00%

Chart 2

Year	Age Ray	Age Michelle	Pre Retirement Inflation Adj Income	Retirement Income Required	Lump Sum Required to Fund	Interest	Balance
1997	42	40	$50,000	$0	$0	$0	$0
1998	43	41	$52,000	$0	$0	$0	$0
1999	44	42	$54,080	$0	$0	$0	$0
2000	45	43	$56,243	$0	$0	$0	$0
2001	46	44	$58,493	$0	$0	$0	$0
2002	47	45	$60,833	$0	$0	$0	$0
2003	48	46	$63,266	$0	$0	$0	$0
2004	49	47	$65,797	$0	$0	$0	$0
2005	50	48	$68,428	$0	$0	$0	$0
2006	51	49	$71,166	$0	$0	$0	$0
2007	52	50	$74,012	$0	$0	$0	$0
2008	53	51	$76,973	$0	$0	$0	$0
2009	54	52	$80,052	$0	$0	$0	$0
2010	55	53	$83,254	$0	$0	$0	$0
2011	56	54	$86,584	$0	$0	$0	$0
2012	57	55	$90,047	$0	$0	$0	$0
2013	58	56	$93,649	$0	$0	$0	$0
2014	59	57	$97,395	$0	$0	$0	$0
2015	60	58	$101,291	$0	$0	$0	$0
2016	61	59	$105,342	$0	$0	$0	$0
2017	62	60	$109,556	$0	$0	$0	$0
2018	63	61	$113,938	$0	$0	$0	$0
2019	64	62	$118,496	$0	$0	$0	$0
2020	65	63	$123,236	$0	$1,807,373	$0	$1,807,373*
2021	66	64	$0	$128,165	$0	$144,590	$1,823,797
2022	67	65	$0	$133,292	$0	$145,904	$1,836,409
2023	68	66	$0	$138,623	$0	$146,913	$1,844,699
2024	69	67	$0	$144,168	$0	$147,576	$1,848,106
2025	70	68	$0	$149,935	$0	$147,848	$1,846,019
2026	71	69	$0	$155,933	$0	$147,682	$1,837,768
2027	72	70	$0	$162,170	$0	$147,021	$1,822,620
2028	73	71	$0	$168,657	$0	$145,810	$1,799,773
2029	74	72	$0	$175,403	$0	$143,982	$1,768,352
2030	75	73	$0	$182,419	$0	$141,468	$1,727,401
2031	76	74	$0	$189,716	$0	$138,192	$1,675,877
2032	77	75	$0	$197,304	$0	$134,070	$1,612,643
2033	78	76	$0	$205,197	$0	$129,011	$1,536,458
2034	79	77	$0	$213,404	$0	$122,917	$1,445,970
2035	80	78	$0	$221,941	$0	$115,678	$1,339,707
2036	81	79	$0	$230,818	$0	$107,177	$1,216,065
2037	82	80	$0	$240,051	$0	$97,285	$1,073,299
2038	83	81	$0	$249,653	$0	$85,864	$909,510
2039	84	82	$0	$259,639	$0	$72,761	$722,631
2040	85	83	$0	$270,025	$0	$57,811	$510,417
2041	86	84	$0	$280,826	$0	$40,833	$270,425
2042	87	85	$0	$292,059	$0	$21,634	($0)
2043	88	86	$0	$0	$0	($0)	($0)
2044	89	87	$0	$0	$0	($0)	($0)
2045	90	88	$0	$0	$0	($0)	($0)
2046	91	89	$0	$0	$0	($0)	($0)
2047	92	90	$0	$0	$0	($0)	($0)

*$ Required

Help Your Clients Construct a College Budget

Chart 3 displays a pie chart indicating how much of the client's retirement income will come from the following sources.

♦   Social Security.

♦   A pension or profit sharing plan at work.

♦   A 401(k) or 403(b) plan.

♦   Personal savings.

Chart 3

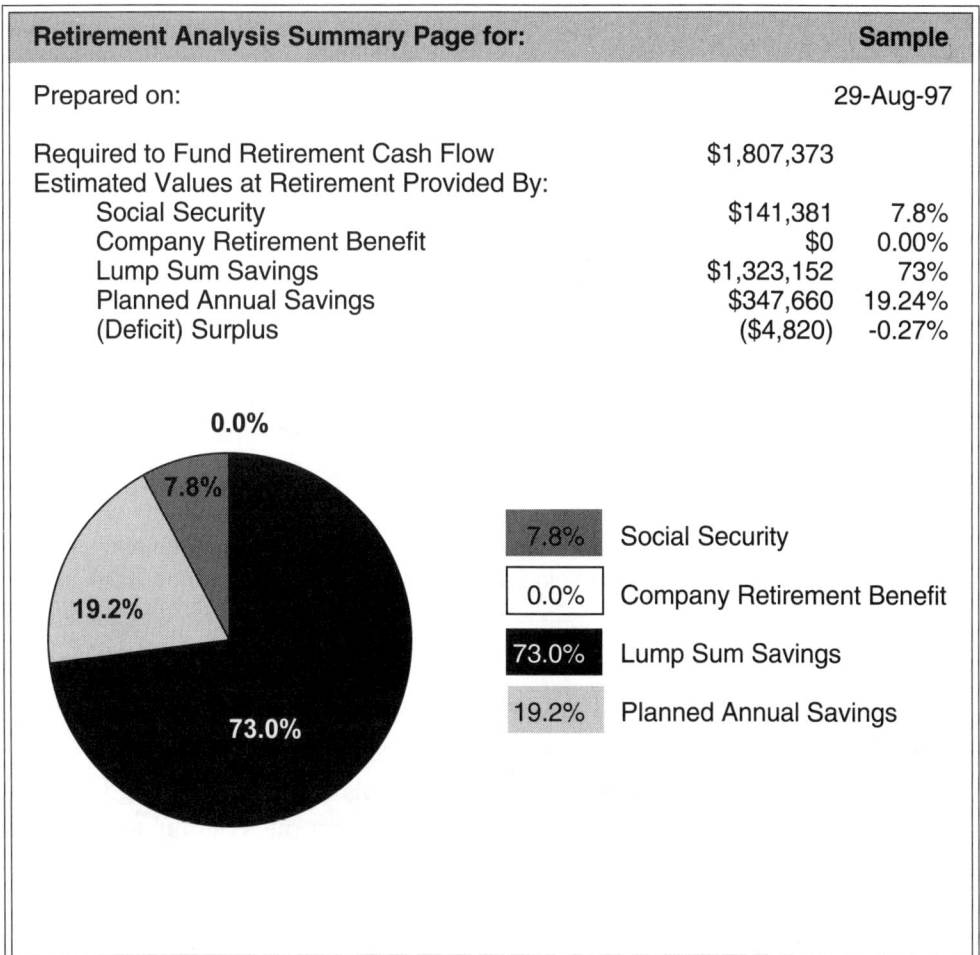

Retirement Analysis Summary Page for:		Sample
Prepared on:		29-Aug-97
Required to Fund Retirement Cash Flow	$1,807,373	
Estimated Values at Retirement Provided By:		
Social Security	$141,381	7.8%
Company Retirement Benefit	$0	0.00%
Lump Sum Savings	$1,323,152	73%
Planned Annual Savings	$347,660	19.24%
(Deficit) Surplus	($4,820)	-0.27%

0.0%
7.8%
19.2%
73.0%

7.8%	Social Security
0.0%	Company Retirement Benefit
73.0%	Lump Sum Savings
19.2%	Planned Annual Savings

The clients need to make some decisions. If they are on target for their retirement goals, or at least close, they can afford to spend more freely for college. If the deficit slice is large, as it is with most clients, the clients need to make some choices. Chart 4 shows the client his options.

1. One option, of course, is to do with less at retirement. Many clients may have to face this option later whether they plan for it now or not.

2. Another option is for the client to postpone retirement. Clients may not have this option if they work for someone else. Those who are self-employed can often defer retirement so this option is worth exploring. Simply changing the retirement age in the software enables you to run a new set of calculations.

Chart 4

Planning Options	26-Aug-97

If your retirement plan is not fully funded, there are four options available to help you:

1 Consider reduing your planned retirement benefit. Although many retirees feel they can live on less, this adjustment should be made only as a last resort.

2 Consider postponing retirement. By retiring a year later, you not only need less money, but you have a longer time period in which to accumulate more. Not all retirees have the option to postpone retirement.

3 Save more money.

4 Improve the return on investment of your existing portfolio and new monies being invested by doing a better job of managing your funds.

3. Option 3 is to look at the investment structure of existing funds to try to improve the long-term rate of return on the portfolio. Many clients don't pay enough attention to their existing retirement funds; they need to make them work harder. Changing assumed investment rates on our software can demonstrate the importance of investing properly.

4.   The final option is to add more annual savings to the retirement pot.

Saving for college and saving for retirement are somewhat mutually exclusive. You can't use the same dollars twice. At this point in the review many clients ask us to help them manage their existing retirement funds. This is something they can do to improve their retirement without diverting funds away from college. We have developed a rather large money management business because of this.

With all of this input, the clients should be able to decide on their college budget strategy. Does this mean the student must sacrifice a quality college because of his parents' budget restrictions? The answer is absolutely not.

Have Your Clients Consider a College Cost Sharing Strategy With Their Student

Here is an example of how a cost sharing arrangement can work effectively. After extensive discussions about retirement, Bob and Sue Smith clarified their thinking regarding college planning. They sat down with their son, Tim, and explained that they had budgeted $10,000 per year for his college education. The Smiths continued that if Tim went to a state college, he would graduate without any loans or financial obligations of any kind along with a very good education; mom and dad would pay the bill.

Bob and Sue went on, however, to tell their student that they did not want to force him to go to a state college. If Tim really wanted to attend a more expensive college, they would work out a cost sharing program. This program would probably include Tim taking on student loans, and trying some creative financing by applying for special scholarships or other cost reduction programs. Mom and dad would be willing to be the banker for additional funds if they were required. They explained to their son, therefore, that any additional loans would be transferred to him after college because they needed to focus on their retirement and their obligation of educating their two other children.

In this case, Tim wanted to attend a $25,000 a year school. He accomplished that by borrowing on the student loan program, and by taking on a Navy ROTC scholarship which required a commitment to the military service after graduation. Mom and dad worked out a way to pay the difference.

Obviously, there was a happy ending to this scenario since mom and dad were able to limit the amount of money for college and Tim was able to meet his needs by attending the school of his choice. By discussing the budget far enough in advance, Bob and Sue were able to enlist the cooperation of their son who looked at other financing avenues and school choices. As we will see in Chapter 5, the choice of the school can have a big effect on the financial options and non-need-based financial aid. Too often we have seen that when the financial aid discussion is put off for a long period of time, students develop different ideas than their parents about where they want to go to school. When parents and students can't get into sync on the choice of a school, an irreconcilable conflict develops. Students wind up with a school choice that does not make them happy and parents find themselves spending more money than anticipated.

5

Teach Your Clients and Their Students How to Select the Proper Colleges

Introduction

How to choose the proper college is a dilemma that faces many parents and students. There are two major objectives to the process.

1.   First and foremost, it is critical that students find colleges that fit them.

2.   Second, it's important that parents can afford these colleges.

Only when both of these criteria are met do you have a successful college selection process. Although many parents dwell on the affordability factor, a college that is economical, or one that awards students lots of financial aid, can be a waste of money if the college doesn't fit the student. When a college doesn' t fit a student, the student is often unhappy, doesn't perform well and drops out of school. All that free money, coupled with the not-so-free money that the parents contribute, is wasted. On the other hand, giving the student an open checkbook could make it very difficult for the parents to later retire.

Fortunately, solving this problem is not all that difficult. There are over 3,000 accredited colleges in the United States. It's important for both parents and students to realize that there is probably more than one college that fits every student and, in fact, it's probable that students can uncover 20 to 30 colleges that fit them and also fit their parents' budget.

There are a number of general factors that students and parents must look at during the college selection process. It's not just the education that makes a college a good value; obviously, students need to learn. However, college is also a growing up process. It's a place where students can develop lifelong friendships which often blossom into business contacts that will be worth substantial dollars later in life. College is likewise a place where special talents can be developed, either on the athletic field or in the arts arena. All of these factors should be considered when picking a college that fits.

As a professional, your job is not to be an expert in the college selection process. There are many college consultants that can offer your clients this kind of in-depth help. There is a process, however, that you must understand and, if you convey it properly to your clients, it will help them get through the college selection process successfully on their own.

It is important to note that the college selection process can cause a great deal of stress in the family. Often parents have difficulty convincing students to seriously look at the college selection process. The primary reason for this is that students often feel their selection of a college and a career are permanent and irrevocable. They don't feel comfortable making that decision in their sophomore or junior year of high school. Students must understand that the decisions they make are not final and there is room for change. By starting the college selection process early, the students will be prepared to make better decisions.

Many times parents and students do not work hard enough during the college selection process. As a financial planning professional, you should emphasize to them that college is expensive. Students will be investing four years of their lives and parents could be spending well over $100,000. Stressing this large investment in time and dollars should help parents and students be more willing to spend the time, effort and dollars now to do it correctly. The process outlined in this chapter will help considerably, but there are several cautions.

♦ First, don't try to narrow the list of colleges too fast. Take the time to review it thoroughly.

♦ Second, apply to at least 10 to 12 colleges. Frequently educators and guidance counselors want students to apply to substantially fewer schools than this. One of the reasons is that it takes time and effort on the part of the guidance department to meet the application requirements of each college. Yet, if we are going to help our clients negotiate a successful college financial aid package, we need to have acceptances at enough schools to give us a chance. You can't negotiate a financial aid package if a student is accepted at only one school.

Start the College Selection Process Early

Students who aren't coached through the college selection process correctly often wait until the last minute at which time they choose a college their friends plan to attend. When parents try to help them broaden or change their decisions, they quickly become interfering parents. We have found that students who start the process early become leaders, take a broader look at the college planning process and tend to choose colleges on a more rational basis.

General Early Planning

Tremendous headway in the college selection process can be made if parents and students start to plan early, no later than the late sophomore or early junior year. Obviously, at this time it's too soon to make final decisions. Students still may not know what majors they want and the remaining years of high school will give them considerable input to help change their decisions. There are some things, however, that parents can do to cut short this process.

First is early career planning or, perhaps a better word, lifestyle planning.

"Quick! What do you want to do with your life? You have fifteen minutes to decide. Not enough time, you say. You're right, of course." Yet, this is often what we expect from students regarding their choice of a college and a major.

Mindy Bingham, in her book entitled *Career Choices – A Guide for Teens and Young Adults,* takes parents and students through a process of thinking ahead about the kind of lifestyle the students may want to live. Key questions the students need to ask themselves include:

- Who am I?

- What do I want?

- How do I get it?

This may involve parent-student discussions on real world lifestyle issues such as:

- The type of house the student wants to live in.

- The type of car the student would like to drive.

- The types of vacations the student may wish to take.

The answers to these questions can be related to the amount of income the students will need in order to support their lifestyle desires. Further discussions can help highlight the kinds of jobs that will create the necessary income. Most students have no concept as to the value of money. They don't know what it takes to buy things. They don't know what people in different professions earn. The sophomore year is a great time for parents to pick up a book like this and talk with students about the type of life they would like to have when they grow up. This will make career planning substantially easier as well as the college planning decisions.

Next, as a financial professional, you should encourage your clients to take their students to visit colleges—even as early as their sophomore year. The purpose is not to pick colleges but to get a feeling about the student's likes and dislikes. This will make it easier later on when decisions must be made. We strongly suggest a summer trip to several types of college campuses. Make sure you include a large college campus, a small college campus, a rural campus, a big city campus and a suburban campus. The goal is to simply walk on campus and look around. This experience will give the students and parents a picture of college life at that type of college. Students can gain a general feeling of where they might fit and where they might not fit.

One of our clients recently visited a college with their daughter. The daughter took one look at the campus and refused to get out of the car stating, "There's no way I'm coming here." This type of visit can give parents and students substantial input in the college selection process about what they like and what they don't like about a specific college campus. College size and college location are often major selection criteria in the decision-making process. Students who have never seen a college campus can't apply any knowledge or experience to that process. Students who have done some prowling on a college campus early in the selection process will have some feelings that will make the decision process easier.

Preparing the Student Resume

Preparing a student resume may seem like a strange activity to go through. After all, the students aren't applying for jobs, or are they? Applying for college is much like applying for a job. Students are going to be asked to explain their strengths, their likes and dislikes and what they hope to achieve. By putting together a resume early on we can help the students mold and record their feelings about what they want.

Figure 5.1 is a sample of a student resume. It is general rather than specific but it does contain a goal of what the student hopes to achieve from the college experience. Preparing a resume will help students make better college choices, complete applications, score better on college interviews and maybe help them receive scholarships. This resume will change several times during the college planning process.

Figure 5.1

Jason T. Smith
123 Main Street
Anytown, USA

Goal: To achieve a Bachelor of Science Degree in Engineering, Chemistry or Physics in May 2002.

Academic Credentials: SAT   Math   690
                           SAT   Verbal   670

                           GPA   3.6/4.0

Athletics: Captain Varsity Swim Team - Anytown High School

           Times: 100 Yard Breaststroke   1:06.7
                      100 Yard Freestyle   0:47.0

Other Activities:

           Student Counsel Vice President
           National Honor Society

Community Activities:

           Anytown Church Fellowship Counsel
           Anytown Homeless Awareness Program

The Computerized Search

Early in the student's junior year it's time to seriously reduce the number of colleges from 3,000 to a manageable number on the student's list. However, it's also important not to cut the list too much too early in the process. The computer and college selection software can help pare the student list quickly. The purpose of using the computer to select colleges is not to have the computer choose those colleges that we will attend, but to choose those colleges that we ought to take a better in-depth look at because they seem to meet our criteria. Helpful college selection materials are listed in Appendix 1. The examples that follow in this chapter use the *Applied Technology* software produced by Princeton Review.

Let's get specific about how we take a student through the college selection process. First remember that there are over 3,000 accredited colleges in the United States. A list of 3,000 contains far too many colleges to read about or even

Figure 5.2

Typical College Selection Criteria	
College Size	1. Very Small (under 1,000) 2. Small (1,000 to 2,000) 3. Medium (2,000 to 5,000) 4. Large (5,000 to 10,000) 5. Very Large (over 10,000)
Environment	**1. Rural** **2. Small Town** **3. Suburb** **4. City** **5. Large Metropolis**
Entrance Difficulty	**1. SAT — Verbal** **2. SAT — Math**
Majors	
Sports	
Activities	
Location by State/Region	
Student Mix	
Cost	
Need-Based Financial Aid	
Scholarships	
Religious Affiliation	
Disability	

attempt to screen. The goal is to have the students develop a list of between 50 and 100 colleges that seem to meet their general needs. This list is large for a purpose. Fifty to 100 schools is ample enough for the human selection process to occur yet small enough to enable us to probe the reference books and scan the Internet for more data. Again, the computer will not make the decisions for us but will simply help us screen the colleges.

Please note that during our initial screening we do not use cost or financial aid as selection criteria. The purpose of developing a list of 50 to 100 colleges is based strictly on the student's wants and needs. Later, we'll apply the financial criteria to help us pare our list to a substantially smaller number of colleges.

Figure 5.2 lists some of the major criteria that students can use to search through the college list.

If students do a good job of visiting colleges during their sophomore year, your clients will find it easy to decide on at least two criteria: environment and size. Decisions on these elements alone will significantly cut our list. For example, suppose our student doesn't want to attend a very small college, but any other size college is acceptable. This decision alone cuts our list from 3,000 colleges to 473.

Figure 5.3

Selection Criteria:
Eliminate colleges with less than 1,000 students.
Number of colleges remaining: 473

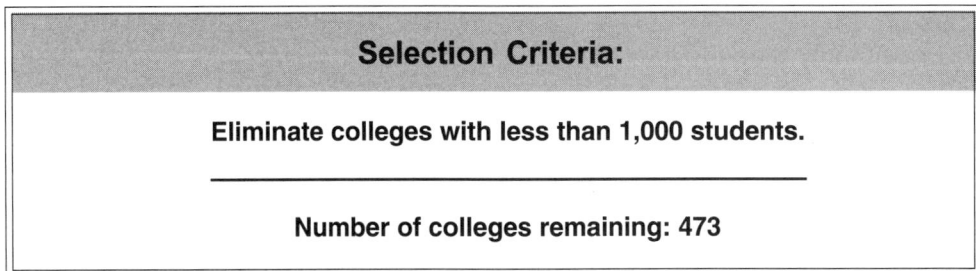

By adding some criteria on environment, we can pare the list even further. Suppose our student indicated that he doesn't want to attend a college which is located in a rural area or a small town, but a college campus in or near a city would be acceptable. By making that decision we've reduced our list of schools from 473 to 358.

Figure 5.4

Selection Criteria:

**Eliminate colleges with less than 1,000 students
and eliminate rural and small town schools.**

Number of colleges remaining: 358

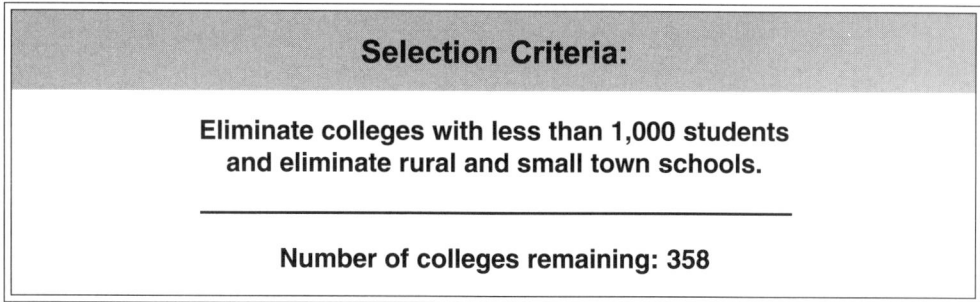

Assume our student is a competitive swimmer and it's very important that the chosen school has a swimming team. Adding the swim team requirement reduces our list to 142 colleges.

Figure 5.5

Selection Criteria:

**Eliminate colleges with less than 1,000 students
and eliminate rural and small town schools.**

Require Men's Swimming Team.

Number of colleges remaining: 142

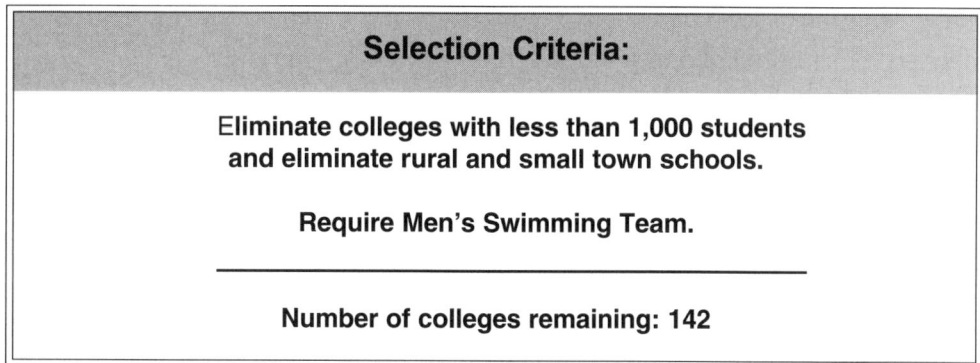

Our student is also very smart and wants to be academically challenged at college so the family decides to choose from only those colleges that have average Math and Verbal SAT scores of 500 and higher. By applying these criteria to our database we further lower the number of colleges to investigate to 100.

Figure 5.6

Selection Criteria:
Eliminate colleges with less than 1,000 students and eliminate rural and small town schools. **Require Men's Swimming Team. and require Math SATs > 500 and Verbal SATs > 500.** --- **Number of colleges remaining: 100**

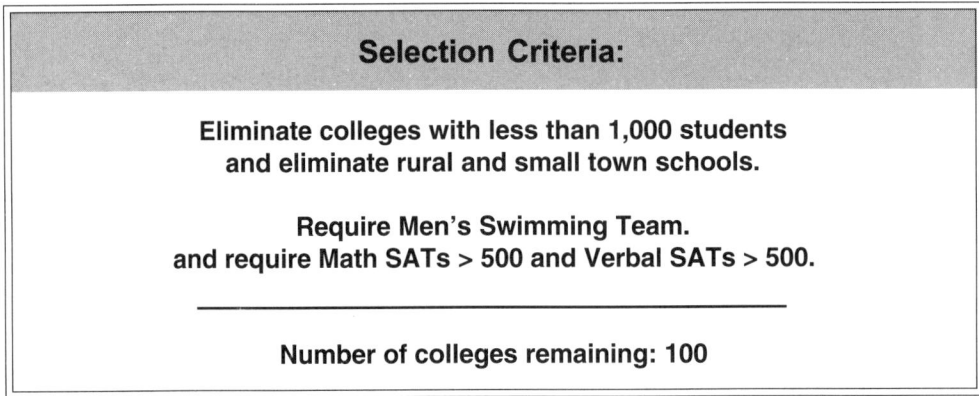

Now let's look at location. Suppose our clients and their student decide to limit their college selection to schools in the New England and mid-Atlantic areas. They specifically confine their search to the states of Delaware, Maryland, New Jersey, Pennsylvania, New York, Washington, DC, Maine, Massachusetts, Rhode Island, Vermont, New Hampshire, Connecticut and Virginia. By eliminating the other states based on geographic preferences, we now have a reduced database containing 66 colleges.

Figure 5.7

Selection Criteria:
Eliminate colleges with less than 1,000 students and eliminate rural and small town schools. **Require Men's Swimming Team. and require Math SATs > 500 and Verbal SATs > 500 and require New England and mid-Atlantic states.** --- **Number of colleges remaining: 66**

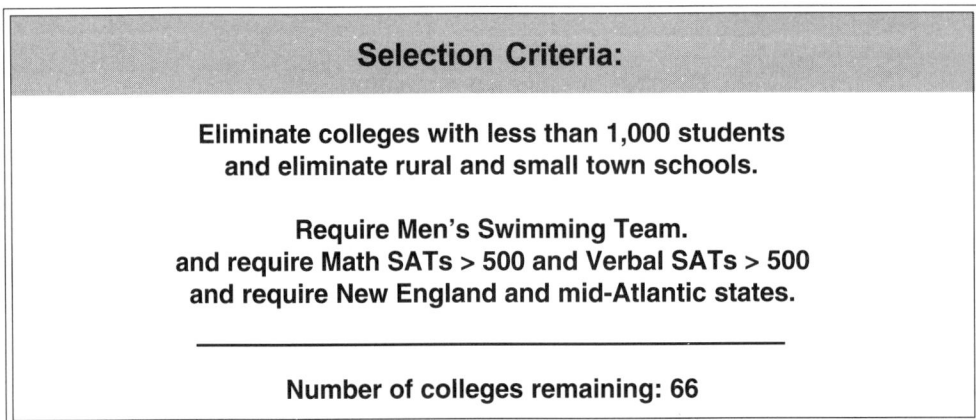

Since this selection procedure yields approximately the right number of colleges, we can stop our screening process. We now have a manageable list on which we will leave room for the financial requirements and other types of research. If we think the list is too small, we may want to review our criteria and broaden our search to retain more schools.

It's now time to print our list of colleges and review it. Since we don't want the computer making decisions for us, this is the opportunity to return any previously eliminated schools to the list. Many students hear of schools that they want to investigate and parents may have preferences. Sometimes we apply selection criteria that we wish to override. It is entirely permissible to restore these schools to our list.

Figure 5.8

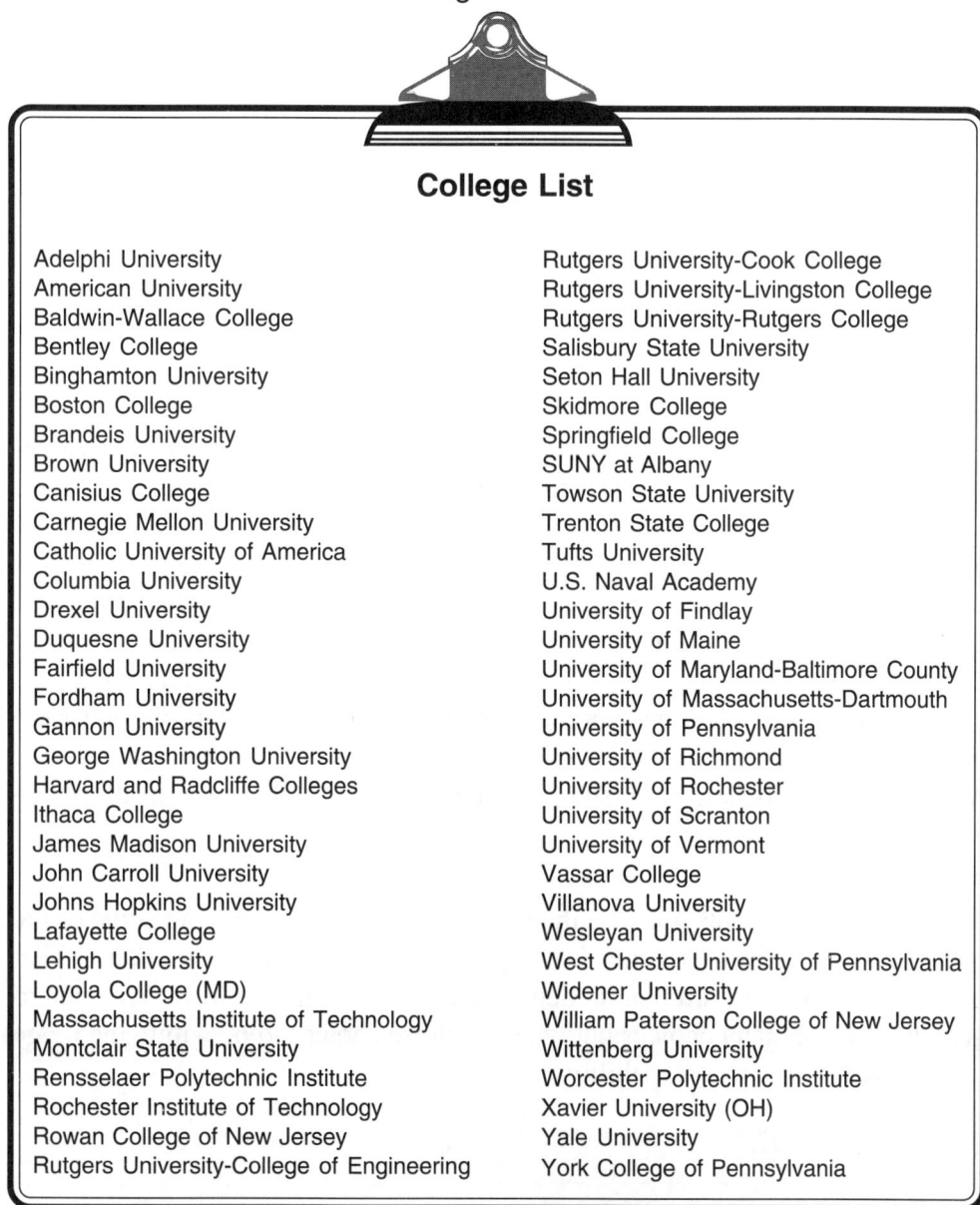

College List

Adelphi University	Rutgers University-Cook College
American University	Rutgers University-Livingston College
Baldwin-Wallace College	Rutgers University-Rutgers College
Bentley College	Salisbury State University
Binghamton University	Seton Hall University
Boston College	Skidmore College
Brandeis University	Springfield College
Brown University	SUNY at Albany
Canisius College	Towson State University
Carnegie Mellon University	Trenton State College
Catholic University of America	Tufts University
Columbia University	U.S. Naval Academy
Drexel University	University of Findlay
Duquesne University	University of Maine
Fairfield University	University of Maryland-Baltimore County
Fordham University	University of Massachusetts-Dartmouth
Gannon University	University of Pennsylvania
George Washington University	University of Richmond
Harvard and Radcliffe Colleges	University of Rochester
Ithaca College	University of Scranton
James Madison University	University of Vermont
John Carroll University	Vassar College
Johns Hopkins University	Villanova University
Lafayette College	Wesleyan University
Lehigh University	West Chester University of Pennsylvania
Loyola College (MD)	Widener University
Massachusetts Institute of Technology	William Paterson College of New Jersey
Montclair State University	Wittenberg University
Rensselaer Polytechnic Institute	Worcester Polytechnic Institute
Rochester Institute of Technology	Xavier University (OH)
Rowan College of New Jersey	Yale University
Rutgers University-College of Engineering	York College of Pennsylvania

The computer selection process is easy and takes very little time. We often have the students prepare several lists until they decide upon one that's satisfactory. Once the list is set, however, we will edit the list by adding financial criteria to the equation.

Screening the List Using Financial Criteria

The time has come to get mom and dad involved in the screening process from a financial point of view. From previous chapters we know a few things about the financial constraints that mom and dad need to put on the college process. In Chapter 3 we completed a financial aid test and we know the kind of financial aid that suits them. Next, in Chapter 4, we explored the college budget with our client. If our client is going to qualify for need-based financial aid then we want to screen the list of colleges to see which ones have the ability to meet our financial needs through need-based aid dollars. If, on the other hand, need-based financial aid is not in the cards, we then need to look at merit-based and other types of financial aid or at lower cost colleges.

Figure 5.9 is a spreadsheet listing the colleges defined from our computer search. We now need to add the financial data by searching through the available reference books. The data in Figure 5.9 was obtained from the *College Money Handbook* published by Peterson's Guides. We simply looked up each college on our list and catalogued the college's comprehensive cost, the college's ability to provide need-based financial aid and the college's ability to offer other kinds of financial aid. If merit-based financial aid or other types of non-need based aid are desired, a call to the college might be in order to acquire more specific data. Parents need to satisfy themselves that the college list price is within their range or that the type of financial aid they are pursuing is likely to reduce their costs to an affordable level.

At this point, our clients may use their parental discretion to cut out some of the colleges because, from a financial standpoint, they don't meet their criteria. That is the reason we don't limit our college search at the computer level. We want to give the student many choices but we want those choices to be within the range of the parents' financial capability.

Figure 5.9

Partial List of Colleges With Financial Criteria

Expected Contribution $18,500
Family Annual College Budget $12,000

College	Budget Bill	% Need Met	% Self-Help	% Gift Aid	Non-Need Aid
Adelphi University	$20,520	100%	44%	56%	Y
American University	$23,137	N/A	44%	56%	Y
Baldwin-Wallace College	$18,156	98%	46%	54%	Y
Bentley College	$23,305	77%	42%	58%	Y
Binghamton University	N/A				
Boston College	$23,075	82%	65%	35%	Y
Brandeis University	$29,821	N/A	N/A	N/A	Y
Brown University	$29,900	100%	36%	64%	Not offered
Canisius College	$18,751	N/A	N/A	N/A	Y
Carnegie Mellon University	$25,580	100%	35%	65%	Y
Catholic University of America	$24,916	90%	51%	49%	Y
Columbia University	$28,698	100%	26%	74%	Not Offered
Drexel University	$21,381	N/A	N/A	N/A	Y
Duquesne University	$19,199	80%	46%	54%	Y
Fairfield University	$25,334	84%	33%	67%	Y
Fordham University	$23,125	79%	27%	73%	Y
Gannon University	$16,404	80%	42%	58%	Y
George Washington University	$27,250	90%	33%	67%	Y
Harvard and Radcliffe Colleges	$30,080	100%	32%	68%	Not Offered
Ithaca College	$24,240	80%	33%	67%	Y
James Madison University	$13,662	70%	82%	18%	Y
John Carroll University	$19,545	87%	33%	67%	Y
Johns Hopkins University	$29,075	95%	31%	69%	Y
Lafayette College	$26,718	82%	23%	77%	Y
Lehigh University	$27,180	97%	27%	73%	Y
Loyola College	$21,990	95%	37%	63%	Y
Massachusetts Institute of Technology	$28,710	100%	37%	63%	Y
Montclair State University	$10,760	90%	58%	42%	Y
Rensselaer Polytechnic Institute	$27,386	N/A	N/A	N/A	Y
Rochester Institute of Technology	$22,776	N/A	41%	54%	Y
Rowan University	$11,259	95%	52%	48%	Y
Rutgers University - College of Engineering	$15,284	82%	42%	58%	Y
Rutgers University - Cook College	$15,288	85%	46%	54%	Y
Rutgers University - Livingston College	$14,436	76%	46%	54%	Y
Rutgers University - Rutgers College	$14,432	84%	45%	55%	Y
SUNY at Albany	$14,080	75%	59%	41%	Y

Data Source: *College Money Handbook*, Peterson's Guides

Book Research and Internet Research

The student must now do some homework; mom and dad may also want to get involved. There are many books and Internet sites (Appendix 1) from which you can accumulate information about the schools on your list. As parents and students sift through this data, they will find many things about schools that they like and some that they absolutely dislike. The dislikes tend to have a greater effect when paring the list. As they go through the list, both parents and students are free to remove any colleges and to add new ones to the list if they find schools that have a particular appeal.

Special Criteria for Athletes

When working with students and parents we frequently find students who have a sport they would like to play. In most cases, the students aren't good enough to be recruited by the major schools. Yet, they still take their sport seriously and are good enough to participate at a less competitive college level. Sports often have a significant impact on college selection. Here is a technique that we've seen used successfully.

Prepare a list of the coaches in the student's sport at the schools on the list. Write them a short letter and append the student's resume making sure the resume highlights the athletic activities. Figure 5.10 is an example.

Figure 5.10

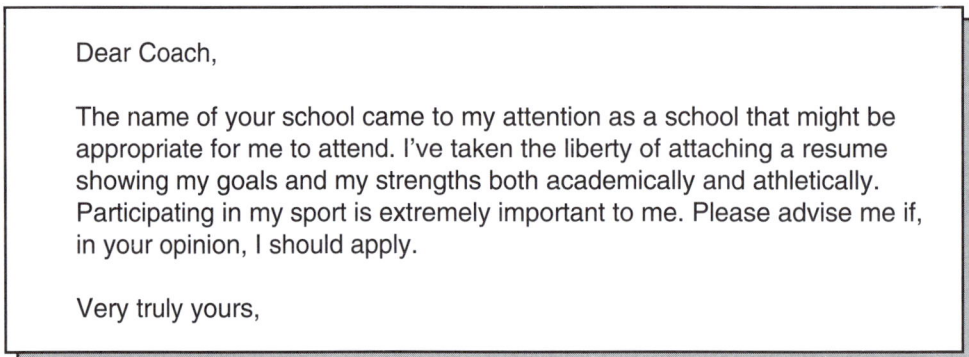

Dear Coach,

The name of your school came to my attention as a school that might be appropriate for me to attend. I've taken the liberty of attaching a resume showing my goals and my strengths both academically and athletically. Participating in my sport is extremely important to me. Please advise me if, in your opinion, I should apply.

Very truly yours,

You can usually tell by the responses from the coaches just what your chances are of participating in the sport at that college. Sometimes you'll receive extremely enthusiastic letters – that's a positive sign. Sometimes you'll get a negative letter or you won't hear from them at all – that's probably a good reason to remove the school from your list if participating in the sport is truely that important. And occasionally students receive unsolicited scholarship offers. So the process does pay off and helps both parents and students obtain additional information for the screening process.

College coaches at many schools are at a significant disadvantage. Although some have scholarship money available, a number of coaches are part-time and have little or no recruiting dollars available. They often do not have the ability to identify the athletes they need. Contact from parents and students can open doors to both admissions and financial aid opportunities.

What We've Learned From Our College Money Radio Program

With the intent of finding ways to pay for college, we launched our radio program in mid-1996. The primary purpose of the show is to encourage students and parents to look at more colleges as part of the decision making process. To help them accomplish that goal, we decided to spotlight a different college each week. Over time we developed three specific types of questions that will help parents, students and colleges focus on the exchange of essential information.

1. First we asked the colleges to describe their typical student on campus. Where did they come from geographically? What kind of different family backgrounds do they have? What are their grades and SAT scores? Are there any special selection criteria used by the college to select students? This information gave our students and parents a chance to look at each college and say, "I can fit there."

2. The second set of questions involved unique features designed to attract students. What are some of the distinct programs? What is the big draw on campus? Do students secure jobs upon graduation? How good is the school's career planning department?

3.   The final questions were money related and were very specific. Does the college award non-need-based financial aid and who receives it? Specifically explain how to apply for the various kinds of scholarships offered by the college and what criteria must be exhibited in order to receive those scholarships.

Three interesting classifications evolved from our interviews.

1.   First, there is a group of prestige colleges. These colleges have many more applicants than they can possibly accept. These colleges offer substantial need-based financial aid but rarely do they offer merit-based financial aid. They also do not need to discount tuition.

2.   The second group is comprised of state colleges and universities. These schools are attractively priced, offer moderate amounts of need-based financial aid and have some merit-based money available. Discounting tuition is not possible because of state regulations.

3.   The third group is composed of private, less well-known colleges. Most of these colleges are not attaining sufficient enrollment but they would like more students and they would like to attract better students. These schools have some need-based money, some merit-based money and will aggressively discount tuition for the right student.

It is this last group, in particular, that offers some interesting opportunities. If your client's student can help one of these colleges improve their statistics with better than average SAT or ACT scores, grades or athletic ability, then that student will qualify as a star at that college. Every student can be a star at the right college by matching his abilities with a college need. Being a star at the right college usually means a better financial aid package or a tuition discount. Next are several examples of what colleges will do to attract the right student.

      ◊   Lehigh University and Clark University, two well-respected colleges, offer a fifth year absolutely free to students who maintain a grade point average of 3.25 or higher.

      ◊   Monmouth University, Long Branch, New Jersey, took its discretionary need-based financial aid money and turned it into

91

merit-based money. Their typical applicant has board scores of approximately 1,100. Now every incoming student who has board scores of 1,100 receives a $4,000 university scholarship. If students have higher board scores they receive bigger scholarship amounts and if they have lower board scores they receive somewhat lower amounts. This is Monmouth's way of attracting the students they want.

◊ Centenary College, Hackettstown, New Jersey, has a nationally respected Equine program. When we first heard about this we thought, "Wonderful, this is just what parents want to hear. They can pay $20,000 a year so their students can play with horses." In fact, students in this program find jobs right out of college in a variety of fields. Centenary has been able to match the special interests of certain students with good career planning opportunities as well as with a good education.

◊ Muskingum College, New Concord, Ohio, took a different approach. They lowered tuition across the board by $4,000. In doing so, they received much national publicity and attracted numerous students. Therefore, they increased their enrollment substantially.

◊ Drexel University in Philadelphia revamped its co-op programs. They shortened some of them so students could participate in a co-op education and still earn their degrees in four years instead of the typical five. In addition, Drexel opted to market to families. Drexel awards scholarships if two members of the same family attend college at the same time. They also have a tuition discount for students whose parents attended the school. All of these techniques give Drexel the opportunity to do a better job of satisfying their enrollment needs.

◊ Grove City College, Grove City, Pennsylvania, is a debt-free college. They have their own student loan programs which offer students larger loans than are possible through the federal government programs and at better rates. In addition, they've kept tuition down thus making the school an exceptional place to attend. As a result, Grove City College can be extremely selective in their admissions process.

◊ Franklin and Marshall College, Lancaster, Pennsylvania, decided they wanted to attract top-notch students, those who might normally attend an Ivy League school. High board score applicants to Franklin and Marshall receive a Marshall Grant renewable for four years and equal to a substantial discount on the price of attending college. In addition, F&M allows all incoming students to apply for a research grant to do independent study. These grants can be extremely attractive to motivated students.

◊ Virginia Wesleyan College, Virginia Beach, Virginia, not only offers an attractive environment to students but also offers a four-year graduation guarantee. If students apply themselves and earn reasonable grades, the school guarantees that the appropriate courses will be available so the student can graduate in four years.

Many students attending state colleges can't register for the required courses and sometimes must extend their curriculum to five or six years in order to graduate.

◊ Maine Maritime Academy, Castelle, Maine, has a very unique program. They teach students engineering on a practical level. Most of their graduates either pilot large oceangoing vessels or run large power plants for utilities or large resort areas. The school frequently rejects high board score applicants and admits students with lower board scores but who also have a flair for practical engineering. The cost of Maine Maritime Academy is extremely competitive and starting salaries are exceedingly high.

◊ The Culinary Institute of America, Hyde Park, New York, trains some of the best chefs in the world. It offers two and four-year programs with new classes starting every three weeks. Graduates average eight job offers each making them particularly employable after their education

The list can go on and on and on. The point we are making is that research pays off. Unfortunately, we don't know of a book that tabulates these special programs and special opportunities. The only way to check is to simply go through the list of colleges that fits your client's student then call the colleges and ask.

How to Select The Proper Colleges

Pare the List to 15 to 25 Colleges

Students and parents working together should be able to pare their computer generated list to 15 to 25 colleges. This breakdown should take place during the student's junior year of high school and absolutely no later than the beginning of the senior year.

This is also the time to consider college visits to shave that list to the final 10 to 12 schools before submitting applications. Although what to look for during a college visit is somewhat beyond the scope of this text, Appendix 4 includes some charts that will help planners and clients highlight the information that is important to them.

Early Decision

One important note involves a concept called "early decision." Early decision is an application process whereby students declare they are applying to their first choice of a college. In the event they are accepted by their first choice, there is a tacit agreement that the students will withdraw all other applications and attend that school. The reason students apply for early decision is because it takes them out of the competitive process and gives them an edge in gaining acceptance to a school they really wish to attend.

Most colleges in their acceptance process rank all of the students who apply to their school based on their acceptance criteria. Then they cut off those students who are below the line. This means that students are competing with one another for the top spots. In the early decision process, students aren't ranked. Rather, they are reviewed based on the college's belief that they will be successful at the school and accepted based on those criteria only, not on competition.

There is one major disadvantage of early decision. When the student declares to a college that he wishes to apply for admission on an early decision basis, and the student indicates to that college that he will attend if accepted, it becomes very difficult to later negotiate with that college for a better financial aid package. If financial aid is important, especially non-need-based financial aid, beware of early decision.

The Application Process

Once again, this book is not designed to analyze the application process in-depth, but we must comment on deadlines and the importance of a complete application. Once you have pared your list of colleges to the 10 or 12 to which you are going to apply, call them and request very specific instructions as to what must be sent in and the date of the filing deadline. Incomplete applications and missed filing deadlines are two of the biggest reasons why students don't get accepted to the colleges of their choice.

6

Plan Your Financial Aid Strategy Early

Introduction

Chapter 2 reviewed several concepts that financial planning professionals need to understand before they help their clients plan for college. Three of those concepts come into play in this chapter.

1. The Trial Financial Aid Test and how it determines which type of financial aid your clients should pursue.

2. The 50%, 47%, 35% and 6% "rules of thumb" and how they affect need-based financial aid.

3. The Federal Methodology and the Institutional Methodology and how they differ.

In this chapter we're going to discuss how some of the routine planning decisions that clients make can affect their financial aid picture. We are also going to investigate some strategies that clients might want to implement to make them more qualified for financial aid.

There are rules we must understand when planning for financial aid.

♦ First, financial aid is an annual process. As income and assets change each year, so will the EFC and the financial aid package.

♦ Second, when we refer to income during the financial aid process, we mean income from the previous tax year. If our client is requesting financial aid for Fall 1999, the system will use the income shown on the client's 1998 federal income tax return. Although using the previous year's income may not be fair, the financial aid administrators can and will use the income tax return as a verification device.

♦ Third, clients' assets, for financial aid form purposes, are tabulated as of the day the form is completed and dated. This allows a financial aid administrator during a random or planned audit to verify the data by requesting copies of bank or investment statements. This procedure sometimes causes problems because a financial aid system administrator uses interest and dividend data from the previous tax year to decide if asset data is recorded properly.

As an example, suppose your client shows $1,000 of interest income on his tax return. Given a current interest rate environment of 4% to 6%, a financial aid administrator would expect savings to be in the range of $15,000 to $25,000. If your client's financial aid form lists different numbers, the administrator may ask for verification.

Basic Financial Aid Planning Issues

Before designing specific strategies to improve the possibility of receiving financial aid, let's look at some things our clients normally do when preparing financially for college and how those things effect financial aid. After examining the answers to the following questions, we may decide to change the way we coach our clients with regard to their college financing strategies.

"Is it a good idea to save money for college?"

The reason this question comes up is that many parents have heard from their neighbors that saving for college precluded them from obtaining financial aid. The tendency for parents who hear this is to say, "We're not going to save for college. We're going to spend our money and be poor so we can get financial aid." The fallacy in this statement is that the financial aid formulas tend to be income driven. Too often we see parents who haven't saved for college and who have growing incomes. Suddenly, when they reach college crunch time, they find they're not going to receive financial aid because their incomes are too high. Since they have no savings, they are in trouble. Figure 6.1 reviews our financial aid planning "rules of thumb."

Figure 6.1

Financial Aid Planning "Rules of Thumb"	
Student's Income	50%
Parent's Income	47%
Student's Assets	35%
Parent's Assets	6%

Let's take an example of saving for college and how it affects financial aid. Recently we conducted a seminar at a local high school. After the seminar we ran a financial aid analysis on the parents of a sophomore student which revealed they had an expected contribution of $10,000 per year. Realizing they had three years in which to do some work, these parents stated, "Wouldn't it be a good idea to save $10,000 for college. That way we will have our first year taken care of. "

Figure 6.2 lays out three options for this family regarding saving for college and shows some interesting results.

1. Option 1: The family can avoid saving for college.

2. Option 2: They can set up an account in the parents' name.

3. Option 3: They can set up an account in the student's name.

Figure 6.2

	Do Not Save	Parent's Name	Student's Name
Original EFC	$10,000	$10,000	$10,000
Applicable "Rules of Thumb"	N/A	6%	35%
New EFC	$10,000	$10,600	$13,500
Savings for College	$0	$10,000	$10,000

Look at what happens.

1. In Option 1, they don't save at all and, assuming everything else remains constant, their Expected Family Contribution stays at $10,000. They have no money set aside for college.

2. In Option 2, they set up an account in the parents' name and save $10,000. We know from applying the 6% rule that the effect of this saving will raise the parents' expected contribution to $10,600. They will, therefore, be eligible for $600 less in financial aid, but they will also have $10,000 in the bank.

3. The last option is to save the money in the student's name. Again, going back to our rules of thumb, we know that the 35% rule applies to student assets. Therefore, the parents' expected contribution will increase from $10,000 to $13,500 and they will also have $10,000 in the bank.

Which, then, is the best option? The answer depends on the financial aid circumstances of the individuals involved.

Suppose the right college for this student is a state college that costs exactly $10,000. In this case, the best savings plan is to put the money into an account in the student's name. The reasoning is that since the family is not going to receive financial aid anyway, financial aid is a moot point. By setting up a custodial account and using the student's tax bracket, we can at least attain some financial leverage by saving tax dollars.

Yet what happens if the right college for this student is a more expensive college, a $25,000 or $30,000 a year college? In that case, we don't want the money in the student's name because we'll loose $3,500 in financial aid by setting up the account that way. It seems logical then that the best choice in this particular case is to save the money in the parents' name. Although we will loose a modest amount of financial aid—$600—we will still have $10,000 in the bank with which to work.

It's almost always better for parents to save for college than not to save for college. The key is to understand your clients' financial aid situation so you can position their savings in order to secure the maximum value out of either the tax savings or through improved financial aid.

"Is it a good idea to have mom return to work to help pay for college?"

More often than not, it's mom who sacrifices her time and energy to return to work in order to help with the college bill while still caring for house and family. The issue here is whether mom's return to work makes sense financially or not. Let's take an example.

Not long ago one of my neighbors, an architect, decided to start his own business. For several years he didn't make much money, but over time his income began to grow. One day he awoke, panicky, realizing his daughter was a junior in high school and he hadn't saved any money for college. After thinking it through he looked at his wife, Ann, and said, "You have a teaching degree. I think you'll have to start teaching again to help pay the college bill."

Here's what happened. Ann was able to find a teaching job starting at $20,000 a year. The college they chose for their daughter was a $14,000 college. At first blush, $20,000 of income to pay a $14,000 college bill looked pretty good. It didn't take long, however, for our clients to realize that when the paychecks came in they had forgotten about federal income tax. Subtracting 28%, or $5,600, they suddenly realized that $20,000 wasn't $20,000–it was only $14,400.

Next, when they saw the Social Security and state taxes that were being taken out they realized they were losing another $2,000 of income. Quickly, the $20,000 was down to $12,400. Yet, $12,400 would still pay a big part of the $14,000 cost. Then they recognized that the extra income was going to have an effect on their ability to obtain financial aid. Applying the 47% rule, 47% of $12,400 is approximately $5,800. After subtracting $5,800 from the after tax income of $12,400, this couple was left with $6,600 for college.

They also noted that Ann had work related expenses: auto expenses, the cost of lunches, clothes, child care expenditures, etc. Taking out another $3,000 to handle these accounts, Ann realized that she was working for a $3,600 contribution towards college. Upon reflection she commented, "Had I known this was all I would net towards college, I would have stayed home."

Figure 6.3 summarizes our example in two columns. The first column looks at a family who qualifies for financial aid. The second column reveals the effect if they do not qualify for financial aid; the difference can be substantial. Planning for mom to return to work can be a mistake if financial aid is in the cards. If, however, need-based financial aid is not in the picture, returning to work can have a positive effect on paying for college.

Figure 6.3

	Qualifies for Need-Based Financial Aid	Does Not Qualify for Aid
Earned Income	$20,000	$20,000
Federal Income Tax @ 28%	$5,600	$5,600
Net	$14,400	$14,400
FICA and State Taxes	$2,000	$2,000
Net	$12,400	$12,400
Lost Financial Aid @ 47%	$5,800	$0
Net	$6,600	$12,400
Work Related Expenses	$3,000	$3,000
Net for College Bills	$3,600	$9,400

"Is it a good idea to have a student work to help pay the college expenses?"

Many parents believe that it's good that their students work. They feel it gives the students a sense of responsibility, the opportunity to earn some money as well as teaches them to appreciate the value of a dollar. When considering financial aid, however, working can backfire. In general, students lose fifty cents of every dollar they earn during the previous year toward their financial aid package for the following year. The two financial aid formulas are somewhat different when dealing with student earnings.

◆ For federal financial aid, there is a $1,750 deductible. In other words, students can earn $1,750 and it will not affect financial aid for federal financial aid purposes.

◆ The Institutional Methodology has no such deductible. Students must show their earnings from dollar one and they lose fifty cents on each dollar from dollar one. In fact, if a student doesn't work, the system plugs in $900 for freshman and $1,000 for upper classmen.

How much should students work? It depends to a large extent on their financial aid circumstances. If the family is not going to qualify for need-based financial aid, it's probably a good idea that the student works. If financial aid is not in the picture, the student can earn an unlimited amount of money and it will have no bearing on financial aid since he doesn't qualify anyway.

We need to be more careful, however, if the student is a financial aid candidate. If the student is going to attend a college that requires only the FAFSA, that indicates the college most likely uses only the Federal Methodology in its calculations. In that case, we encourage the student to work and earn up to $1,750 per year with no effect on financial aid. If, on the other hand, the college the student chooses requires the filing of the Profile Form, then that is an indication the college uses the Institutional Methodology. In that case, having a student work will cost us in financial aid from dollar one. If our student doesn't work at all, we'll be penalized $900 to $1,000 dollars so we might as well earn that much. Earning more will cost the student financial aid dollars at the rate of fifty cents for each dollar the student earns.

One of the dilemmas we frequently observe is that parents let their students buy cars during their senior year of high school. Since the students are expected to work to pay for their own car insurance, the dollars earned are not saved for college. As a result, the student receives less financial aid and there is no money in the bank.

"What happens if our student works and saves his earnings in his own bank account?"

Another dilemma occurs when students save their money. Remember, student income reduces financial aid by fifty cents on the dollar, but assets in the student's name reduces financial aid by only thirty-five cents on the dollar. It is highly possible that when students earn money and save it in their own name, they can lose as much as eighty-five cents for every financial aid dollar they're trying to get.

⚷ If a student must work, and if the student is going to save money, one trick is for the student and parent to open a joint savings account and use the parent's Social Security number. In that situation, funds in the account are treated for financial aid purposes as the parent's money. The student, as a joint owner, has the ability to withdraw money as needed but it won't feel like he's lost control of his own bank account.

Strategies to Obtain More Financial Aid

One of the things I hope you see is that financial aid often makes us do things that go against our normal grain. It appears the financial aid system is telling us not to work and not to save money and, whatever we do, don't have our children work in order to pay for their own education. The traditional values of working and saving for college seem to be at odds with the financial aid system. This often frustrates our clients. With some planning, however, we can outthink the system. The following strategies can be used to give your clients an edge.

Strategy 1: Reposition client assets.

There are many financial professionals who use college planning as an opportunity to earn money through the repositioning of assets. Many of them claim that by repositioning assets they can improve a client's financial aid picture. Does this really work? The answer is, it depends.

First, let's look at the typical types of assets parents deal with when filing financial aid forms. Figure 6.4 represents how the two financial aid formulas treat assets.

Figure 6.4

Asset Description	Federal Methodology	Institutional Methodology
Family Home	No	Yes
Family Farm (lived on)	No	Yes
Family Farm (not lived on)	Yes	Yes
Second Home or Vacation Home	Yes	Yes
Cash, Savings, Checking	Yes	Yes
Stocks, Bonds, Mutual Funds	Yes	Yes
Annuities, Variable Annuities	No	Maybe
Retirement Funds - Qualified	No	No
Retirement Funds - Nonqualified	No	Maybe
Stock Options	No	Maybe
Business	Yes	Yes
Life Insurance Cash Values	No	Maybe

The Federal Methodology allows you to procure money from Uncle Sam. Federal Methodology rules are predictable and liberal so when colleges use the Federal Methodology, the results of repositioning assets are predictable. But what kind of money do students get from Uncle Sam? Unfortunately, most of Uncle Sam's money comes in the form of student loans and work-study programs. Although there are some grant programs available, they tend to be very limited and are not worth much money. For example, last year the federal Pell Grant program gave a maximum award of $2,700 to low income families. As the family income approached $42,000, however, the amount of the award was reduced significantly.

Since federal financial aid rules are predictable, putting money into annuities or life insurance cash values causes that money to disappear as an asset of the family. Therefore, using cash value life insurance and annuities to hold assets can qualify a family for more federal financial aid. Keep in mind, though, that most federal financial aid comes in the form of loans and jobs, not scholarships and grants. Much of the real free money, the scholarships and grants, comes out of the pocketbooks of the colleges that have substantial endowments.

Prior to 1992, colleges and Uncle Sam used the same rules for doling out financial aid. But in 1992, the colleges and Uncle Sam disassociated themselves from each other, both choosing to use separate formulas and different interpretations as to what constitutes assets and income. We talk with our clients about colleges using the golden rule when it comes to awarding financial aid. Yet it's not the Golden Rule in the Bible but another golden rule–*"He Who Has The Gold Makes The Rules."*

Colleges award their financial aid packages using their own rules. Where annuities and life insurance cash values are excluded from assets when applying for federal financial aid, colleges often ask about them and many times will not exclude them from their financial aid calculations. Whether or not you get away with asset repositioning depends upon how astute a particular college or university is, or how strong your client's bargaining power is. Parents become very upset with advisors who tell them to buy an annuity because it will hide money from the colleges as well as secure more financial aid for them, only to find the colleges asking about annuities and adding back into the formulas that money. Not only did the strategy fail, but now the client has an additional problem. In order to take money out of the annuity or the life insurance policy, the parent must pay substantial penalties.

Since we're trying to build long term client relationships, not destroy them, we must be extremely careful when using asset repositioning. A level load annuity is one of the tools that we often use in that situation. These annuities pay a small commission and do not have a front-end load or surrender charge. This gives you the opportunity to take a chance that the college won't ask the right questions and allows the client to put the money into the annuity where it can benefit them through increased financial aid. If you're wrong, you can make the client whole by simply taking money out of the annuity without penalty or cost. Although the 10% penalty on income growth will still apply, that is not much of a problem considering the client is making money and will simply reduce his investment income.

Strategy 2: Reduce investment income.

Investment income alone could have a substantial negative effect on financial aid. Dividends and interest in a parent's name fall under the 47% rule; Dividends and interest in the student's name fall under the 50% rule. Income producing assets actually hit the financial aid system with a double wallop. First, the assets themselves reduce financial aid by 6% if they are in the parent's name, or 35% if they are in the student's name. Second, the investment income reduces financial aid by either 47% or 50%. Figure 6.5 illustrates how this works.

Figure 6.5

		Parent		Student	
		"Rules of Thumb"	Lost Financial Aid	"Rules of Thumb"	Lost Financial Aid
Asset Value	$20,000	6%	$1,200	35%	$7,000
After-tax Investment Income	$1,000	47%	$470	50%	$500

Annuities work well here. Even if the college counts the asset value of the annuity in the financial aid calculation, there is no investment income, thus a lower EFC. Again, we need to be concerned about liquidity. Level load annuities with no surrender charges work well but care must be taken if the client needs to withdraw dollars from the annuity. That withdrawal will trigger taxable income which, in turn, will cause a change in the EFC.

Strategy 3: Shift assets from children to parents.

Sometimes a professional can catch a client's mistake early enough to take corrective action. Suppose your client has been saving money in a Uniform Gifts to Minors Act account (UGMA) for his student and has accumulated $10,000. He then realizes his student is likely to receive need-based financial aid. The attorneys tell us that when a custodial account is funded an irrevocable gift is made. (Also, in many instances, the student is usually not old enough to make a return gift to the parent.) The attorneys likewise tell us that the custodian of an account has the right to make expenditures on behalf of the minor as long as the custodian meets certain criteria. (Check your particular state laws.) Generally, however, it appears that the custodian can spend the student's dollars on items such as private school tuition, summer camp, computers, music lessons, etc. With care you can have your client spend the student's money while replacing the savings in a parent owned account. This can have the dramatic effect as shown in Figure 6.6. If it is not possible to spend all of the student's money before college, remember that financial aid is an annual event. Spending the student's money on the first year of college can increase the student's eligibility for financial aid during the second and later years.

Figure 6.6

	Student's Name	Parent's Name	Difference
Savings	$10,000	$10,000	
"Rules of Thumb"	35%	6%	
Lost Financial Aid	$3,500	$600	$2,900

A word about relative bargaining power.

We discussed the "golden rule" colleges use when awarding their private funds. The stronger the student's credentials are, the more likely it is that the college will bend some rules in favor of the student.

A client has twin daughters they wanted to send to an expensive, prestigious northeastern college. After applying for financial aid, the school turned them down cold. They were told the reasons were high income and an account in each daughter's name worth $35,000. The client contested the financial aid decision arguing that bad advice from a financial planner was the reason for the UGMA accounts instead of saving the money under their own name. When the parents discussed sending their daughters to a state college, the financial aid administrator opted to treat the students' cash as the parents' cash. The financial aid recalculation meant a $10,000 grant for each student.

In this case, a financial aid officer didn't want to lose two students so he bent the rules under the "golden rule" concept.

Strategy 4: Manage capital gains.

The sale of investments can also trigger capital gains. Capital gains are treated by the financial aid system as income. Currently, the financial aid system looks at the tax return from the year prior to the time students receive financial aid. Therefore, 1997's tax return will affect 1998's financial aid. If we are going to liquidate assets in order to pay for college, the timing of that liquidation is important.

First, a few facts. Suppose our clients have saved for college and several years ago they invested $20,000 in a mutual fund. That fund has now grown to $50,000 with a cost basis for tax purposes of $25,000. Their student will start college in September, 1999.

Since the 1998 tax return will determine the parents income for financial aid purposes, the clients should liquidate their mutual funds in 1997 to avoid losing the financial aid due to the capital gains. An alternative is to delay the investment sale until the student's senior year of college, after the last financial aid package is awarded. Please note that clients need to consider income tax implications on the sale of investment assets as well as the financial aid aspects.

Strategy 5: Reduce cash by paying off debts.

Cash, CDs, money market funds all reduce a client's ability to qualify for financial aid. It is sometimes wise to prepay expenses before completing financial aid forms. Some expenses to consider paying include:

♦ Mortgage payments

♦ Credit card balances

♦ Elective surgery

♦ New car purchase

♦ Car repairs

Strategy 6: Prepay the mortgage.

For federal financial aid purposes, the family home is not considered as an asset available to pay college costs. For this reason, home equity disappears. A parent with substantial cash could reduce his EFC by using that cash to prepay the mortgage. The disadvantage is that the parent's liquidity is reduced. Should the parent need cash to pay college bills or other expenses, it would be difficult to retrieve that cash. To recover the cash it might require that the parent takes out a second mortgage at some unknown interest rate and incurrs a loan acquisition expense.

There is also a potential problem of credit changes. As parents take on college loans, their ability to borrow decreases. Great care needs to be taken before you recommend this strategy to your client since liquidity issues often become significant during the college years.

It is also important to realize that the Institutional Methodology does take the house into consideration, so prepaying your mortgage does not improve your financial aid circumstances at all. If the school of choice uses the Profile Form, it is a clear indication that the Institutional Methodology will be considered and that the family home will be a part of the formula. Sometimes schools that use the Federal Methodology also follow up with an additional questionnaire. It is possible that they may include the family home in the calculation of the EFC as it pertains to using their own private endowment funds.

Strategy 7: Plan to have two students in college at the same time.

Another planning strategy for need-based financial aid money is to have two students in college at the same time. Most parents feel that the financial aid system attempts to squeeze out of them everything it possibly can in order to have them pay for college. As a professional, you will agree after you finish this book. In spite of that, there is a bright side. When there are two students from a family attending college at the same time, there is no more to squeeze. In fact, the financial aid system doesn't expect families with two or more students in college at the same time to pay much more. What happens is the expected contribution of the parent is allocated almost equally between the two students going to college. Figure 6.7 displays how a family with a $12,000 expected contribution receives no financial aid when the first child attends a state college costing $10,000. However, with two students in college at the same time, the parents still have an expected contribution of the same $12,000, but it is now considered $6,000 for Student 1 and $6,000 for Student 2. Suddenly, both students become eligible for financial aid.

Figure 6.7

	One Student in College	Two Students in College	
		Student 1	Student 2
College Cost	$10,000	$10,000	$10,000
EFC per Student	$12,000	$6,000	$6,000
Financial Aid	$0	$4,000	$4,000

There are times when it is appropriate to delay for a year or two sending a student to college in order to have that student join a sibling in school. This occurs when students aren't sure whether they should go to a four-year college or instead attend a community college in order to improve their grades. Trying to match two children in college at the same time can often pay big dividends in terms of financial aid.

A note of caution. Many colleges scrutinize the situation when families have two or more students attending college at the same time to confirm the circumstances. Also, some colleges take the time to investigate the actual college costs in terms of allocating the expected contribution among the students.

For example, let's suppose we have an expected contribution of $12,000. We have one student going to a $4,000 community college and a second student attending a $20,000 private school. Some colleges will allocate the $12,000 EFC on a 50/50 basis, or $6,000 for each student. Some colleges will actually look at the true cost of college and allocate $4,000 toward the student who is going to the $4,000 community college and $8,000 toward the student who is attending the more expensive college. When this situation occurs, the actual financial aid picture is not as good as when the colleges allocate equally.

Strategy 8: Parents attending college.

Students attending college at the same time are not limited to being adolescents in order to qualify for financial aid. Parents can count as students but colleges are watching carefully to make sure that parents aren't abusing the situation. One trick is for the parent to choose the cheapest community college and the cheapest curriculum available and then enroll himself as a full time student. The parent also indicates on the financial aid form that he is attending college full time. As soon as the financial aid is awarded, the parent drops out of school and applies for a refund. But colleges have smart financial aid people and now they check when and where the parent returns to school. Consequently, a parent attending college does not automatically entitle the family to more financial aid. Notwithstanding, there are circumstances where a parent legitimately returns to school and colleges will often look at that when determining the financial aid package. The next example is a case in point.

Not long ago one of the women who worked for me decided to return to school full time. She had completed two years of college before she married and raised a family. But she always regretted that she had quit college early to have children and to put her husband through law school. To make a long story short, she, her son and her daughter all enrolled in full-time classes at the same college. In this particular case, the college recognized three students in college and understood that it was a legitimate situation. Financial aid was awarded appropriately.

Strategy 9: In the case of divorced parents, plan to have the poorer parent be the custodial parent.

For federal financial aid, in the case of divorced parents, the system only takes into account the finances of the family of the custodial parent. This can present an interesting planning option, especially when the parents live in the same vicinity, talk with one another and one of the parents has substantially more income and assets than the other.

The basic idea is to have the poorer parent become the custodial parent. This strategy can work providing the chosen school asks only for the FAFSA form. If the school requires the Profile Form, there is a divorced/separated statement that must be filed indicating the financial status of the non-custodial parent. In that case, the school is likely to bring in both sets of parents and the strategy fails.

When a custodial parent remarries, the income and assets of the stepparent are included in the financial aid calculations even though the stepparent may not have any legal obligation to support the student.

Strategy 10: Characterize assets as business assets if possible.

Business assets under $420,000 are discounted by the financial aid system. Figure 6.8 describes the discount.

Figure 6.8

Business Net Worth	Discount Factor
$0 to $85,000	40%
$85,001 to $250,000	50%
$250,001 to $420,000	60%

Suppose your client owns a small business, a sole proprietorship, for example. His only asset is $50,000 in cash. For financial aid purposes, this cash is valued at $20,000 and increases the EFC by only $1,800. Personal assets that can be reclassified as business assets can yield significant improvements in acquiring financial aid.

Conclusions

As we've seen, it's fairly easy to maneuver financial data in order to secure federal financial aid. We need to keep in mind, however, that most of the financial aid we receive from Uncle Sam comes in the form of loans and work-study programs. Grants are small and usually not of much significance.

Money coming from the colleges' private endowment funds can be significant and often comes in the form of grants and scholarships. This kind of money is worth going after. Colleges, however, are much more astute in screening financial data when making their financial aid calculations. The professional really needs to think through the value of asset repositioning. Usually when you try to secure financial aid, you wind up tying up assets and making them nonliquid. For college financial aid there's no guarantee that the strategies are going to work. Because of this, as a general rule, we recommend that you look at the situation from the standpoint of sound planning first and financial aid second. If repositioning the client's assets makes sense financially, without taking into account financial aid, it may give us the chance to secure financial aid without hurting our client. In that case, the strategy probably should be implemented especially if it can be done in such a way so it can be reversed if the strategy does not work.

There are also diminishing returns to financial aid planning. If a client has not used all of his Asset Protection Allowance (see Chapter 3), repositioning his assets will not change the EFC. Low income and asset families may see smaller percentage affects on the EFC by implementing our financial aid strategies because the financial aid formulas are not linear at those lower levels of income and assets.

Keep in mind that one of the goals of college financial planning is to seize the opportunity to build long-term relationships with clients. If properly handled, these long-term relationships will allow us to control the management of their retirement plans and help them with future estate planning and life insurance needs. Inferior financial and college planning can ruin relationships very quickly.

7

Filling Out Financial Aid Forms Correctly

Introduction

Now that you have helped your client's family determine their expected contribution, helped them apply to the proper colleges and helped them plan a financial aid strategy, it is time to look at completing the actual financial aid forms. Even though you have helped your client with some financial aid planning, there are still some decisions that must be made at the form level. Understanding the basic concepts underlying each type of financial aid form can help you guide your client through this daunting process.

In most cases, you don't want to prepare the form yourself because that is a very time consuming and tedious job. However, you can coach your client through the process and you can provide a form review service. If you actually complete a federal financial aid form on behalf of your client, you are legally obligated to sign the form as a preparer. Your client also needs to know that forms signed by preparers are likely to be scrutinized more carefully by financial aid administrators.

Reasons Why Your Client Should Fill Out the Financial Aid Forms

Obviously, the primary reason is that your client wants to obtain need-based financial aid. Yet, believe it or not, your client may need to complete the financial aid forms so he can be refused financial aid. Getting turned down allows clients to apply for unsubsidized college loans in the name of their student. In addition, there are a number of colleges that will require completed financial aid forms in order to receive merit-based financial aid.

The Forms

There are four basic types of financial aid forms:

1. The Free Application for Federal Student Aid;

2. The Profile Form;

3. College Specific Forms; and

4. Foreign Student Financial Aid Applications.

The Free Application for Federal Student Aid Form

The Free Application for Federal Student Aid (FAFSA) is the form used to apply for:

♦   Federal Pell Grants.

♦   Federal Supplemental Education Opportunity Grants (FSEOG).

♦   Federal Subsidized and Unsubsidized Stafford Loans.

♦   Federal Perkins Loans.

♦   Federal Work-Study Programs.

♦   Title VII and Public Health Act Programs.

Almost every college requires that the FAFSA form be filed in order to obtain any financial aid. Every college is anxious to have students apply for these programs because the money that is awarded comes from an external source—the federal government. Many colleges require only the FAFSA form and they may use it as a tool to allocate funds from their own private resources. Data from the FAFSA form is processed through the Federal Methodology, a formula originally legislated in 1992, and updated annually.

The FAFSA form is available from high school guidance offices, college financial aid offices and the Department of Education web site in late November or early December each year for use after January 1 of the following year.

The Profile Form

Many colleges and some private foundations require that the student submits the Profile Form in addition to the FAFSA form. The Profile Form is a product of the College Scholarship Service (CSS), which is a division of the College Board which, in turn, is an association of member colleges. Some colleges feel they need additional information about the students before they award financial aid. The Profile Form allows for customized questions from different colleges. The Institutional Methodology is the formula corresponding to the Profile Form.

Using the Profile Form is a two-step process. Step 1 is to register the student who then completes a data form by answering sixteen questions and including a list of colleges and scholarship organizations. The form can be filed by mail, telephone or through the Internet. There is a registration fee and a per organization filing fee as well. After the student registers, he or she will receive a customized packet of forms; Step 2 involves completing and filing these customized forms.

The Profile Forms are available from high school guidance offices, college financial aid offices or can be down loaded from the College Board web site.

College Specific Forms

Many colleges require their own financial aid form. Contact the colleges directly for information about these special forms.

Foreign Student Financial Aid Applications

Foreign students can also file for financial aid directly from the colleges. There is a special College Scholarship Service form for this including a certification of finances. Most foreign students are not eligible for federal financial aid.

The Supplements

There are three supplemental forms that might be required:

1. The Business/Farm Supplement;

2. The Divorced/Separated Supplement; and

3. The Graduate/Professional Student Supplement.

The Business/Farm Supplement.

This form is required when your client indicates that he or she owns part or all of a closely held business. Business values are considered an asset available to pay for college although they are discounted substantially. The form is essentially a balance sheet and a profit and loss statement that does not consider soft assets like goodwill. The form requires two years of past data and estimates for the following year. Unlike the FAFSA form, which excludes farm values if your client lives on the farm, the Profile Form treats the farm as a business and requires that the Business/Farm Supplement be completed.

Figure 7.1

Discounts of Business Assets for Financial Aid		
Amounts From	To	Discount %
$1	$85,000	40%
$85,001	$250,000	50%
$250,001	$420,000	60%
Over $420,001		100%

The Divorced/Separated Supplement

Generally, all financial aid forms should be completed by the custodial parent. If a custodial parent has been divorced and remarried, the income and assets of the new spouse (the stepparent) are required as financial data on the form. If a student wants to attend a college that requires only the FAFSA form, there is no requirement to submit financial data from the non-custodial parent.

This situation is generally not true, however, in the event the Profile Form is required. In that case, the non-custodial parent must also submit financial data by completing the Divorced/Separated Supplement. If the non-custodial parent has remarried, financial data from the new spouse is also required. Even if the divorce agreement does not require payments from the non-custodial parent, that does not preclude the need for completing the supplement. We have occasionally noticed that when a custodial parent has remarried, the college may, at its discretion, waive the supplement. Generally, however, if your client is divorced, be prepared to complete the Divorced/Separated Supplement.

The Graduate/Professional Student Supplement

This supplement provides graduate students a place to list their undergraduate indebtedness. Colleges can also gather additional data about the financial circumstances of the student and spouse, if married.

Responses From the Financial Aid System

The financial aid system responds to students and parents with two forms:

1.   The Student Aid Report (SAR); and

2.   The College Scholarship Service (CSS) Data Confirmation Report.

The Student Aid Report (SAR) is a vehicle that provides students and parents with a chance to correct data. Data from the original FAFSA form is processed by a computer system using the Federal Methodology to calculate the Expected Family Contribution. Students and parents should review the data summary carefully. If corrections are required because data is incorrect, changes must be made on the SAR and resubmitted to the processing service.

The CSS Data Confirmation Report is similar to the SAR. It gives parents and students a chance to correct data for the Institutional Methodology calculations. The CSS Data Confirmation Report does not provide the EFC for the Institutional Methodology; it is only used for data correction.

Which Forms Are Required?

Almost all colleges require the FAFSA form. Most private colleges also require the Profile Form while some colleges require additional information on their own forms. It is critical that your client contacts each college to determine which forms are required and the deadlines for filing. Financial aid officers process complete files. If your client fails to file all of the forms required by the deadline, his file is considered incomplete. This can mean that the financial aid people are awarding your client's financial aid dollars to other students. *Make sure your clients file the proper forms on time!*

Family Situations Affect How Clients Should Approach the Forms

If your clients are divorced, own their own business or have older students, they can sometimes choose a special strategy for filing financial aid forms. The strategy must also take into account whether it is the college or the government that is supplying the financial aid.

For example, suppose your client is divorced, shares custody of the student with the other parent and lives in the same community. The colleges the student is applying to require only the FAFSA form. In this case, we want the poorer parent to be the custodial parent and file the financial aid form.

Caution: If both parents have remarried, the stepparent's income and assets will be included on the financial aid forms. Running several Trial Financial Aid Tests on both sets of parents can be helpful in developing a final strategy. If a college requires the Profile Form, a Divorced/Separated Supplement will be required. Sometimes, but not always, both sets of financial data will be considered, thus eliminating this strategy as a planning option. Sometimes college specific forms will also include questions about the non-custodial parent.

Independent student status is another option. It works only when the FAFSA form alone is required. An independent student can apply for aid based upon his own financial statement and does not require any parental financial data. In order for a student to be considered independent, the student must meet any one of the following requirements.

- The student is over the age of 24.

- The student is a veteran of the U.S. military service.

- The student has completed an undergraduate degree.

- Both of the student's parents are deceased and the student is a ward of the court.

- The student has dependents other than a spouse.

Again, please remember these requirements are for federal financial aid only. Colleges make student independence difficult. They feel strongly that it is the parent's obligation to pay for college. The key is to look at which forms are required.

If your client owns a business he can try to characterize personal assets as business assets in order to discount their value for financial aid purposes. A business owner might also defer billing near the end of the year, thus lowering income for financial aid purposes. Although this defers the income into the following year and may create a financial aid problem in that year, it gives your client some control that can be used to maximize financial aid in the critical years. C Corporation owners can actually lower personal income by borrowing from their corporations. From a financial aid standpoint, this converts income dollars (the 47% rule) to discounted asset dollars (the 6% or less rule).

We will discuss other strategies in Chapter 12.

Preparing to Complete the Forms

Before attacking the forms, you should have a completed federal income tax return and a current list of assets. Although financial aid forms can be completed using estimates, financial aid administrators will eventually require copies of the client's federal income tax return. If actual income tax return numbers differ from the data submitted, modifications will be made to the financial aid package. A student accepting admission at a college because he or she has received a great financial aid package could be surprised.

Reviewing the four rules of thumb on how income and assets affect financial aid will also be helpful(Chapter 6). Running a Trial Financial Aid Test before submitting the form will give your client a tentative result even before filing. Your client might then take the time to re-evaluate the numbers on the form. Trial Financial Aid Tests can also act as a cross check of the Student Aid Report. If the Expected Family Contribution on the SAR does not agree with your calculations, you must carefully reexamine the input data.

Seven Mistakes Parents and Students Make When Completing Their Financial Aid Forms

Before examining the financial aid forms, one should keep in mind a few common mistakes that are made when applying for financial aid. A surprisingly high percentage of forms are returned without being processed and that will delay your clients financial aid award.

1. Unsigned forms. Forms require the signatures of the parents and the student.

2. Unmet deadlines. College deadlines for financial aid are different than those listed on the FAFSA form.

3. The required forms are not filed. Many colleges only require the FAFSA form while others require the Profile Form and supplements. The student and parents filing the FAFSA form might find that their application sits on the desk of the financial aid officer who is waiting to receive additional forms. Meanwhile, while your client's application is sitting in the "Incomplete" pile, the financial aid officer is doling out financial aid dollars to other students. Your clients must check with the college financial aid office to make sure they understand which forms need to be filed and the filing deadline.

4. The residence is overvalued. Most people are proud of their house and overvalue their home. A more realistic approach is to take a quick sale value of the house, subtract closing costs, and consider the net proceeds. Colleges red flag low value homes. Financial aid forms contain questions about the purchase price and the date of purchase. Homes that have not appreciated in

value by 3% or more will probably be red flagged for questions. This does not mean colleges won't listen to realistic appraisals for low value homes. The 6% rule applies to home values; a $10,000 error means $600 of lost aid each year.

5. The business is overvalued. Financial aid forms request the value of a business which is owned by the family of the student. Usually the financial aid people are looking for the liquidation value of the business (cash less liabilities). Goodwill is not considered a business asset. There is a supplement for families that have business assets that will be required.

6. Retirement assets are included. Retirement assets are not included as values available for college. Therefore, the clients' pension, IRAs, HR-10s, etc. are not included on the forms. Some colleges will ask about these assets in order to take a look at the overall financial strength of a parent, but we have not yet seen colleges utilize them as part of the EFC process.

7. The financial aid forms do not agree with the federal income tax forms. Take the time to verify that the information on the financial aid forms agrees with the federal income tax returns. Most colleges will question discrepancies and often will amend the student's financial aid award.

This last point leads to an interesting story.

Some time ago two women walked into our office and complained that they did not have any money, did not have any income and yet kept getting turned down for financial aid. When I asked to examine their federal income tax return, I saw earned income of a $100,000 and unearned income exceeding $1.5 million. I knew why they didn't receive any financial aid. Then I was given the facts.

I was told the $1.5 million was gambling winnings. What I hadn't seen on the form were the $2.5 million of gambling losses. The husband had tried to cover his losses by embezzling funds from his company, mortgaging the family home to the hilt and running up thousands of dollars of credit card bills. When he was caught and sent to jail for embezzlement, he lost his $100,000 a year job.

These two young ladies truly had no income and no assets. When they tried to express that on the FAFSA form, the financial aid people returned the form to them to correct the discrepancies between the FAFSA form and the federal income tax return that was also submitted. Colleges awarding federal aid dollars go through periodic audits themselves and can lose their financial aid resources if they are not diligent.

If financial aid forms do not match the federal income tax returns the financial aid forms are going to be returned until the errors are corrected. The correct way to approach this problem is to fill out the financial aid form to match the federal income tax return and be rejected for financial aid. Then ask for an exception at the college level. In this case, a letter from the Philadelphia district attorney explained the circumstances which allowed the financial aid officer to design a super financial aid package. I am happy to report this young lady is attending school on a full need-based scholarship.

8

Compare and Evaluate Every Financial Aid Award

Introduction

By the first or second week in April, every high school senior who plans on going to college should have his financial aid package. Now, here is the big question, "Is it the right financial aid package?" How do you know that aid package is the best your chosen college can do for you? Informed professionals, parents and students do know.

Predetermining the Need-Based Package

There is a process for determining your client's need-based financial aid expectations and checking the financial aid package. The process requires you to know four things:

1. The Expected Family Contribution calculations using the Federal Methodology (Chapter 3).

2. The Expected Family Contribution calculations using the Institutional Methodology (Chapter 3).

3. The percentage of need met by the student's college of choice (Chapter 2, Concept 9).

4. The percentage of grants vs. loans and jobs normally given at the student's college of choice (Chapter 2, Concept 9).

If you know these four things you should be able to verify the accuracy of the financial aid package. Next, Figure 8.1 is a worksheet designed to help you and your client evaluate each college's financial aid offer.

Figure 8.1

Need-Based Financial Aid Package Review Worksheet

Name of College	Expected Values			
	Federal Methodology	Institutional Methodology	Actual Award	Variance from Dominant Methodology
College Budget Bill			***************	***************
EFC			***************	***************
Financial Need			***************	***************
% Need Met			***************	***************
Expected Offer				
% Gift				
% Self-Help Work Study Student Loans				

Example One: The XYZ Private College

Suppose our client's student has chosen to apply to the XYZ Private College. The student has been accepted and our client just received a letter with the following financial aid package.

Figure 8.2

XYZ Private College Financial Aid Package for Academic Year 1997-98	
General University Scholarship	$7,000
Student Loan (Stafford Loan)	$2,500
Total Award	$9,500

Is this a good offer or isn't it? In order to answer that question, we must return to the basics. We can gather information on the financial aid strength of this college by referencing the book entitled Peterson's *College Money Handbook* that was mentioned in Chapter 2. Figure 8.3 summarizes the data we discovered about this fictitious college.

Figure 8.3

XYZ Private College College Financial Aid Strength Data	
1. The comprehensive cost or college budget bill	$22,500
2. The percentage of expected need met	100%
3. The percentage of gift aid	60%
4. The percentage of self-help (loans and jobs)	40%

We need the Expected Family Contribution calculations using the Federal and Institutional Methodologies. These numbers were calculated when we completed the Trial Financial Aid Test in Chapter 3. For this example, we will assume the EFC is:

♦   Federal Methodology = $10,500

♦   Institutional Methodology = $13,000

We also know that this college is likely to use the Institutional Methodology as their basis for financial aid decisions because the college required the Profile From the College Scholarship Service.

Our worksheet, Figure 8.4, summarizes this data in a useful form.

Figure 8.4

Need-Based Financial Aid Package Review Worksheet				
Name of College	XYZ Private College			
	Expected Values			
	Federal Methodology	Institutional Methodology (X)	Actual Award	Variance from Dominant Methodology
College Budget Bill	$22,500	$22,500	***************	***************
EFC	$10,500	$13,000	***************	***************
Financial Need	$12,000	$9,500	***************	***************
% Need Met	100%	100%	***************	***************
Expected Offer	N/A	$9,500	$9,500	$0
% Gift	N/A	60% $5,700	$7,000	+ $1,300
% Self-Help Work Study & Student Loans	N/A	40% $3,800	$2,500	- $1,300

To recap, first we take the $22,500 college budget bill from the college and subtract the $13,000 EFC we previously calculated using the Institutional Methodology. That leaves us with a financial need number of $9,500. Referencing the *College Money Handbook*, our resource mentioned earlier for financial aid information, we find that this particular college usually meets 100% of the expected need. Therefore, we expect our total financial aid offer to be equal to

$9,500. Further, again from the *College Money Handbook*, we know that approximately 60% of the financial aid packages awarded are in the form of gift aid, which are scholarships and grants. Consequently, we expect gift aid to total $5,700. The self-help, or work-study portion, is 40% according to our resource, the *College Money Handbook*. Therefore, we should expect about $3,800 in loans and jobs.

In looking at our financial aid picture, we've received a $9,500 grant so our expectations for total financial aid have been met. It appears as though the college is meeting our full need and giving us everything expected from it. In addition, they have been generous and given us a $7,000 grant which exceeds our $5,700 expectation. Consequently, it looks as if this is a great financial aid package and we should probably not contest it.

Example Two: The ABC Private University

Our student also applied to a second private university that we will call ABC Private University. This school has a college budget bill of $23,000 and never requested the Profile Form. Therefore, we expect the financial aid calculations will be made using the Federal Methodology. Our EFC using the Federal Methodology is $10,500 which we calculated by employing our Trial Financial Aid Test and confirmed with the results of the Student Aid Report. Accordingly, there is a financial need of $12,500.

Furthermore, we expect that our financial need will not be fully met because this school, according to the *College Money Handbook,* only meets 80% of the financial need. Our expected offer, therefore, should be $10,000. When we break down that amount into the percentages of gift and self-help aid from this college, 40% and 60% respectively, we expect our gift aid to be $4,000 and our work-study aid and/or student loan aid to be $6,000. When looking at our actual award, this college gave us a $9,000 financial package which is $1,000 less than we expected. However, it did give us more gift aid than we anticipated, a total of $6,000 vs. $4,000, but not as much of a student loan, $3,000 instead of $6,000. Since this package is less than we expected, it makes sense to call the college and ask them why.

Figure 8.5

Need-Based Financial Aid Package Review Worksheet				
Name of College	**ABC Private University**			
	Expected Values			
	Federal Methodology	Institutional Methodology	Actual Award	Variance from Dominant Methodology
College Budget Bill	$23,000	$23,000	***************	***************
EFC	$10,500	$13,000	***************	***************
Financial Need	$12,500	$10,000	***************	***************
% Need Met	80%	80%	***************	***************
Expected Offer	$10,000	N/A	$9,000	- $1,000
% Gift	40% $4,000	N/A	$6,000	+ $2,000
% Self-Help Work Study Student Loans	60% $6,000	N/A	$3,000	- $3,000

When challenging a financial aid package please keep in mind that no college expects to "negotiate" financial aid with anyone. They will, however, listen to reason. Using the previous example, we must coach our client to call the college and ask, "We don't understand. According to the calculations we made and according to our resource books, we should be receiving a $10,000 financial aid package but we were only awarded $9,000. Did we do something wrong?" These statements inform the college that your client is financially aware and understands the financial aid process. It puts the college on notice that there is a challenge to their financial aid package.

Compare and Evaluate Every Financial Aid Award

Will they increase the financial aid package? That depends upon several factors.

♦ First, sometimes colleges simply have a bad year financially. Perhaps their endowment funds didn't earn as much as they did the pervious year. Maybe there are other reasons why they are short of financial aid dollars and are not able to meet all of the needs. Sometimes, schools just can't meet the needs because they don't have the funds, for whatever reason.

♦ Second, it depends upon how badly the college wants the student. Relative bargaining strength—if the college truly wants the student, it will likely ante up the difference. If the student is marginal for admission to the school, the college may decide not to meet the additional need.

It is important, however, to coach your client to ask the question. Colleges do not become angry with parents when they ask intelligent questions. In this particular case, not asking means accepting the lower financial aid offer. By challenging the amount of the award, perhaps we'll secure more financial aid for our client.

Comparing Financial Aid Packages Among Colleges

Comparing what a college awards in financial aid with what we expect it to award is only one way of enhancing a financial aid package. Another way is to compare one college's aid package with another college's aid package. It is perfectly permissible to do that, but for it to pay off it must be done tactfully.

Recalling the chapter on college selection (Chapter 5), we made the recommendation that most students should apply to ten or twelve schools. One of the reasons for this is that you need to be accepted to more than one school if you're going to use leverage to obtain more financial aid. One acceptable form of this leverage is to take a financial aid offer from a competitive college and send it to the college you really want your student to attend. Usually the best way to handle this is to telephone the financial aid officer. The conversation might go something like this:

"Mr./Ms. Financial Aid Officer, we have received a financial aid offer from another school that sounds too good to be true. It's substantially better than the one we received from your school. If we took the time to fax it to you, would you do us a favor and review it and make sure that we understand it before we act on an offer that might not be in our student's best interest?"

Most financial aid officers will look at competitive offers and often, based upon the competitive strengths of the students, will up the ante. In other words, if the college genuinely wants your client's student, it will often match or exceed comparable offers from other schools.

Occasionally, however, a financial aid officer may refuse to upgrade your client's financial aid package after it is compared with one from a school he believes does not meet the same standards as his own college. Colleges do have peer groups with whom they compete. They love to steal from their peers and more competitive schools. They also know there are other schools they compete favorably with based upon reputation and they don't need to compete on a monetary basis with those schools.

Special Circumstances for Athletes

It is important to use coaches if the student is an athlete. Coaches have a vested interest by interceding with the financial aid department. Also, be aware that athletic awards often come together late in the process.

Not too long ago, the daughter of one of our clients was recruited heavily by a number of schools; she played softball and was a catcher. At her favorite school, though, she was the second choice. Even though she received a financial aid package, the full scholarship was given to another student who the college hoped would be their catcher on their softball team. Late in April, however, the coach found out that his first choice for catcher was going to attend another school. Quickly, the full scholarship opened up and our client's daughter received a call early in May. The gist of the call was, "Name your price—we need you."

Summary

♦ Don't be afraid to challenge need-based awards, but do your homework first. Know the financial aid strength of the colleges on your list.

♦ Use competitive offers from peer groups and more competitive schools as leverage to improve a financial aid package.

♦ Plan to position the student during the college selection stage. The relative strength of the student is important when negotiating a financial aid package. Keep in mind, every student is a star at the right college.

♦ Remember the golden rule: *"He Who Has the Gold Makes the Rules."* Colleges can and will bend the rules when giving out their own private financial aid dollars. This aid is usually in the form of grants and scholarships, i.e., really free money. The colleges bend the rules for the students they actually want at the expense of those they want less.

♦ Finally, no college will negotiate financial aid….but they will listen to reasonable concerns and will often adjust their offers.

9

Putting Together the College Financing Package

Introduction

Usually by May of the senior year, high school students have chosen a college and their parents have negotiated for the best financial aid package. Yet, the financial aid that is secured is almost never enough. There remains a gap between the cost of college and the financial aid package that needs to be filled. There's a sense of urgency, too, because the bills will be sent early in August and they are due and payable before the semester begins. The remainder of this chapter lists the sources of funds you, as a financial services professional, can use to help your clients find the money they need to pay the college bills.

Taking Advantage of Tax Credits

The Taxpayer Relief Act of 1997 created two new tax credits that may be useful to some families. They are called the Hope Scholarship Credit and the Lifetime Learning Credit. The Hope Scholarship Credit applies to expenses paid after December 31, 1997 for education furnished in academic periods beginning after such date. In order to take advantage of the credit, a student must be enrolled at least part-time at an eligible institution. The Hope Scholarship Credit may also be elected only during the first two years of the student's post-secondary education. The student may be the taxpayer, the taxpayer's spouse or the taxpayer's dependent. The amount of the credit is equal to 100% of the first $1,000 of qualified educational expenses and 50% of the second $1,000 of qualified educational expenses paid during the taxable year. The maximum credit for 1998, therefore, is $1,500. Qualified educational expenses generally consist of tuition payments. Excluded specifically are course expenses such as books, room and board, activity fees and athletic fees. Most parents sending their students to normal college courses will incur at least $1,500 worth of expenses in each of the first two years and, thus, should be able to utilize the Hope Scholarship Credit. However, there are some exclusions.

The Hope Scholarship Credit is a per person credit; therefore, parents with two children in college at the same time can take a credit for qualified educational expenses for each student.

The Lifetime Learning Credit is somewhat different. It represents a "per family" credit. The Lifetime Learning Credit applies to expenses paid after June 30, 1998 for an education furnished in academic periods beginning after such date. It is available in an amount equal to 20% of the first $5,000 of qualified educational expenses paid by a taxpayer on behalf of such taxpayer, his spouse or dependents for a maximum credit of $1,000. After the year 2002, this credit will increase to 20% of $10,000, or a maximum credit of $2,000. Under the Lifetime Learning Credit, qualified educational expenses include not only post-secondary education, but also course work at schools to acquire approved job skills.

There are some significant limitations that will exclude our clients from taking advantage of either the Hope Scholarship Credit or the Lifetime Learning Credit. First is income. In order to obtain the maximum credit, the client's modified adjusted gross income must be under $40,000 for a single parent and under $80,000 for parents who are married and file a joint return. After the year 2001, these amounts will be indexed. Credits will be phased out completely for the single parent at $50,000 and for the married couple at $100,000. In addition to the income exclusion, parents must be careful to use these credits only for qualified educational expenses which normally includes tuition. Specifically excluded are payments for unrelated academic course expenses such as books, room and board, and activity and athletic fees. In addition to the income limitation, credits are also disallowed if distributions are made from an education IRA in the same year.

Unfortunately, credits come after the end of the tax year. If you believe that your client will be eligible for either the Hope Scholarship Credit or the Lifetime Learning Credit, you should inform your client to change his withholding immediately so he can accelerate his cash flow to help pay the college bills.

Pay-As-You-Go Strategies

Obviously, one "pay-as-you-go" strategy is to increase the family income but, as we've discussed in previous chapters, we must be careful that the clients we represent don't diminish their financial aid by increasing their short-term current earnings. Remember that income received this year will affect next year's financial aid package. For those clients who do not qualify for need-based financial aid, increasing the family income is a viable option to help them pay for college.

A second item, however, under pay-as-you-go strategies, is using college budget payments. Most colleges will allow parents to pay for college on a monthly basis. Often these budget plans do not incur interest but simply charge a flat administrative fee, usually $40 or $50. Most colleges that employ budget payments require that the parents make those payments beginning in May. Thus, they are prepaying some of their expenses and they are not receiving interest on the part of the payment that is made early. Payments then continue through the following May and there is no interest charged. If the amount of the college bill is fairly small, using this kind of payment plan is usually quite helpful to parents and often allows them to refrain from borrowing for college.

Using Savings and Investments to Pay the College Bill

Most parents have saved some money for college. There are four factors, however, that need to be considered before parents use those savings to pay the college bills.

1. Taxes.

2. Financial aid.

3. Opportunity costs.

4. Emergency funds.

Let's examine emergency funds first. Many of our clients are going to live on a shoestring when they send their children to college. Budgets are, obviously, going to become tight and cash flow is going to become stressed. It is extremely important that clients keep some reserves in emergency funds so, if they do run into trouble, they can take care of their emergency needs. Before you let your clients exhaust their college savings, make sure they have thought through their needs for emergency funds and are retaining such funds for their own use. Cash value life insurance and 401(k) balances can often be used to enhance emergency funds. It is easy to borrow money when you don't need it, but as clients accumulate debt it becomes more difficult to borrow.

Next is opportunity costs. To some degree, whether or not we liquidate savings and investments depends upon what we see as the return on those investments. In the last few years, investments in the stock market have easily yielded 15% to 20% and higher returns. Is it wise to have your clients spend their resources, which are earning these outstanding returns, when money can be borrowed from the parent loan program (discussed later in this chapter) at 9% or less?

Third, taxes become an issue. When we liquidate funds that have been invested at a profit, we will need to pay taxes on those gains. Timing when those taxes are paid could be an important consideration as to how you advise your clients about liquidating their college savings plans.

Also, when we liquidate funds at a profit, those capital gains also cause capital gains income which have an effect on the following year's financial aid. Remember, income follows the 47% rule.

Let's look at an example that will clarify this point.

> Suppose we have diligently saved for college and put aside $25,000. That amount has now grown to $50,000. Along the way we have paid taxes on some dividends which we have reinvested. If our cost basis is $30,000, we have a $20,000 gain. At 47%, that gain will reduce the following year's financial aid by approximately $9,400.

Sometimes it is beneficial to keep the savings in a parent's name until after college is over and forgo those gains because of the taxes and financial aid considerations. Many parents, without proper advice, will simply dip into their savings accounts and deplete them first, not thinking at all about emergency funds, taxes, opportunity costs or financial aid. You, as a financial services professional, can have a big impact on their thinking.

Loan Sources

Unfortunately, most parents will have to borrow funds for at least part of their college bills. Here are some of the loan options that are available to parents.

- Student loans.

- Parent college loans.

- Home equity arrangements.

- Retirement plan loans.

- Life insurance loans.

In the past we had to carefully evaluate the cost of these loans. Some of these loans were cheaper than others because of the tax deductible interest. Fortunately for some of our clients, the Taxpayer Relief Act of 1997 reduced the cost of borrowing by making college loan interest deductible.

College Loan Interest Deductibility

Starting in 1998, interest on student loans paid during the first 60 months that interest payments are required is deductible as a deduction for AGI. The 60-month period does not have to be consecutive which then allows for periods of deferment should a student go on to graduate school. Refinancing college loans will not begin a new 60 months. Eligible loans include those for attendance at post-secondary schools as well as institutions conducting internship or residency programs. Loans must be for the qualified higher educational expenses of the taxpayer, taxpayer's spouse, or dependent, who is enrolled in at least one-half of the normal academic load of a full-time student.

The following limitations apply:

1. The maximum deduction allowed is $1,000 in 1998, $1,500 in 1999, $2,000 in 2000, and $2,500 in 2001 and thereafter.

2. The interest deduction is phased out for a single taxpayer with a modified AGI of $40,000 to $55,000, and married taxpayers filing jointly with a modified AGI of $60,000 to $75,000. Married taxpayers filing separate returns do not qualify. After 2002, the $40,000 and $60,000 threshold amounts are indexed for inflation.

3. No deduction is allowed for anyone who is claimed as a dependent on another's return.

4. Education loans from relatives and related parties within the purview of Section 267(b) and Section 707(b)(1) do not qualify.

Many parents with higher incomes will not be able to deduct loan interest. Most students coming out of college will have lower incomes and will qualify for interest deductions.

Student Loans

First, let's look at student loan programs. In general, we feel that student loans are probably the best source of college money to go after. Unfortunately, many parents, as we indicated in Chapter 4, don't want their students taking on college loans; we think that is a mistake. First of all, student loans give children a vested interest in their education. If they know that borrowing money is part of the college cost, they tend to do better.

Second, student loans are bargains. There are two kinds of student loans that are prevalent: The Perkins Loan, which we can't apply for because it is included as part of a financial aid package; and Stafford Loans, which come in two forms: subsidized loans which are part of a financial aid package, and unsubsidized loans which are available to all students.

There are additional student loans as well. Some of them are state specific loans and some of them are college specific loans. State specific loans and college specific loans are beyond the scope of this text, but in Appendix 1 there is a list of state agencies that can provide you with more information about state specific loans. College specific loan information must come directly from the college.

Stafford Loans are an extremely good source of college money and they warrant an in-depth discussion.

Stafford Loans

A Federal Stafford Loan is a loan that is made available to both graduate and undergraduate students to help pay for their college education. There are both need-based (subsidized) loans and non-need-based (nonsubsidized) loans available. The crucial difference between the two loans is that the government pays the interest for the subsidized loan during deferments, as well as during college attendance, while the student pays all of the costs associated with the unsubsidized loan.

The federal government does not make the loans. Instead, they are made through financial institutions such as a bank, savings and loan association or credit union. Many colleges act as a direct lender. The government's involvement is in the form of state guaranty agencies which insure the loans, and the federal government which reinsures them.

Any student, whether independent or dependent, may apply for a Stafford Loan regardless of his income or his parents' income. It is important to fill out a FAFSA form before applying for a Stafford Loan because it must be determined whether the student is eligible for a federal Pell Grant since the amount of grant aid received will affect the amount of the Stafford Loan. An application can be obtained from a local bank, the college or the state guaranty agency. After the student's portion is completed, the application is sent to the college which certifies enrollment, cost of the education (tuition, room and board and expenses), the student's academic standing, any financial aid already received and the student's financial need.

It is important to note that a college or university has the right to refuse to certify a loan application, or to certify the loan for less than a student is actually eligible to receive. As long as the college presents its reasons and explains them in writing, their decision is final.

Most colleges and universities will make Stafford Loan applications available to their students, or one can be obtained from a local bank or savings and loan. If none of these sources offers an application, the guaranty agency in each state should be contacted for an application or list of participating lenders. Once the loan is approved, disbursements will be made payable to either the student or the college, or both.

What Is the Cost of a Stafford Loan?

What is the true cost of a Stafford Loan? Loan costs vary depending upon how much a student borrows, the interest rate and whether the loan is subsidized or unsubsidized. In addition to the amount borrowed, there is a three percent origination cost and a lender may require a one percent guarantee fee. Both fees are designed to offset program costs and will be deducted proportionately from each loan disbursement made to the student.

What Determines a Student's Loan Limits?

A student's status, academic year and program determine the maximum amount of the loan. Students who are claimed as dependents by their parents can borrow a varying amount each year. A first-year student can borrow up to $2,625 for educational costs. A second-year student may borrow up to $3,500 and those who have completed at least two years may borrow up to $5,500 a year. These amounts are based upon enrollment for a full academic year. For part-time students, the maximum loan amount is reduced.

Independent undergraduate students may borrow more than indicated above but a portion of that amount must be in unsubsidized Stafford Loans. Independent status is usually granted to students who support themselves, are 24-years old or older, are students whose parents are deceased and are, therefore, wards of the court, are married, are veterans of the U.S. armed forces, or are students who have legal dependents other than a spouse. Independent students in their first year of undergraduate study may borrow up to $6,625, $4,000 of which must be in unsubsidized loans. Second-year students may borrow up to $7,500, of which at least $4,000 must be in unsubsidized loans. Those who have completed two years may borrow up to $10,500 a year, of which $5,000 must be in unsubsidized loans. As with dependent student loans, maximum amounts are based upon full academic year status.

All graduate students are considered independent students and their parents' income does not play a role in determining their financial need for federal funds.

A graduate student may borrow up to $18,500 a year, at least $10,000 of which must be in unsubsidized Stafford Loans.

There are maximum loan limits. A dependent student can borrow a maximum of $23,000, and an independent undergraduate can borrow no more than $46,000. The maximum amount a graduate or professional study student can borrow is $138,500, $65,000 in subsidized Stafford Loans and $73,000 in unsubsidized Stafford Loans. These tremendous amounts include any federal loans accrued during the student's undergraduate study as well.

What Are the Interest Rates?

Interest rates for Stafford Loans are variable but capped at 8.25%. Rates are set each June at 3.1 points over the three-month U.S. Treasury Bill. A student's lender will inform the student of the interest rate and any change in that rate. Interest begins to accrue from the moment a loan is granted although no payments are made until after a student has graduated. For those students who qualify for subsidized Stafford Loans, interest payments are paid by the federal government while the student is attending college and when the loan is in deferment. A student who borrows unsubsidized Stafford Loans is responsible for the interest payments while in school or during deferments. Many lenders will let the interest accumulate while a student is attending college rather than require payments. The interest due will be added to the principal amount borrowed so the principal that must be repaid will increase.

When Does Repayment Begin and What Are the Terms?

In most cases, the repayment of a loan begins six months after a student graduates, leaves college or reduces his requirements to less than half-time status. There is a one-time only grace period and students with unsubsidized loans are responsible for interest payments. A student may apply for a loan deferment at any time including prior to when the repayment is scheduled to begin. Since loans are made through independent lenders, circumstances under which a deferment may be granted vary from one institution to another. Generally, a loan may be deferred while attending graduate school, participating in the Peace Corps or during times of financial hardship. The student should contact the lending institution for details.

Again, interest will accumulate on unsubsidized Stafford Loans. If a student does not qualify for a loan deferment, a forbearance may be granted to those who cannot make payments. A forbearance is a period during which neither principal or interest payments must be made although interest will accumulate on both unsubsidized and subsidized loans. This forbearance may last up to three years but the borrower must reapply for it each year. An automatic forbearance will be granted if loan payments are at least twenty percent of the borrower's gross income, although it must be requested by the borrower.

There are several repayment options available to both new student borrowers and those who have already acquired federal education loans and wish to re-finance. The standard plan, under which a student repays the loan in equal monthly installments, takes up to ten years to complete but it is the quickest and overall least expensive for those who can afford the payments. Deferments or forbearance is an option for those who cannot make the payments.

The lender must also give their borrowers the option of either a graduated or income sensitive repayment plan. Under a graduated plan, a student's monthly payments will gradually increase, it is hoped, as the student's financial situation improves. Monthly payments for an income sensitive plan will vary according to the borrower's financial situation although monthly payments must at least cover the cost of interest. While these programs may circumvent the need for a loan deferment or forbearance, they may take anywhere from ten to thirty years to repay.

Borrowers may consolidate federal loans into one loan and, therefore, one monthly payment. These payments, made in equal installments, may also take up to thirty years to repay. As in the standard plan, forbearance and deferment under an Individual Education Account allow for both a borrower's and spouse's loans to be consolidated together. The IEA offers standard, graduated, extended and income contingent repayment plans. These options are lengthy but more convenient.

Income Contingent Repayment plans allow borrowers to determine the size of their monthly payments based upon their income and expenses. A low income can allow them to make only minimal monthly payments—lower than needed to meet the accrued interest. After twenty-five years, the unpaid balance will be forgiven, but the remaining balance will be treated as taxable income which could result in a tremendous tax bill. While the payments are extremely low, the potential cost could be continual debt especially if the tax on the forgiven loan cannot be paid.

A loan will be forgiven or canceled in only certain cases. A loan may be forgiven if the college or university the student is attending closes before a degree is awarded. Interest and principal payments the student already made may also be refunded. Loans may be canceled if the student dies or becomes permanently disabled. The lender will determine other circumstances for granting cancellations or forgiveness.

In recent years, some lenders have given increased incentives to students to repay their loans on time. A typical program is:

♦   A ¼ point reduction in loan interest if the loan payment is taken directly out of the graduate's checking account.

♦   A rebate of most loan acquisition costs if payments are made on time for two full years.

♦   A 2 point reduction in loan interest if loan payments are mode on time for four full years.

These incentives reduce student loan costs to bargain levels. Add loan interest deductibility, which we will describe later, and you can see that these loans are worth considering. Since all lenders do not give these incentives, shopping for loans becomes important.

Why should a student assume the responsibility of a Federal Stafford Loan? Some have no choice since it is a part of their financial aid package offered by their particular college or university. For others who do not qualify for financial aid, it is a way to cover costs they and their parents cannot afford. This is, after all, the student's education–why should all debts associated with it be taken on by only the parents? Stafford Loans give students a chance to contribute to their own future.

Home Equity Arrangements

Once we have exhausted our ability to use student loans, the next best place to borrow money from will be a home equity loan. The interest on home equity loans is generally tax deductible to most parents and that can make it cheaper to borrow the money. Also, because home equity arrangements are collateralized, interest rates are usually lower. There are several approaches that you can take to help your clients plan.

One approach is to secure a fixed interest loan for a certain period of time and take out all of the money in advance. The advantage to this is that your client knows the terms in advance. He knows what interest rate he will pay because it's locked in and he knows the exact term of the loan so he can think ahead about what he needs to do. Usually this kind of loan demands that the client thinks ahead for the entire four-year college problem when planning the loan strategy.

One of the disadvantages of this kind of loan, however, is that your client will have significant cash remaining as an asset. This cash must be managed and, in addition, could have a negative effect on financial aid if the client's student is attending a college that uses the Federal Methodology. The reason for this is because the home equity does not appear as an asset for financial aid when using the Federal Methodology. Therefore, we are pulling cash out of an asset that doesn't count and turning it into a cash asset that does count against the family for financial aid purposes. If the client is going to a school where the Profile Form is used and the Institutional Methodology is the dominant methodology, it won't matter. We simply reduce the home equity and replace it with cash, and the two assets cancel out each other.

The second type of home equity arrangement is a credit line. The advantage here is that the client doesn't have to take all of the money in advance and doesn't need to pay the interest on all the money in advance. The primary disadvantage here is the client doesn't know what his interest rate will be since it will fluctuate over time. This kind of home equity credit line won't have an adverse effect on obtaining financial aid because as money is pulled out of the home, it is used almost immediately. In fact, this arrangement does have a positive effect on securing financial aid because it reduces the home equity under the Institutional Methodology. Unused credit lines can also be cancelled thereby frustrating your clients college plan.

When exploring home equity arrangements, keep in mind that your planning is limited to what you can borrow on the home. In many cases this is 80% of the total equity in the house. Often this is not enough to provide significant funds to pay the total college bill. Some lending institutions will, however, give 125% equity loans. These loans usually come at the price of a higher interest rate. As a planner, you need to balance the tax deductibility of interest coming out of the home equity type arrangement with the security considerations for the family and the cost of borrowing.

Federal PLUS Loans

Another form of borrowing is parent loans. Uncle Sam has created a loan program to help parents pay for college that is called the Federal PLUS Loan Program.

What is a PLUS loan?

Comparable to the Stafford Loan that is available to students, the PLUS loan is a parent loan that is also sponsored by the federal government. The PLUS loan (Parent Loan for Undergraduate Students) is taken out by the parents of the dependent student to cover the entire cost of college, including tuition and living expenses, minus any financial aid for which the student is eligible. Under the Stafford Loan, students may only borrow a limited amount each year but which increases as they continue their education. Like the Stafford Loan, the PLUS loan can be repaid over a period of ten years at low interest rates and may be deferred or canceled in certain cases. Unlike the Stafford Loan, there is no grace period before payments begin; the first payment is due sixty days after the disbursement of the loan.

PLUS loans are non-need-based; anyone can apply, regardless of income. The only requirement is that the borrower meets federal standards of credit worthiness which are, reportedly, more lenient than other non-federally guaranteed programs. It may actually be easier to borrow a PLUS loan than other loans and at a lower rate of interest. In the case where the intended borrower does not meet the set credit requirements, the loan may still be granted if an endorser, who does meet the requirements, is found to co-sign the loan.

What is the true cost of a PLUS loan?

The principal amount varies, of course, from case to case, depending upon the cost of the college or university attended and the amount of money requested. (Parents may borrow less than the total amount of the education if they so wish.) The interest rate is variable but capped at 10% for loans borrowed through July, 1994, and 9% for loans borrowed after July, 1994. The interest rate is set each May by the federal government which places it at 3.1% above the twelve-month U.S. Treasury Bill.

The principal and interest are not the only costs associated with a PLUS loan, however. There is a 1% guarantee fee which is mandated by Congress to offset the cost of the program. There is also a 3% origination fee which is included to fund the program benefits such as death/disability insurance and deferments. Both fees are deducted from the disbursement check and paid to the federal government. These fees must be included by the college when it determines the cost of the education and may be included in the requested amount of the loan.

How does the loan work?

Although the law does not require the family to complete a FAFSA form in order to receive a PLUS loan, *many colleges are requiring the family to complete the FAFSA form.* A PLUS loan application must be completed and submitted and a credit check will be performed on the potential borrower. Based on the estimated cost of attendance (which includes tuition, room and board, fees, books, supplies, equipment, transportation and commuting expenses) minus the estimated (not guaranteed) financial assistance the student can receive, a requested loan amount will be submitted. *A student's eligibility for grants, work-study programs and other funds will be affected by a PLUS loan so these should be estimated before figuring the loan request.* It is at the institution's discretion whether or not to certify a loan application and at what amount; it can be for an amount less than the borrower's eligibility.

The cost of attendance will also be determined by the academic institution as will the disbursement terms. At an institution without academic terms, disbursements will be made at the commencement and midpoints of the enrollment period. The loan may be disbursed by check, co-payable to the borrower and the institution, and sent to the institution, or it may be sent, with the borrower's approval, by electronic transfer to the institution. Repayment of the loan will begin sixty days after the final disbursement.

PLUS loans are generally repaid in monthly installments over a period of ten years, barring any deferments. The minimum annual payment for all federal loans is $600 or the amount of interest due, whichever is greater. There is a late fee of no more than 6% for any payments more than ten days late.

There is a Federal Consolidation Loan program available for those who wish to consolidate the federal education loans they received from different lenders or loan programs. This consolidation would result in one monthly payment and the repayment period could exceed the usual ten years. Under certain recruitment programs for the military, a portion or all of a PLUS loan may be repaid by the Secretary of Defense. Loans may also be deferred or canceled under certain circumstances.

Can the PLUS loan be deferred or canceled?

A PLUS loan will be automatically cancelled if the borrower, or the student for whom the loan was borrowed, dies. If the borrower or student sustains a permanent disability the loan will be cancelled as long as the condition that caused the permanent disability did not occur before the loan application. If the disability is the result of a pre-existing condition, a doctor's confirmation of significant deterioration after the loan application was made must be submitted. Since a PLUS loan is signed for by only one parent, it will not be canceled if the borrower's spouse dies or becomes disabled. A deferment may be granted if a death or disability results in a borrower's economic hardship.

A loan may also be canceled if a student cannot complete his studies at the intended institution, whether because the institution closes or the student's eligibility was falsely certified by the institution. A PLUS loan *may be* canceled, but it is not a guaranteed cancellation, should the borrower declare bankruptcy.

A borrower should be aware that, although monthly payments may be deferred, interest will continue to accrue and be added to the principal of the loan if it is allowed to be capitalized. For loans disbursed after July, 1993, deferments will be granted only in cases where 1) the borrower is enrolled at least part-time at an eligible institution, or 2) while pursuing a graduate fellowship or a rehabilitation training program for the disabled for an undetermined amount of time. A loan may be deferred for up to three years while the borrower 1) conscientiously seeks full-time employment, but is unable to find it, or 2) experiences an economic hardship for a reason approved by federal regulations.

A potential borrower should be aware of the consequences of defaulting on a PLUS loan. The total amount of the loan will become due if:

♦ The student fails to enroll a least part-time at the institution mentioned on the application;

♦ The loan proceeds are used for anything other than the student's education;

♦ The application is falsified to allow the borrower to receive a loan greater than one for which he or she is eligible; or

♦ The loan is in default.

A refusal to make payments for more than six months without applying for and receiving a deferment will signal a default. Defaulting on a PLUS loan can result in the loss of federal or state income tax refunds, legal action, assessment of collection charges including legal fees, loss of a professional license, ineligibility for other federal student aid funds, ineligibility for deferments, negative credit reports and wage garnishment. As the PLUS loan is a federal program, it is subject to government stricture.

What effect will the recent tax changes by Congress have on the program? While federal grants and loan repayment programs (such as Americorps) may come under the attack of zealous cost-cutters, federal loan programs are the more secure bet.

Plus loan interest may be deductible for some parents if they meet the income restrictions for deductibility of college loans. For many of our upper-middle and upper income clients, however, PLUS loans will not be deductible. There are some advantages, though, to using the PLUS loan. First, interest rates are capped at 9%—they can never go higher. Second, the PLUS loan has built-in life insurance. Since only one parent signs for the PLUS loan, the loan is cancelled due to the life insurance if the signing parent dies or becomes disabled. This can be a significant benefit especially when you are dealing with uninsurable parents.

Figure 9.1

PLUS Loan Summary	
Non-need-based loan	Yes
Loan limit	The cost of college less any other financial aid the student might receive.
Special requirements	Credit worthiness
Interest rate	Variable, set each May at 3.1% above the 12 month T-bill.
Interest rate cap	10% for loans issued through July, 1994; 9% for those loans issued after July, 1994.
Current interest rate July, 1996 to June, 1997	8.72%
Guarantee Fee	1%
Origination Fee	3%
Repayment	Begins 60 days after the final disbursement. May be deferred or canceled in some circumstances.

Finally, PLUS loans are easy to obtain. It is a signature loan; it is not asset based and all that parents must show is good credit. One of the dangers of using PLUS loans is that it is easy for parents to accumulate more loans than perhaps it is wise for them to take on. Part of the exercise that you as a financial professional need to make sure your clients explore is the ability to repay any debt prior to retirement. Remember, college is a retirement problem.

State Specific and College Specific Loans

In addition to Stafford and PLUS loans, many colleges and some states have attractive loan programs. Some may have lower interest rates while others may offer better terms. Appendix 1 contains a contact list for each state. Information on college loan programs must come from each individual college.

Other Resources

There are two other resources that bear mentioning. One is utilizing money from a 401(k) plan or tax sheltered annuity to pay for college. Although the advantage of using these funds is that a client is using his own money and is paying interest, in effect, to himself, there are several disadvantages.

First, this represents retirement money and, since college is a retirement problem, parents need to think twice before they reduce their retirement benefits. Second, this is money that is invested and growing on a tax deferred basis. Any money that is borrowed is taken out of the investment pot and is no longer earning interest and growing tax deferred. Losing this financial leverage can be significant. Third, there is a trap in borrowing from 401(k)s especially. 401(k) loans need to be repaid over a five-year or shorter time period. This means high monthly cash flow payments at a time when maybe the parents should spread out their cash flow. If parents default on loans it is easier to default on their 401(k) loan since it does not effect their credit; after all, it is their money. However, when a parent defaults on his 401(k) loan, he triggers a taxable distribution. Income tax must be paid on that distribution in that year. In addition, penalties may apply. This kind of premature distribution could be extremely costly to parents.

Life insurance cash values are another resource that could be available for college. Here again, although life insurance loans are cheap and the initial impulse is to use them first, their use to pay the college bills diminishes a parent's life insurance at a time when a parent is financially vulnerable. Also, one of the advantages of a life insurance loan is that the insurance company must give it to you. Thus, it is great emergency fund money. Perhaps the life insurance cash value should be held back in case a parent finds himself into trouble.

The discussion of life insurance leads us nicely into the final comment that we want to make with regard to borrowing for college. When parents borrow for college, they put the family as a whole at risk in the event of a catastrophe, and parents don't often plan for catastrophes. College cash flow planning is an extremely good time to review your client's life and disability insurance needs. It is often difficult to get parents to face up to these issues. They are not interested in life insurance and disability insurance at this time. They are interested in paying for college and the last thing they believe they need to spend money on is insurance premiums. But we have seen too many families almost lose their home because of improper planning simply because the breadwinner died or became disabled. It is extremely important to make your clients sit down and review their family's security at this time in their planning.

Summary

When you sit down with a family to help plan their college cash flow, make sure you look at what is necessary to get them out of debt prior to their retirement. Unfortunately, parents are pressured to borrow to pay for college. Students are accepted at some great colleges and the parents are, naturally, proud. So it's easy to borrow money to send the students to those colleges. But, borrowing restraint, debt reduction, and life and disability insurance are all key parts of the college cash flow problem.

10

Saving for College the Right Way

Introduction

Having gone through the first eight steps, you have a good idea of what your clients will experience if they don't save enough money and don't save it the right way. Perhaps this will give you some incentive to convince your client's to save money for college.

During the last seventeen years we have helped over 40,000 families pay for college. Most parents come to us in a state of crisis when their student is in the junior or senior year of high school. They have bigger college aspirations than initially planned and very little money. In fact, out of the 40,000 families we've helped, less than 10, not 10%, had enough savings.

Several years ago, a major magazine asked us to report on the college savings status of business executives earning $100,000 to $200,000. Sadly, the average savings were equal to about one year of college costs; not one year per student, but one year for the entire family. The lack of savings cuts down the college selection options of the family so many times students end up at their second or third choice schools. Although you can still help your clients by following the first eight steps, your clients will be better off if you convince them to save.

Why Parents Don't Save Enough for College

Most parents know that college costs a lot of money. Unfortunately, saving for college competes with other dollars used by the family for everyday living expenses and retirement savings. Parents also spend considerable amounts of money to develop their children's skills so they will be able to compete for college admissions. Music lessons, summer camp and athletic coaching are just a few. It is not surprising, therefore, that parents do not save enough.

Procrastination is another big reason. College seems so far away when the children are young. Time passes quickly and suddenly students are in high school.

Of those parents who do plan, most underestimate the cost of college. They forget about the tax implications. Many don't understand the impact of college inflation and how much more it is than regular inflation.

Our profession often attacks the college savings process in a manor that demoralizes parents. We show them big numbers without giving them realistic options. As an example, we project future college costs and calculate the savings required to meet those costs. Often those numbers are so big that parents can't handle them; they just walk away and do nothing.

Review the charts in Appendix 7. We have duplicated one of those as Figure 10.1 as an example of a high-priced Ivy League-type of college. If our client wants his student to attend this type of college, he must accumulate $376,311 and, at a net 8% after taxes rate of return, he will need to save $936 per month, every month, starting immediately and lasting through the end of college. And that's for only one student. Although we think the projections are accurate and the calculations are correct, most parents can't make that kind of commitment, so they do nothing.

➤ Note: College cost projections, college inflation and monthly saving requirements are discussed in Appendices 6 and 7.

There is room for the financial services professional to make a significant impact by persuading our clients to attack the college problem early, but we must give our clients realistic options. The following example is an approach we have found to be effective. This approach involves several steps.

♦ Project future college costs for the entire family.

♦ Calculate the savings requirements to complete the job.

Figure 10.1

Projected College Costs and Savings Requirements

ASSUMPTIONS:
  PLANNED SAVINGS STARTS SEPTEMBER   1997
  PLANNED WITHDRAWALS START SEPTEMBER   FRESHMAN YEAR
  SCHOOL CATEGORY (1=LOW, 2=Med/Low, 3=MEDIUM, 4=Med/High, 5=HIGH) 5
  PROJECTED AFTER-TAX GROWTH ON SAVINGS   6.00%   8.00%   10.00%

Notes:
  Assume funding through August of the last year of college
  College costs are total costs based on college budget bill plus misc. costs reported by parents.
  Cost Categories - 1= Low for State schools(in-state resident), 5 = High for Ivy League, 2-4 = Medium range for Private

PROJECTED FRESHMEN YEAR	PROJECTED FRESHMAN COST	PROJECTED SOPHOMORE COST	PROJECTED JUNIOR COST	PROJECTED SENIOR COST	PROJECTED FOUR YEAR COST	APPROX. MO. SAVINGS REQ 6.00%	APPROX. MO. SAVINGS REQ 8.00%	APPROX. MO. SAVINGS REQ 10.00%
1997						n/a	n/a	n/a
1998	$35,888	$37,882	$39,986	$42,206	$155,962	$2,512	$2,483	$2,454
1999	$37,882	$39,986	$42,206	$44,550	$164,624	$2,142	$2,096	$2,050
2000	$39,986	$42,206	$44,550	$47,540	$174,282	$1,884	$1,824	$1,764
2001	$42,206	$44,550	$47,540	$50,730	$185,026	$1,696	$1,623	$1,553
2002	$44,550	$47,540	$50,730	$54,134	$196,954	$1,555	$1,471	$1,392
2003	$47,540	$50,730	$54,134	$57,766	$210,169	$1,446	$1,353	$1,265
2004	$50,730	$54,134	$57,766	$61,642	$224,272	$1,359	$1,257	$1,161
2005	$54,134	$57,766	$61,642	$66,524	$240,065	$1,290	$1,180	$1,077
2006	$57,766	$61,642	$66,524	$71,791	$257,723	$1,237	$1,118	$1,007
2007	$61,642	$66,524	$71,791	$77,476	$277,433	$1,197	$1,068	$950
2008	$66,524	$71,791	$77,476	$83,612	$299,403	$1,166	$1,028	$903
2009	$71,791	$77,476	$83,612	$90,233	$323,112	$1,141	$993	$861
2010	$77,476	$83,612	$90,233	$97,378	$348,699	$1,120	$963	$824
2011	$83,612	$90,233	$97,378	$105,089	$376,311	$1,104	$936	$79
2012	$90,233	$97,378	$105,089	$113,411	$406,111	$1,090	$913	$761
2013	$97,378	$105,089	$113,411	$122,392	$438,270	$1,080	$893	$733
2014	$105,089	$113,411	$122,392	$132,084	$472,975	$1,072	$874	$708
2015	$113,411	$122,392	$132,084	$142,543	$510,429	$1,066	$858	$685
2016	$122,392	$132,084	$142,543	$153,831	$550,849	$1,062	$843	$664
2017	$132,084	$142,543	$153,831	$166,012	$594,470	$1,060	$830	$644
2018	$142,543	$153,831	$166,012	$179,159	$641,545	$1,060	$818	$625

♦ Show parents what happens if they rely on the other ways of funding college costs such as:

  ◊ Pay-as-you-go,

  ◊ Borrowing.

♦ Develop a composite plan of saving, pay-as-you-go, cost sharing with the student and borrowing that is tailored to the specific needs of the client.

♦ Implement the plan.

Case Study: Dr. Learner

Dr. Learner and her husband are both age 44. They have two children, Hilary age 10, and Craig age 7. This situation is typical of many families we counsel today. These adults are having children later in life and they will retire either when the children are in college or shortly thereafter. In this case, Craig will finish college in the year 2014 and Dr. Learner and her husband plan to retire in the year 2017. This situation presents a significant dilemma. The Learners will need to amortize any remaining college debt over four years which means high monthly payments if they don't pre-fund enough of their college expenses.

The Learners already have $50,000 set aside for college and they can save $1,100 per month. They plan to send their children to the best schools especially since both of the Learners are graduates of Ivy League colleges.

Our first step in the savings process is to generate a college cost forecast by using Lotus spreadsheets. Chart 3 of our presentation illustrates the college cost forecast for the Learners. As you can see, they are facing college bills over $277,000 for Hillary (#1) and over $348,000 for Craig (#2). The total college bill will exceed $626,000.

When we discussed the nine concepts in Chapter 2, we outlined the four ways to pay for college which are summarized on Chart 4. The first three options, saving, pay-as-you-go and borrowing, are valid but we don't want to depend upon financial aid. Our client has a high income and is not likely to receive help other than from merit scholarships or negotiated tuition discounts. Since we can't forecast those benefits we will complete our analysis without including them. Should the Learners be lucky enough later on to receive financial aid, these benefits will reduce their cash flow during college or give them more money that they can use for their own retirement.

Chart 5 represents how much the Learners must save for college if they start immediately and it includes the $50,000 they have already saved. The chart also shows that if the Learners save $18,059 and earn an after-tax yield of 8%, they will be able to pre-fund the entire college bill.

If the Learners decide not to save for college, they could try and pay the college costs out of their current income during the college years. But in order to do that they would have to earn substantially more in order to pay the taxes in their 39% tax bracket and have enough remaining for college. Chart 6 summarizes this data and demonstrates to the Learners that in order to have $626,132 to pay for college they must earn in excess of $870,000 and pay over $244,000 in taxes. This chart can often be a motivating factor in convincing parents to save.

Chart 7 is another motivating sheet. It depicts how the Learners could ignore saving for college and ignore the pay-as-you-go system and borrow the money. However, if they did borrow they would borrow in excess of $626,000, pay over $365,000 in interest at 9% and have annual payments in excess of $247,000 per year in order to amortize their college loans. This is because the Learners have only four years between the end of Craig's college days and their retirement.

Chart 8 summarizes the Learners' options. It reveals they can:

◊   Save $18,059 per year until Craig graduates from college;

◊   Increase their income by an average of $124,332 per year during college to pay the taxes on the additional income as well as the college bills;

◊   Borrow throughout the college years and have annual payments in excess of $247,803 in order to amortize the amount borrowed between the time Craig graduates from college and the start of their retirement;

◊   Use a combination of the three.

The end result is that the Learners asked us to design a composite plan of saving, pay-as-you-go and borrowing in order to give them a workable plan.

The Lerner Presentation

Chart 1

Prepared on:	**01-Nov-97**
Prepared for:	**Dr. Learner**
Prepared by:	**Raymond D. Loewe, CLU, ChFC** **College Money** **112B Centre Blvd.** **Marlton, NJ 08053** **(609) 596-4700**
Subject:	**College Funding Analysis**

The analysis that follows has been prepared especially for your family. The purpose of this analysis is to help you design a plan to handle anticipated future college costs in a reasonable and effective manner. You should understand that any analysis of this type is for planning purposes only. The projections imply no guarantees. Projections are based on future college cost data, interest and inflation assumptions, and personal data you supplied, all of which can change over time. If used properly, however, this analysis can help you be better prepared to handle college for your family.

Chart 2

**College Planning Model
Data Verification as of:**   **01-Nov-97**

Parent Data:
* Client name   Dr. Learner
* Age of older parent   44
* Plan end (year of older parent retirement or sooner)   2017
* Year oldest student starts college   2007
* Year youngest student finishes college   2014
* After-tax savings earnings rate   8.00%
* Loan interest rate   9.00%
* Parent tax bracket   39.00%
* Savings already set aside for college $50,000

Plan Design Data:
Planned monthly college savings $1,100.00
Planned annual increase in monthly savings (percentage)   4.00%
Planned annual payments during college $13,200

Student Data:

Student #	1	2	3	4	5	6
Student Name	Hillary	Craig	–	–	–	–
Undergrad Start Year:	2007	2010	0	0	0	0
School Cost Code*	5	5	0	0	0	0
# Undergrad Years	4	4	0	0	0	0
Last Year Undergrad	2011	2014	0	0	0	0
Grad Start Year	2011	2014	0	0	0	0
School Cost Code*	5	5	0	0	0	0
# Grad School Years	0	0	0	0	0	0
Last Year Grad	2011	2014	0	0	0	0

* School Cost Codes
  1 Low Cost (eg. state college for in-state resident)
  2 Low Medium (eg. lower cost private college)
  3 Medium Cost (eg. average private college)
  4 High Medium (eg. higher cost private college)
  5 Highest Cost (eg. Ivy League)

Chart 3

TABLE I - College Cost Forecast

The first step in developing a good college plan is to forecast what college is likely to cost for your family.

The following table projects future college costs for each member of your family based on the types of colleges you selected for each student and our college cost model.

Age Older Parent	Year	COLLEGE COSTS FOR STUDENT						TOTAL COSTS
		#1	#2	#3	#4	#5	#6	
44	1997	$0	$0	$0	$0	$0	$0	$0
45	1998	$0	$0	$0	$0	$0	$0	$0
46	1999	$0	$0	$0	$0	$0	$0	$0
47	2000	$0	$0	$0	$0	$0	$0	$0
48	2001	$0	$0	$0	$0	$0	$0	$0
49	2002	$0	$0	$0	$0	$0	$0	$0
50	2003	$0	$0	$0	$0	$0	$0	$0
51	2004	$0	$0	$0	$0	$0	$0	$0
52	2005	$0	$0	$0	$0	$0	$0	$0
53	2006	$0	$0	$0	$0	$0	$0	$0
54	2007	$61,642	$0	$0	$0	$0	$0	$61,642
55	2008	$66,524	$0	$0	$0	$0	$0	$66,524
56	2009	$71,791	$0	$0	$0	$0	$0	$71,791
57	2010	$77,476	$77,476	$0	$0	$0	$0	$154,952
58	2011	$0	$83,612	$0	$0	$0	$0	$83,612
59	2012	$0	$90,233	$0	$0	$0	$0	$90,233
60	2013	$0	$97,378	$0	$0	$0	$0	$97,378
61	2014	$0	$0	$0	$0	$0	$0	$0
62	2015	$0	$0	$0	$0	$0	$0	$0
63	2016	$0	$0	$0	$0	$0	$0	$0
64	2017	$0	$0	$0	$0	$0	$0	$0
65	2018	$0	$0	$0	$0	$0	$0	$0
66	2019	$0	$0	$0	$0	$0	$0	$0
67	2020	$0	$0	$0	$0	$0	$0	$0
68	2021	$0	$0	$0	$0	$0	$0	$0
69	2022	$0	$0	$0	$0	$0	$0	$0
70	2023	$0	$0	$0	$0	$0	$0	$0
71	2024	$0	$0	$0	$0	$0	$0	$0
72	2025	$0	$0	$0	$0	$0	$0	$0
73	2026	$0	$0	$0	$0	$0	$0	$0
74	2027	$0	$0	$0	$0	$0	$0	$0
75	2028	$0	$0	$0	$0	$0	$0	$0
76	2029	$0	$0	$0	$0	$0	$0	$0
77	2030	$0	$0	$0	$0	$0	$0	$0
78	2031	$0	$0	$0	$0	$0	$0	$0
79	2032	$0	$0	$0	$0	$0	$0	$0
80	2033	$0	$0	$0	$0	$0	$0	$0
81	2034	$0	$0	$0	$0	$0	$0	$0
82	2035	$0	$0	$0	$0	$0	$0	$0
83	2036	$0	$0	$0	$0	$0	$0	$0
TOTALS		$277,433	$348,699	$0	$0	$0	$0	$626,132

Chart 4

There Are Only Four Ways To Pay For College

Now that you know what college cost projections look like for your family, you need to realize that there are only four ways to pay for college:

Option 1:   Save or pre-fund college in advance.

Option 2:   Pay for college out of current income when you get there.

Option 3:   Borrow during the college years and pay for it later.

Option 4:   Let someone else pay for college. (eg. financial aid, wealthy grandparents, etc.)

The analysis that follows will help you plan by examining options 1, 2, and 3 individually and in combination with each other. We will not explore financial aid because financial aid rules change over time. It is important, however, to build flexiblity into every plan so you don't miss out on future financial aid eligibility.

Chart 5

TABLE II - How Much You Need To Save To Pre-fund College (Start Now Through Last Year)

Present Value of Future College Costs	$227,903
Current Savings Committed to College	$50,000
Additional Lump Sum Required Today to Fund College	$177,903
Annual Savings Required to Pre-fund	$18,059
After Tax Interest Assumption	8.00%

Age Older Parent	Year	College Costs	Acct Bal Yr Start	Annual Savings Yr Start	Interest Income Yr End	Acct Bal Yr End
44	1997	$0	$50,000	$18,059	$5,445	$73,503
45	1998	$0	$73,503	$18,059	$7,325	$98,887
46	1999	$0	$98,887	$18,059	$9,356	$126,302
47	2000	$0	$126,302	$18,059	$11,549	$155,909
48	2001	$0	$155,909	$18,059	$13,917	$187,885
49	2002	$0	$187,885	$18,059	$16,476	$222,420
50	2003	$0	$222,420	$18,059	$19,238	$259,717
51	2004	$0	$259,717	$18,059	$22,222	$299,997
52	2005	$0	$299,997	$18,059	$25,445	$343,501
53	2006	$0	$343,501	$18,059	$28,925	$390,484
54	2007	$61,642	$390,484	$18,059	$27,752	$374,653
55	2008	$66,524	$374,653	$18,059	$26,095	$352,283
56	2009	$71,791	$352,283	$18,059	$23,884	$322,435
57	2010	$154,952	$322,435	$18,059	$14,843	$200,384
58	2011	$83,612	$200,384	$18,059	$10,786	$145,618
59	2012	$90,233	$145,618	$18,059	$5,875	$79,319
60	2013	$97,378	$79,319	$18,059	$0	($0)
61	2014	$0	($0)	$0	$0	($0)
62	2015	$0	($0)	$0	$0	($0)
63	2016	$0	($0)	$0	$0	($0)
64	2017	$0	($0)	$0	$0	($0)
65	2018	$0	($0)	$0	$0	($0)
66	2019	$0	($0)	$0	$0	($0)
67	2020	$0	($0)	$0	$0	($0)
68	2021	$0	($0)	$0	$0	($0)
69	2022	$0	($0)	$0	$0	($0)
70	2023	$0	($0)	$0	$0	($0)
71	2024	$0	($0)	$0	$0	($0)
72	2025	$0	($0)	$0	$0	($0)
73	2026	$0	($0)	$0	$0	($0)
74	2027	$0	($0)	$0	$0	($0)
75	2028	$0	($0)	$0	$0	($0)
76	2029	$0	($0)	$0	$0	($0)
77	2030	$0	($0)	$0	$0	($0)
78	2031	$0	($0)	$0	$0	($0)
79	2032	$0	($0)	$0	$0	($0)
80	2033	$0	($0)	$0	$0	($0)
81	2034	$0	($0)	$0	$0	($0)
82	2035	$0	($0)	$0	$0	($0)
83	2036	$0	($0)	$0	$0	($0)
TOTALS		$626,132	N/A	$306,999	$269,133	N/A

Chart 6

TABLE III - Paying for College From Current Income During the College Years

This method puts undue stress on family finances during the college years. Usually a nonworking spouse returns to work to increase family income. Table III shows the extra income required during the college years to pay tax on the additional earnings and have enough left over to pay for college.

WARNING! Current financial aid formulas reduce aid eligibility as family income increases.

Tax bracket assumed for this analysis: 39.00%

AGE OF OLDER PARENT	YEAR	COLLEGE COSTS	INCOME TAXES	PRETAX INCOME REQ
44	1997	$0	$0	$0
45	1998	$0	$0	$0
46	1999	$0	$0	$0
47	2000	$0	$0	$0
48	2001	$0	$0	$0
49	2002	$0	$0	$0
50	2003	$0	$0	$0
51	2004	$0	$0	$0
52	2005	$0	$0	$0
53	2006	$0	$0	$0
54	2007	$61,642	$24,040	$85,683
55	2008	$66,524	$25,944	$92,468
56	2009	$71,791	$27,999	$99,790
57	2010	$154,953	$60,432	$215,384
58	2011	$83,612	$32,609	$116,220
59	2012	$90,233	$35,191	$125,423
60	2013	$97,378	$37,977	$135,355
61	2014	$0	$0	$0
62	2015	$0	$0	$0
63	2016	$0	$0	$0
64	2017	$0	$0	$0
65	2018	$0	$0	$0
66	2019	$0	$0	$0
67	2020	$0	$0	$0
68	2021	$0	$0	$0
69	2022	$0	$0	$0
70	2023	$0	$0	$0
71	2024	$0	$0	$0
72	2025	$0	$0	$0
73	2026	$0	$0	$0
74	2027	$0	$0	$0
75	2028	$0	$0	$0
76	2029	$0	$0	$0
77	2030	$0	$0	$0
78	2031	$0	$0	$0
79	2032	$0	$0	$0
80	2033	$0	$0	$0
81	2034	$0	$0	$0
82	2035	$0	$0	$0
83	2036	$0	$0	$0
TOTALS		$626,132	$244,191	$870,323

Chart 7

TABLE IV - Borrowing to Pay for College

Borrowing is often a necessary college financing alternative, but it converts the college problem into a retirement problem. The Table IV shows the cash flow burden placed on the family that relies on borrowing and then attempts to amortize debt between the end of college and the start of retirement.

Annual payment required: $247,803

Older Parent Age	Year	Family College Costs	Amounts Borrowed	Loan Interest	Levelized Loan Payment	Loan Balance
44	1997	$0	$0	$0	$0	$0
45	1998	$0	$0	$0	$0	$0
46	1999	$0	$0	$0	$0	$0
47	2000	$0	$0	$0	$0	$0
48	2001	$0	$0	$0	$0	$0
49	2002	$0	$0	$0	$0	$0
50	2003	$0	$0	$0	$0	$0
51	2004	$0	$0	$0	$0	$0
52	2005	$0	$0	$0	$0	$0
53	2006	$0	$0	$0	$0	$0
54	2007	$61,642	$61,642	$0	$0	$61,642
55	2008	$66,524	$66,524	$5,548	$0	$133,713
56	2009	$71,791	$71,791	$12,034	$0	$217,539
57	2010	$154,953	$154,953	$19,579	$0	$392,070
58	2011	$83,612	$83,612	$35,286	$0	$510,968
59	2012	$90,233	$90,233	$45,987	$0	$647,188
60	2013	$97,378	$97,378	$58,247	$0	$802,813
61	2014	$0	$0	$72,253	$247,803	$627,263
62	2015	$0	$0	$56,454	$247,803	$435,913
63	2016	$0	$0	$39,232	$247,803	$227,342
64	2017	$0	$0	$20,461	$247,803	$0
65	2018	$0	$0	$0	$0	$0
66	2019	$0	$0	$0	$0	$0
67	2020	$0	$0	$0	$0	$0
68	2021	$0	$0	$0	$0	$0
69	2022	$0	$0	$0	$0	$0
70	2023	$0	$0	$0	$0	$0
71	2024	$0	$0	$0	$0	$0
72	2025	$0	$0	$0	$0	$0
73	2026	$0	$0	$0	$0	$0
74	2027	$0	$0	$0	$0	$0
75	2028	$0	$0	$0	$0	$0
76	2029	$0	$0	$0	$0	$0
77	2030	$0	$0	$0	$0	$0
78	2031	$0	$0	$0	$0	$0
79	2032	$0	$0	$0	$0	$0
80	2033	$0	$0	$0	$0	$0
81	2034	$0	$0	$0	$0	$0
82	2035	$0	$0	$0	$0	$0
83	2036	$0	$0	$0	$0	$0
TOTALS		$626,132	$626,132	$365,081	$991,213	

Chart 8

Prepared on:	**01-Nov-97**
Prepared For:	**Dr. Learner**
Prepared By:	**Raymond D. Loewe, CLU, ChFC** **College Money** **112B Centre Blvd.** **Marlton, NJ 08053** **(609) 596-4700**
Subject:	**Report Summary:**

Report Summary:
For most families, none of the above alternatives are realistic. A better approach is to look at combinations of saving, pay-as-you-go, and borrowing. Using a combination plan will spread the financial pressure over a period of time making it more bearable. Before we investigate combination plans, let's recap each individual approach.

Option 1:
You can try to prefund college by saving each year beginning now and saving through your youngest student's last year of college. To accomplish this will require annual saving of: $18,059

Option 2:
You can wait until college begins and try to increase your income enough to pay taxes on the additional income and have enough remaining to pay your college bills. To do this would require an average annual increase in income over the entire college period of: $124,332

Option 3:
You can do nothing until college is over, borrow what you need throughout college and repay loans between the time college ends and your first year of retirement. This would require annual payments of: $247,803

Note:
Whatever you decide, it is critical to start early to avoid a potential retirement problem. Even a modest start can reduce future borrowing.

Working Out a Composite Plan

After presenting our preliminary analysis to the Learners, they did not feel they would be able to save the required $18,059 each year. They did believe, however, they could continue to make annual payments of $13,200 throughout the college years. We prepared a new report showing them what would remain for them to borrow if they continued with that plan. The results are shown in Chart 9. By saving or paying $13,200 through the end of college, the Learners would have loan payments of $50,845 for four years. They were concerned that going into retirement they wouldn't be able to handle those payments so they asked us for other options.

We suggested that the Learners consider having their children take out student loans. Students under the current student loan program can borrow approximately $17,000 over four years of college. With two students this means they could borrow $34,000 towards their college costs.

In order to demonstrate this strategy we created a new plan (Chart 10) for them illustrating $18,000 payments during the college years. These payments would consist of $13,200 from the Learners and an average of $4,800 from their students in the form of student loans over the seven year college period. Even with this plan, the Learners would have loan payments of $37,516. This was still too much and they asked us for further suggestions.

Chart 9

A Composite College Funding Plans for: Dr. Learner   01-Nov-97

1. Add new savings to your college funding account this year in the amount of: $13,200
2. Increase college savings each year until college starts at the rate of: 0.00%
3. Once college starts make transfers from current income each year of: $13,200
4. Borrow the balance and repay loans prior to retirement @ interest of: 9.00% $50,845
5. Invest net proceeds @ an interest rate of: 8.00%

Age of Older Parent	Year	Total College Cost	Save	Transfer	Loan Pmts	Net Interest	Acct Bal
44	1997	$0	$13,200	$0	$0	$0	$63,200
45	1998	$0	$13,200	$0	$0	$5,056	$81,456
46	1999	$0	$13,200	$0	$0	$6,516	$101,172
47	2000	$0	$13,200	$0	$0	$8,094	$122,466
48	2001	$0	$13,200	$0	$0	$9,797	$145,464
49	2002	$0	$13,200	$0	$0	$11,637	$170,301
50	2003	$0	$13,200	$0	$0	$13,624	$197,125
51	2004	$0	$13,200	$0	$0	$15,770	$226,095
52	2005	$0	$13,200	$0	$0	$18,088	$257,382
53	2006	$0	$13,200	$0	$0	$20,591	$291,173
54	2007	$61,642	$0	$13,200	$0	$23,294	$266,025
55	2008	$66,524	$0	$13,200	$0	$21,282	$233,983
56	2009	$71,791	$0	$13,200	$0	$18,719	$194,110
57	2010	$154,952	$0	$13,200	$0	$15,529	$67,886
58	2011	$83,612	$0	$13,200	$0	$5,431	$2,906
59	2012	$90,233	$0	$13,200	$0	$232	($73,895)
60	2013	$97,378	$0	$13,200	$0	($6,651)	($164,723)
61	2014	$0	$0	$0	$50,845	($14,825)	($128,703)
62	2015	$0	$0	$0	$50,845	($11,583)	($89,442)
63	2016	$0	$0	$0	$50,845	($8,050)	($46,647)
64	2017	$0	$0	$0	$50,845	($4,198)	$0
65	2018	$0	$0	$0	$0	$0	$0
66	2019	$0	$0	$0	$0	$0	$0
67	2020	$0	$0	$0	$0	$0	$0
68	2021	$0	$0	$0	$0	$0	$0
69	2022	$0	$0	$0	$0	$0	$0
70	2023	$0	$0	$0	$0	$0	$0
71	2024	$0	$0	$0	$0	$0	$0
72	2025	$0	$0	$0	$0	$0	$0
73	2026	$0	$0	$0	$0	$0	$0
74	2027	$0	$0	$0	$0	$0	$0
75	2028	$0	$0	$0	$0	$0	$0
76	2029	$0	$0	$0	$0	$0	$0
77	2030	$0	$0	$0	$0	$0	$0
78	2031	$0	$0	$0	$0	$0	$0
79	2032	$0	$0	$0	$0	$0	$0
80	2033	$0	$0	$0	$0	$0	$0
81	2034	$0	$0	$0	$0	$0	$0
82	2035	$0	$0	$0	$0	$0	$0
83	2036	$0	$0	$0	$0	$0	$0
TOTALS		$626,132	*******	$92,400	$203,379	$148,353	n/a

Chart 10

A Composite College Funding Plans for: Dr. Learner   01-Nov-97

1. Add new savings to your college funding account this year in the amount of: $13,200
2. Increase college savings each year until college starts at the rate of: 0.00%
3. Once college starts make transfers from current income each year of: $18,000
4. Borrow the balance and repay loans prior to retirement @ interest of: 9.00% $37,516
5. Invest net proceeds @ an interest rate of: 8.00%

Age of Older Parent	Year	Total College Cost	Save	Transfer	Loan Pmts	Net Interest	Acct Bal
44	1997	$0	$13,200	$0	$0	$0	$63,200
45	1998	$0	$13,200	$0	$0	$5,056	$81,456
46	1999	$0	$13,200	$0	$0	$6,516	$101,172
47	2000	$0	$13,200	$0	$0	$8,094	$122,466
48	2001	$0	$13,200	$0	$0	$9,797	$145,464
49	2002	$0	$13,200	$0	$0	$11,637	$170,301
50	2003	$0	$13,200	$0	$0	$13,624	$197,125
51	2004	$0	$13,200	$0	$0	$15,770	$226,095
52	2005	$0	$13,200	$0	$0	$18,088	$257,382
53	2006	$0	$13,200	$0	$0	$20,591	$291,173
54	2007	$61,642	$0	$18,000	$0	$23,294	$270,825
55	2008	$66,524	$0	$18,000	$0	$21,666	$243,967
56	2009	$71,791	$0	$18,000	$0	$19,517	$209,693
57	2010	$154,952	$0	$18,000	$0	$16,775	$89,516
58	2011	$83,612	$0	$18,000	$0	$7,161	$31,065
59	2012	$90,233	$0	$18,000	$0	$2,485	($38,682)
60	2013	$97,378	$0	$18,000	$0	($3,481)	($121,541)
61	2014	$0	$0	$0	$37,516	($10,939)	($94,964)
62	2015	$0	$0	$0	$37,516	($8,547)	($65,995)
63	2016	$0	$0	$0	$37,516	($5,940)	($34,418)
64	2017	$0	$0	$0	$37,516	($3,098)	$0
65	2018	$0	$0	$0	$0	$0	$0
66	2019	$0	$0	$0	$0	$0	$0
67	2020	$0	$0	$0	$0	$0	$0
68	2021	$0	$0	$0	$0	$0	$0
69	2022	$0	$0	$0	$0	$0	$0
70	2023	$0	$0	$0	$0	$0	$0
71	2024	$0	$0	$0	$0	$0	$0
72	2025	$0	$0	$0	$0	$0	$0
73	2026	$0	$0	$0	$0	$0	$0
74	2027	$0	$0	$0	$0	$0	$0
75	2028	$0	$0	$0	$0	$0	$0
76	2029	$0	$0	$0	$0	$0	$0
77	2030	$0	$0	$0	$0	$0	$0
78	2031	$0	$0	$0	$0	$0	$0
79	2032	$0	$0	$0	$0	$0	$0
80	2033	$0	$0	$0	$0	$0	$0
81	2034	$0	$0	$0	$0	$0	$0
82	2035	$0	$0	$0	$0	$0	$0
83	2036	$0	$0	$0	$0	$0	$0
TOTALS		$626,132	********	********	$150,064	$168,068	n/a

Chart 11

A Composite College Funding Plans for: Dr. Learner   01-Nov-97

1. Add new savings to your college funding account this year in the amount of: $13,200
2. Increase college savings each year until college starts at the rate of: 4.00%
3. Once college starts make transfers from current income each year of: $22,800
4. Borrow the balance and repay loans prior to retirement @ interest of: 9.00% $6,856
5. Invest net proceeds @ an interest rate of: 8.00%

Age of Older Parent	Year	Total College Cost	Save	Transfer	Loan Pmts	Net Interest	Acct Bal
44	1997	$0	$13,200	$0	$0	$0	$63,200
45	1998	$0	$13,728	$0	$0	$5,056	$81,984
46	1999	$0	$14,277	$0	$0	$6,559	$102,820
47	2000	$0	$14,848	$0	$0	$8,226	$125,894
48	2001	$0	$15,442	$0	$0	$10,071	$151,407
49	2002	$0	$16,060	$0	$0	$12,113	$179,580
50	2003	$0	$16,702	$0	$0	$14,366	$210,648
51	2004	$0	$17,370	$0	$0	$16,852	$244,870
52	2005	$0	$18,065	$0	$0	$19,590	$282,525
53	2006	$0	$18,788	$0	$0	$22,602	$323,915
54	2007	$61,642	$0	$22,800	$0	$25,913	$310,986
55	2008	$66,524	$0	$22,800	$0	$24,879	$292,141
56	2009	$71,791	$0	$22,800	$0	$23,371	$266,521
57	2010	$154,952	$0	$22,800	$0	$21,322	$155,690
58	2011	$83,612	$0	$22,800	$0	$12,455	$107,334
59	2012	$90,233	$0	$22,800	$0	$8,587	$48,488
60	2013	$97,378	$0	$22,800	$0	$3,879	($22,211)
61	2014	$0	$0	$0	$6,856	($1,999)	($17,354)
62	2015	$0	$0	$0	$6,856	($1,562)	($12,060)
63	2016	$0	$0	$0	$6,856	($1,085)	($6,290)
64	2017	$0	$0	$0	$6,856	($566)	$0
65	2018	$0	$0	$0	$0	$0	$0
66	2019	$0	$0	$0	$0	$0	$0
67	2020	$0	$0	$0	$0	$0	$0
68	2021	$0	$0	$0	$0	$0	$0
69	2022	$0	$0	$0	$0	$0	$0
70	2023	$0	$0	$0	$0	$0	$0
71	2024	$0	$0	$0	$0	$0	$0
72	2025	$0	$0	$0	$0	$0	$0
73	2026	$0	$0	$0	$0	$0	$0
74	2027	$0	$0	$0	$0	$0	$0
75	2028	$0	$0	$0	$0	$0	$0
76	2029	$0	$0	$0	$0	$0	$0
77	2030	$0	$0	$0	$0	$0	$0
78	2031	$0	$0	$0	$0	$0	$0
79	2032	$0	$0	$0	$0	$0	$0
80	2033	$0	$0	$0	$0	$0	$0
81	2034	$0	$0	$0	$0	$0	$0
82	2035	$0	$0	$0	$0	$0	$0
83	2036	$0	$0	$0	$0	$0	$0
TOTALS		$626,132	******	******	$27,423	$230,628	n/a

Chart 11 depicts our last attempt at a solution for the Learner family. It includes annual savings payments of $13,200 but increases them by 4% per year until the beginning of college. The Learners expected their income would keep pace with inflation and they felt they could handle the increasing payments. They also believed they could continue their final payments of about $18,000 throughout the seven years of college. Adding $4,000 from the contributions of the students' loans gave them a total of $22,000 in payments during the college years. That left the Learners with four annual payments of about $7,000 for parental loans they would personally incur in order to complete the undergraduate expenses for their students. The Learners believed that was a workable plan and directed us to implement it.

Other Options

The Learners are a high income family and they have the ability to save substantial amounts of money. They also have high aspirations for their children's education and did not wish to compromise their objectives. For other families, we might start with a lower college cost category in order to make our numbers work. Sometimes the only option is to direct parents to save what they can. Yet many parents can't save enough to reach even the minimum college costs. We have found, however, that any savings are better than doing nothing.

Saving for college can be compared to buying a house; the bigger the down payment, the less money that must be borrowed. Any savings that is put towards the college bill can make the difference between students attending the college of their choice or choosing a less favorable alternative. Lower income parents who can't save as much may still have the ability to qualify for need-based financial aid but they will have significantly more flexibility if they have some savings.

Now that we've established how to achieve a savings commitment, the next job is to decide which savings vehicles to use and how to title accounts in order to minimize taxes, financial aid and protect the family savings in the event the student decides not to attend college. The final page of our report, Chart 12, discusses seven key factors which we would ideally like to have in our college savings plan. They are:

1. Avoid the "kiddie tax."

2. Allow for controlled taxation of savings growth.

3. Allow for controlled taxation during the withdrawal phase.

4. Provide flexibility to deal with future financial aid eligibility.

5. Allow multiple investment options that consider:

   a) Staying ahead of college inflation rates;

   b) Diversifying risk; and

   c) Making changes to investments at a reasonable cost as markets and needs change particularly as the withdrawal phase nears.

6. Consider self-completion in the event of death or disability of all breadwinners.

7. Pay yourself first.

Chapter 11 discusses savings vehicles and account titling options that can help us achieve these goals.

Summary

It's not good enough to forecast college costs and calculate how much to save. If we want our clients to have a successful savings plan we must make sure that plan is implemented. That means making certain goals are realistic and being creative by blending savings, borrowing, pay-as-you-go and cost sharing into the plan.

Chart 12

Prepared On:	**01-Nov-97**
Prepared For:	**Dr. Learner**
Prepared By:	**Raymond D. Loewe, CLU, ChFC** **College Money** **112B Centre Blvd.** **Marlton, NJ 08053** **(609) 596-4700**
Subject:	**Planning Recommendations:**

1 Begin a savings plan as quickly as possible.
You don't have to save everything right now. Saving even small amounts is more important than not saving. Early savings enjoy the benefit of compound growth.
This means that every dollar you save now will result in more than a dollar that won't have to be borrowed later.

2 Make sure that your savings plan considers the following key features:
a. Your plan should avoid the "kiddie tax."
b. Your plan should allow for controlled taxation of savings growth.
c. Your plan should allow for controlled taxation during the withdrawal phase.
d. Your plan should provide flexibility to deal with future financial aid eligibility.
e. Your plan should allow multiple investment options that consider:
    1 Staying ahead of college inflation rates
    2 Diversifying your risk; and
    3 Making changes at reasonable cost both as markets change and as your needs change, particularly as you get close to the withdrawal phase.
f. Your plan should consider self-completion in the event of the death or disability of all breadwinners.
g. Your plan should consider a "pay yourself first" option that allows automatic, systematic plan deposits.

3 Complete a Trial Financial Aid Test now.
A Trial Financial Aid Test can help you assess your potential future eligibility for financial aid. Knowing your likelihood of qualifying for future financial aid will help you judge the desirability of planning on a pay-as-you-go philosophy during the college years.

4 Review your retirement plans, now.
College is part of the retirement problem. Without proper thought, you are likely to invade retirement funds to pay for college or are likely to over borrow for college and be caught repaying college loans at a time you should be saving for your own retirement.

5 Review your plan at least annually.

11

Savings Vehicles and Account Titling

Seven Factors in the Ideal College Savings Plan

At the end of chapter 10, we outlined seven key factors that go into a successful college plan. In this chapter we will discover that some savings vehicles are better than others in meeting these goals. Sometimes combining savings vehicles with account titling strategies can enhance the process even more. Let's look at those seven key features again as we review the savings vehicle types and the account title strategies in this chapter. Ideally, your plan should:

1. Avoid the "kiddie tax."

The "kiddie tax" applies to children who have not attained the age of 14 by the end of the taxable year, and who have over $1,400 (in 1998) of unearned income. The tax is the greater of:

- ♦ The tax the child would pay at his own tax rate; or

- ♦ The sum of i) the tax he would pay on net unearned income at the parent's top rate, plus ii) the tax he would pay on all other income (other than "net unearned income") at his own rate.

2. Allow for controlled taxation of savings growth.

If we can avoid paying taxes as the money grows, the growth is actually accelerated because we generate earnings on dollars that otherwise would not be available. The power of tax deferral can be substantial.

3. Allow for controlled taxation during the withdrawal phase.

Often money we thought was ours is reduced by capital gains taxes. Capital gains income can also cause loss of financial aid dollars.

4. Provide flexibility to deal with future financial aid eligibility.

Income generated upon the liquidation of an asset can reduce financial aid. Some assets reduce financial aid more than others and some don't affect financial aid at all. For example, retirement assets generally don't count at all, children's assets count more than the parents' assets and business assets are usually discounted.

5. Allow multiple investment options that consider:

    ♦   Staying ahead of college inflation rates;

    ♦   Diversifying risk; and

    ♦   Making changes to investments at reasonable cost as markets and needs change particularly as the withdrawal phase nears.

In general, some investments are riskier than others. Less risky investments usually won't generate returns high enough to offset college inflation. Clients can often reduce their risk if their time horizon is extended and if they diversify their portfolio.

6. Consider self-completion in the event of death or disability of all breadwinners.

Life and disability insurance has an important role in the college plan.

7. Consider a "pay yourself first" option that allows for automatic, systematic plan deposits.

Financial pressures often cause families to end the college savings plan when things get tight. Frequently, the plan is never restarted. Plans that have deposits automatically deducted from a payroll check or a checking account tend to be disrupted less often.

Some Financial Products Suitable for College Savings Vehicles

When choosing a suitable financial product to fund your clients' college needs, consider the following:

♦ Most parents do not save enough for college.

♦ College inflation has outpaced the cost of living substantially over the past 50 years, and there is every indication that trend will continue.

Therefore, if parents want to get ahead with a college savings plan, they cannot be too conservative. It is important that college savings funds be invested in order to realize above average returns whenever possible. Although we must evaluate every client's risk tolerance when designing a savings program, allowing your client to be too conservative will not keep him ahead of college inflation. What follows is a nonexclusive list of options that you should consider for college funding solutions.

Certificates of Deposit, Savings Accounts and Money Market Accounts

In general, these accounts are extremely low risk and, therefore, appeal to many parents. They are suitable for short-term college savings plans when dollars will be needed quickly and the investment risk cannot be tolerated. These savings vehicles will generally not keep pace with college inflation. As such, we don't recommend them as part of a long-term funding plan of five years and over except as a temporary holding vehicle between permanent investments.

Growth Mutual Funds

Growth mutual funds are a good vehicle to have in a college savings plan for the following reasons. Growth mutual funds diversify risk by spreading the investment dollars over many different stocks. They require little management and there are enough growth mutual funds with good track records from which to choose.

There are two reasons why growth mutual funds are often preferable to other types of mutual funds.

1. First, given a long enough planning horizon, growth funds should generate a good, overall after-tax rate of return which will help keep college accounts ahead of college inflation.

2. Growth mutual funds tend to pay less dividend income than other types of mutual funds. Therefore, they will help control taxation during the accumulation phase, often helping to compound investment growth and helping to reduce the "kiddie tax."

A potential disadvantage can occur during the withdrawal phase. Large taxable capital gains can reduce proceeds due to taxes which can have an adverse effect on financial aid.

Mutual Fund Portfolios

Mutual fund portfolios make a good college savings vehicle, especially as college savings increase. They provide diversification and professional management and, if there is a large amount of money, funds can be mixed and matched to meet any family's goals and risk tolerance. Figure 11.1 shows three basic portfolios corresponding to the three stages of the college planning cycle.

If you are experienced with asset allocation, you can make the portfolios you design for your clients more complex and more sophisticated. A traditional college funding strategy using mutual funds for most parents involves being fairly aggressive with investments when the children are very young and making investments more conservative as the children approach college age. Figure 11.1 illustrates some typical examples as to how such a strategy might change over time. This is only an example. Specific strategies depend upon the parents' resources and on the risk-taking ability of each family.

Stage One is the Accumulation Stage that usually occurs from the birth of the child until he is fourteen-years old. When children are in this age group, the mutual fund selection can be weighted heavily toward stocks with the emphasis on long-term capital growth. In addition to potentially higher returns, stocks tend to spin off lower annual incomes than bonds. Thus, whether the funds are put into a custodial account or invested in the parents' name, annual taxes will be lower.

Stage Two is a Conservation Stage. Normally, as children grow older, funds are transferred away from aggressive growth and toward more stable investments since cash will be needed in a shorter period of time. The Conservation Stage depicts how a portfolio for children 14 to18-years old might be structured.

Stage Three is the Liquidation Stage. As payment of the college bill becomes imminent, parents must move into a more conservative stage. The Liquidation Stage shows a higher percentage of bonds and cash and a much lower percentage of stocks.

Each portfolio must be designed for the particular family involved. It must take into account the family's goals and objectives, the time horizon available for planning and the risk the family is willing to take. Professionals should encourage parents with younger children, however, to take more risks because it is the only way they will stay ahead of rapidly rising college costs.

Often, parents who have put together successful portfolios of mutual funds make a critical mistake as their children approach college—they liquidate their mutual funds at the wrong time. If a student will be eligible for financial aid, special care must be taken when timing the liquidation of a mutual fund portfolio. When mutual funds are sold at a profit, that profit not only becomes taxable but it also generates income that will have an adverse effect on financial aid. This is over and above the value of the portfolio as an asset which will also have an adverse effect on financial aid.

One strategy parents can implement, especially when redeeming shares of an appreciated mutual fund portfolio that will create a substantial capital gain, is to consider liquidating the portfolio early in the student's junior year. This will keep capital gains income from adversely affecting financial aid. Another option is to hold the securities until the student's senior year in college, borrowing temporarily to meet college cash flow needs. Two types of loans should be considered: a home equity loan, and the federal PLUS loan. The choice will be based upon tax deductibility of interest, availability of home equity, relative interest rates at the time and the parents' preference.

Figure 11.1

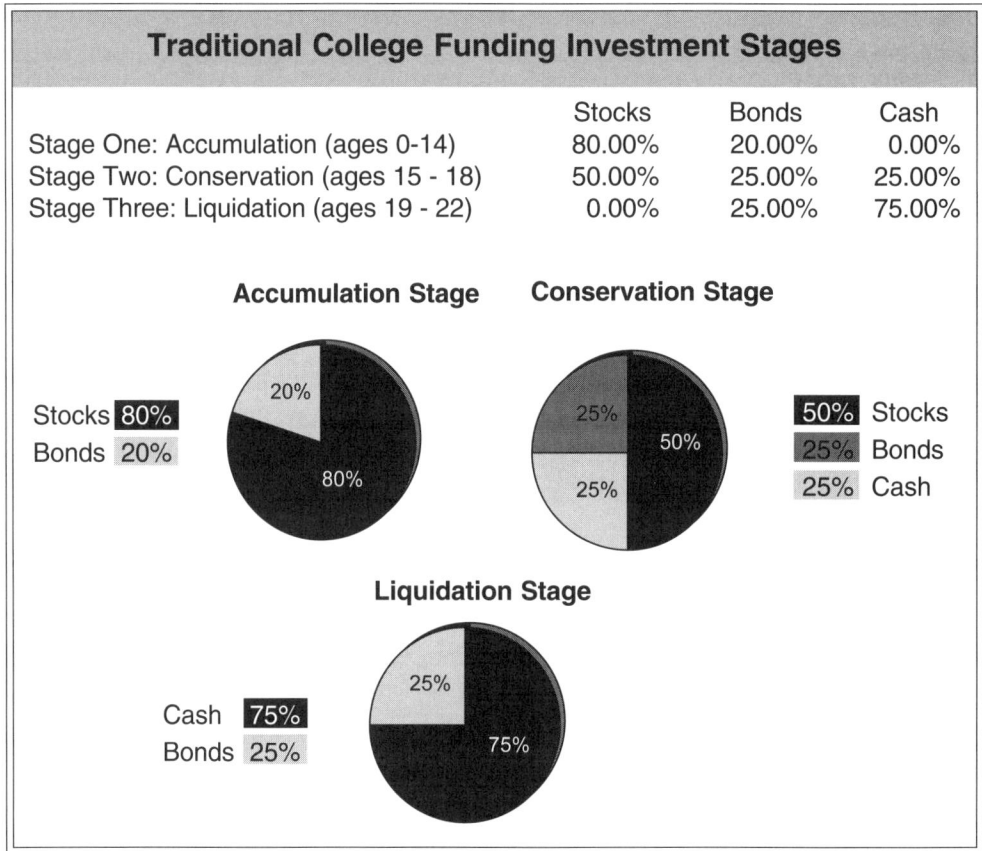

Traditional College Funding Investment Stages

	Stocks	Bonds	Cash
Stage One: Accumulation (ages 0-14)	80.00%	20.00%	0.00%
Stage Two: Conservation (ages 15 - 18)	50.00%	25.00%	25.00%
Stage Three: Liquidation (ages 19 - 22)	0.00%	25.00%	75.00%

Accumulation Stage

Stocks 80%
Bonds 20%

20%
80%

Conservation Stage

50% Stocks
25% Bonds
25% Cash

25%
50%
25%

Liquidation Stage

Cash 75%
Bonds 25%

25%
75%

Prepaid Tuition Plans

Forty-two states have passed enabling legislation for a prepaid tuition plan. The following states have plans in place as of April, 1998.

1. Ohio
2. Michigan
3. Florida
4. Massachusetts
5. Pennsylvania
6. Virginia
7. Texas
8. Nevada
9. Utah
10. Arkansas
11. W. Virginia
12. Minnesota
13. Louisiana
14. Mississippi
15. Alabama
16. Tennessee

Generally, a prepaid tuition plan allows parents, grandparents, relatives and just about anyone else to buy shares of a year of college at a discount. The shares are theoretically redeemable at college time for tuition at an eligible college. Shares are supposed to earn interest at a rate equal to college inflation. Shares grow tax deferred until they are used and are then taxed to the student on a pro rata basis using an exclusion ratio. In the event the student wishes to attend college at a school that is ineligible, the shares will be redeemed at their purchase price including a minimal interest rate. If the student decides not to attend school, the shares can be rolled over to another student or redeemed. If they are redeemed, taxation of the proceeds can depend upon the state of issuance, but gains are usually taxable.

There are two factors that are extremely important when evaluating these programs.

1. These shares are designed to keep pace with college inflation, not beat it.

2. Eligible schools are usually schools within the state.

You should ask the following questions before investing in a prepaid tuition plan.

♦   What is the likelihood the student will attend college in the state?

♦   Can the family investment portfolio generate a better rate of return than the college inflation rate proscribed to the prepaid tuition plan?

♦   What is the likelihood of obtaining financial aid?

♦   Will the family move to another state?

Although some families will appreciate the ease of buying these plans and the guarantees afforded by them, prepaid tuition plans have many more disadvantages than advantages. Remember, if the student attends an ineligible school under the plan, the redemption amount is subject to a reduced return penalty. Many colleges consider prepaid tuition plan dollars as a student asset, thus reducing financial aid awards accordingly. Some colleges consider distribution from a prepaid tuition plan as they would a scholarship from an outside source and reduce financial aid on a dollar for dollar basis.

On the plus side, if withdrawals are made from a prepaid tuition plan in a given year, the family is not excluded from using the Hope Scholarship or Lifetime Learning Credit, as they are by using Education IRAs. There is a trend to make these plans more flexible and transferable across state lines. Some states are proposing plans that are not linked to college inflation with returns comparable to returns earned on employee pension funds. These plans have the potential to become tax abusive because they would give parents the ability to shift substantial taxes to lower income students. Some state plans allow parents to invest tens of thousands of dollars in a plan and have students pay the taxes (plus penalties) in a lower tax bracket even if the student doesn't use the money for college. Prepaid tuition plans are becoming more interesting but still have substantial limitations for long-term college savings.

A possible use of prepaid tuition plans that bears consideration is as a short-term hedge against college inflation. Consider liquidating a savings portfolio in the student's junior year of high school. If the student is reasonably sure that he will attend an eligible college, and if the student is not likely to qualify for need-based financial aid, then consider purchasing prepaid tuition units. This strategy removes short-term market risk while insuring that funds keep pace with college inflation.

The Taxpayer Relief Act of 1997 clarified the gift tax treatment of contributions to a prepaid tuition plan. The gift will be treated as a gift of present interest at the time the gift was made. If the donor makes a gift in excess of the $10,000 annual exclusion, the donor can elect to spread the amount over a five-year period beginning with the year of the initial contribution. If the beneficiary rolls over the value of the prepaid account to another beneficiary in a generation below the current beneficiary, the rollover will be treated as a taxable gift. If the rollover stays in the same generation, there is no taxable gift.

The "CollegeSure" CD

The CollegeSure CD is a unique college funding vehicle put together by the College Savings Bank of Princeton, New Jersey. Professionals may have mixed feelings about the value of these bond-like savings instruments, but they are certainly worth mentioning and have a place in college planning.

The CollegeSure CD is an FDIC insured savings certificate. CollegeSure CDs are purchased in units representing a percentage of either typical current state college costs or typical current private college costs. The College Savings Bank guarantees that these unit values will maintain their purchasing power as a percentage of a year of college, regardless of actual college inflation. CD performance is indexed to college inflation via a special index prepared annually by the College Board. Although this planning device seems to be too good to be true as a college planning vehicle, it is important for professionals to understand how it works.

The CDs issued by the College Savings Bank actually tend to pay the going CD rates. Units are purchased at a premium or a discount, depending upon how the College Savings Banks feels inflation for college will run over the planning horizon. Thus, the CollegeSure CD acts somewhat like a zero coupon bond that is purchased at a premium or discount, depending upon the forecast of college cost inflation.

The College Savings Bank touts the CollegeSure CD as the closest thing available today to a national prepaid tuition program. As a professional, you may use the CollegeSure CD to varying degrees, depending upon your comfort level with it as an investment. It is certainly, however, a tool that you should be familiar with as part of the college planning process. To receive more information about the CollegeSure CD, contact:

>The College Savings Bank
>5 Vaughn Drive
>Princeton, NJ 08540
>Telephone (800) 342-6670

Annuities: Fixed, Indexed and Variable

Annuities offer another savings vehicle. They are insurance company products that allow parents to make lump sum or annual deposits. Fixed annuity deposits are invested in the general funds of life insurance companies. The insurance company takes the investment risk and pays out an appropriate return. Fixed annuities normally will not keep pace with college inflation.

Deposits in variable annuities are invested in variable accounts that are managed as mutual funds. Unlike fixed annuities, where funds are invested in the general account of the insurance company, variable annuities are separate accounts and are not subject to the creditors of the insurance company. Thus, with variable annuities, there is less of a concern over the financial solvency of the underlying insurance carrier.

The advantage of variable annuities over mutual funds is that investments grow on a tax deferred basis within the annuity account which provides a faster compounding because funds are not reduced by the impact of current taxes. Disadvantages of variable annuities include extra management fees, that is, the cost of the tax deferred shell and the fact that taxes must eventually be paid along with a 10% penalty tax if the funds are removed from the annuity before the parent reaches the age of 59½.

Variable annuities can have advantages over mutual funds in several different circumstances. If a parent will be over the age of 59 ½ at the time that monies are removed from the annuity shell to pay for college, the 10% penalty tax will not apply. A second advantage of variable annuities is that the compounding, as a result of the tax deferral, can overcome the 10% penalty if the time period for investing is long enough. Whether or not variable annuities are appropriate in a given situation depends upon many factors. Also, each variable annuity must be evaluated carefully for its performance potential. The fees in a variable annuity can have a substantial negative effect if a product does not perform. If applied properly, however, variable annuities can be a worthwhile college planning tool.

A third form of annuity is the indexed annuity. Indexed annuity returns are tied to the performance of an index such as Standard & Poor's 500 index. As such, they can provide above average returns and also guarantee against losses. Generally, the long-term returns of indexed annuities will be somewhere between that of fixed and variable annuities.

Many professionals use annuities because they believe that annuities hide money from the financial aid system. That is not always true. The Federal Methodology treats annuities as retirement money and, therefore, it is not counted as an asset for financial aid. However, the Institutional Methodology expects annuities to be disclosed. Annuities can help financial aid because the investment income is zero as long as withdrawals are not made. If you are trying to maximize financial aid, a safe approach is to find a no surrender charge annuity or make sure that surrender charges disappear prior to any withdrawal of funds for college.

Life insurance: Fixed or Variable

For the sophisticated client, life insurance is a product worth investigating for college planning, especially when there is a ten-year or longer planning horizon for college and/or the need for additional life insurance. Fixed life insurance has fixed returns that may not keep up with college inflation. Variable life, however, can meet all of the key criteria that should be incorporated into any good college savings plan that we listed at the beginning of this chapter.

♦ The plan will avoid the "kiddie tax." Variable life accumulates dollars on a tax free basis, therefore, even if funds are owned on behalf of the child, there is no income generated from the plan and, therefore, no "kiddie tax" during the accumulation period.

♦ The plan will avoid taxes completely during the accumulation period; life insurance values grow tax free.

♦ The plan will allow for the control of taxation during the withdrawal period. Variable life gives the advantage to families that monies can be withdrawn as a loan and, therefore, are not subject to tax. If the plan is properly designed to mature as a death claim, no income taxes will be paid.

♦ The plan offers above average investment returns since mutual funds underlie the investment in the plan. This gives a family a chance to earn those above average returns by taking the appropriate risks.

♦ The plan can be diversified to reduce risk. Most variable life programs offer a multiplicity of mutual funds, including stock funds, bond funds, money market funds and balanced funds. Therefore, asset allocation models can be built into a variable life plan.

♦ The plan is generally liquid. As college approaches, providing the plan is designed properly, substantial funds are available in the plan that can be withdrawn, subject to taxes, or borrowed upon, thus avoiding taxes.

♦ The plan allows for self-completion in the event of death or disability. Many parents don't have enough life insurance and if life insurance is needed, variable life can offer additional death benefits at a reasonable cost.

♦ The plan can allow for automatic and systematic contributions. One of the problems with any savings plan is that parents stop in the middle of the plan. An insurance plan can use a check-a-matic plan whereby the plan acts as a pay yourself first plan.

As with any plan, there are also accompanying disadvantages. Most variable life plans have high costs associated with them, that is, the cost of life insurance, the cost of the insurance company's profit and the cost of managing the mutual funds. For many high tax bracket parents, however, these costs are more than compensated for by the tax benefits. Another disadvantage is surrender penalties that can last up to ten years. Because of these reasons, variable life must be looked at closely from the standpoint of the investment planning horizon. These plans tend to work when there are a number of years between the time when the investments start and the time when the funds will be needed for college; conversely, they tend not to work when the planning horizon is short. However, coupling variable life plans with the new college parent loans can make this liquidity, or lack of liquidity, feature less troublesome.

Finally, a major cost of this plan is the cost of life insurance. If parents need additional life insurance anyway, the cost of the insurance is outweighed by its need. A second way of minimizing the cost is to overfund the plan by purchasing a minimum amount of life insurance and a maximum amount of cash value in the plan. The professional must be aware of the federal guidelines in this area.

Again, some planners will like variable life and some will not, but as a college planning tool it is worth taking a good, long look at for each client.

U.S. Savings Bonds

U.S. Savings Bonds offer some unique advantages when they are used to pay for college. They also have special restrictions that must be adhered to in order to take advantage of them. As an investment, U.S. Savings Bonds are extremely conservative. Backed by the full faith of the U.S. Government, these bonds are very safe. Returns vary over time, but they tend to be at the low or moderate end of the spectrum. Many parents find savings bonds to be too conservative an investment for college funding because the bonds do not provide them with the returns they need in order to accumulate the kind of cash they need to pay for college.

On the tax side, however, savings bonds generally accumulate interest income on a tax deferred basis, thus offering the advantage of having money compound faster than other investment vehicles that might be subject to current income taxes. In addition, parents can escape paying taxes completely on the interest from savings bonds under certain circumstances.

♦ Bonds must be purchased in the parent's name beginning in 1990 or later.

♦ Bonds cannot be issued in the name of the child.

♦ Bonds must be redeemed in a year in which the owner pays qualified higher education expenses, which includes tuition and fees to an eligible institution. Room and board is not a qualified educational expense.

♦ Eligible institutions include colleges, universities, technical institutes, and vocational schools.

Interest on qualifying bonds will be fully exempt from federal income tax only if the qualified higher education expenses paid during the year are equal to or more than the redemption proceeds. If tuition and fees are less than the bonds cashed, the exemption is proportional to the percentage of the value that was used for tuition and fees.

For parents to receive the full benefit of the tax free status of the bonds, their incomes must be below certain threshold levels set by the U.S. Government. Levels for 1998 are $78,350 for married couples filing jointly and $52,250 for single parents. Parents who wish to qualify for tax exclusions must have modified adjusted gross incomes below the threshold level. Modified adjusted gross income generally represents adjusted gross income from the parents' tax form plus any gains on the bond. Therefore, to determine whether or not parents actually qualify for the exclusion, parents must surrender the bonds, add the taxable gain to their income, and calculate their adjusted gross income. It is this income, including the gain, that must be below the threshold levels in order for the exclusion to apply.

There is also an upper threshold level for each bondholder. Parents whose modified adjusted gross incomes exceed these thresholds will not qualify for the exemption at all. The upper threshold for 1998 is $108,350 for married parents filing jointly and $67,250 for single parents.

Unfortunately, income from the liquidation of savings bonds, whether taxable or non-taxable, will have a negative effect on financial aid. So while savings bonds, with their income tax exemption, may work for lower and middle income families, they will probably not work well for higher paid clients and those who might qualify for need-based financial aid.

Titling College Savings and Investment Accounts

How parents title savings and investment accounts depends largely on four factors that sometimes conflict with one another.

1.   Taxes.

2.   Control issues.

3.   Financial aid.

4.   Investment costs.

Let's discuss tax issues first. Generally speaking, students are in a lower tax bracket than their parents. Therefore, parents can save taxes by putting money in their child's name rather than their own. Sometimes parents can create a third party tax bracket by setting up a trust. In some cases, trusts are in a lower tax bracket than both the students and parents. Dollars not taxed or taxed in a lower bracket compound faster which creates a larger college account.

Second, we need to consider control issues. Ordinarily, when parents give money to children they lose control of that money to some degree. Usually they give up ownership either currently or at some predefined time in the future, usually the child's age of majority which, in most cases, is age 18. If a child decides not to attend college, that money becomes the property of the child and he or she might not use the money for the purpose intended by the parents.

The next issue we must consider involves financial aid. In general, money in a child's name is counted more heavily by colleges toward paying for an education than money in a parents' name. Thus, a student who has money in his or her name might receive less financial aid than if the money were titled in the parents' name. Dollars in a trust can be considered a parents' money or a student's money, depending upon the terms of the trust or a particular college's rules governing financial aid. In some cases, trust dollars are not considered an asset for financial aid purposes.

The final decision factor involves investment costs. Trusts, in particular, might involve an attorney's fee to create and administrative fees to operate. Often excessive costs diminish or override other benefits.

Putting together the best combination of tax benefits, financial aid benefits, control factors and costs is the goal of good college planning. Although individual circumstances dictate individual planning, some general rules of thumb apply.

♦ Keep money in the parents' name until a child reaches age 14. This money will likely be taxed back to the parents anyway because of the "kiddie tax."

♦ When the child reaches age 14, complete a financial aid test. If the student is likely to qualify for financial aid, evaluate whether or not financial aid is more important than tax savings. If it is, keep the money in the parents' name. If it is not, then parents can make gifts to children either into custodial accounts or some other vehicle in order to take advantage of tax savings over financial aid benefits.

A third factor that must be evaluated before a transfer is made is whether the student is likely to attend college. In other words, is this money likely to be used for the purpose for which it was intended?

Sometimes large funds are put into the student's name only to have the student not only not go to college but to use that money to feed a drug habit or spend it on something else the parents would not normally desire. If control of funds is an issue, leaving money in the parents' name may be more important than both taxes and financial aid.

The following paragraphs relate to some tools that can be used for college planning. Each should be considered in terms of taxes, control, financial aid and costs.

UGMA AND UTMA Accounts

Uniform Gift to Minors Accounts (UGMA) and Uniform Transfer to Minor Accounts (UTMA) are two of the simplest vehicles that parents can use to accumulate money for college. Let's examine the use of these accounts considering the four criteria that we outlined above: taxes; control issues; financial aid; and investment costs.

From a tax standpoint, UGMAs allow children over the age of 14 to pay taxes on unearned income on their accounts at their own tax bracket. This often allows parents to accumulate dollars faster since investment earnings are taxed at a lower rate. For children under the age of 14, the "kiddie tax" diminishes the value of such accounts. However, there still may be some advantages to having unearned income of $1,400 or less generated by these accounts. The Internal Revenue Code allows transfers to minors under UGMA to be free of gift tax, providing that gifts from any one donor do not exceed $10,000 in any given year. Since custodial accounts represent gifts of present interest, money can pass free of gift taxes. Consequently, two parents can give up to $20,000 per year without incurring gift taxes.

From a control standpoint, UGMA accounts have both advantages and disadvantages. While children are minors, the custodian, usually the parent, has full control over the use of the money in the account. The primary disadvantage is that the age of majority in many states is 18-years old. The students gain complete control of the accumulated values in their accounts as they approach their college years. Because the money belongs to the student outright at the time of majority, the student can use the money for things other than the intended use, which is college. When parents are not sure of the maturity of their children, they may wish to keep control of the money and not use the UGMA, or custodial account, as it is sometimes called.

Money in custodial accounts is treated as the student's money by the financial aid system and there are substantial, adverse financial aid consequences. The 35% rule applies. Thus, a student's potential aid award can be reduced in the first year by 35% of the value of his or her accounts. Dollars in these accounts are readily visible to colleges since the interest shows up on the student's income tax return. In almost every case, a financial aid officer will request an income tax return from the student before granting a final financial aid award.

Finally, investment costs do not represent an adverse factor because custodial accounts can be set up with no administrative costs.

Planning Notes

In general, income from a UGMA is taxed to a minor; however, if this income is used to discharge a legal obligation of a parent, it may be taxed back to the parent. Parents must be careful how they spend custodial account money.

A strategy for avoiding the "kiddie tax" can be used with custodial accounts. If investment vehicles can be found that generate little or no taxable interest income while the children are under the age of 14, but have substantial capital appreciation that can be realized after the children reach age 14, then custodial accounts can be used. Generally, however, if there is any suspicion that a student can be the beneficiary of substantial financial aid, custodial accounts should be avoided.

In almost every case, financial aid advantages dwarf tax advantages when using custodial accounts. Figure 11.2 and Figure 11.3 illustrates how $13,000 invested in a custodial account and $13,000 invested in a parent's name compare on account growth net after-taxes vs. the financial aid benefits. Figure 11.2 assumes a parent in the 15% tax bracket; Figure 11.3 assumes a parent in the 39% tax bracket. Both figures show the dominance of financial aid benefits over tax benefits, regardless of the tax bracket. Keep in mind that financial aid packages sometimes include loans. It's not good enough to plan a savings strategy to secure more financial aid; you must help your client use the techniques from the previous chapters to obtain a good financial aid package.

Figure 11.2

Tax Savings vs. Financial Aid Losses by Using Custodial Accts

Initial Account Deposit	$13,000
Assumed Pretax Interest	10.00%
Assumed Parent Tax Bracket	15.00%
Assumed Student Tax Bracket	15.00%
Financial Aid Factor for Student Savings	35.00%
Financial Aid Factor for Adult Savings	5.60%

Years	Interest	Total Taxes Student	Account Balance Student	Lost Fin. Aid Student	Account Balance Adult	Lost Fin. Aid Adult	Lost Fin. Aid Difference	Acct. Bal Difference
			$13,000	$4,550	$13,000	$728	$3,822	$0
1	$1,300	$98	$14,203	$4,971	$14,105	$790	$4,181	$98
2	$1,420	$116	$15,507	$5,428	$15,304	$857	$4,571	$203
3	$1,551	$135	$16,923	$5,923	$16,605	$930	$4,993	$318
4	$1,692	$156	$18,459	$6,461	$18,016	$1,009	$5,452	$443
5	$1,846	$179	$20,125	$7,044	$19,548	$1,095	$5,949	$578
6	$2,013	$204	$21,933	$7,677	$21,209	$1,188	$6,489	$724
7	$2,193	$232	$23,895	$8,363	$23,012	$1,289	$7,075	$883
8	$2,390	$261	$26,024	$9,108	$24,968	$1,398	$7,710	$1,056
9	$2,602	$293	$28,333	$9,917	$27,090	$1,517	$8,400	$1,243
10	$2,833	$328	$30,839	$10,794	$29,393	$1,646	$9,148	$1,446
11	$3,084	$365	$33,558	$11,745	$31,891	$1,786	$9,959	$1,667
12	$3,356	$406	$36,508	$12,778	$34,602	$1,938	$10,840	$1,906
13	$3,651	$450	$39,709	$13,898	$37,543	$2,102	$11,796	$2,166
14	$3,971	$498	$43,181	$15,113	$40,734	$2,281	$12,832	$2,447
15	$4,318	$550	$46,949	$16,432	$44,197	$2,475	$13,957	$2,753
16	$4,695	$607	$51,037	$17,863	$47,953	$2,685	$15,178	$3,084
17	$5,104	$668	$55,473	$19,416	$52,029	$2,914	$16,502	$3,444
18	$5,547	$735	$60,286	$21,100	$56,452	$3,161	$17,939	$3,834

UGMA vs. UTMA

All states have adopted either the Uniform Gifts to Minors Act or the Uniform Transfers to Minors Act. There are two basic differences between the acts.

1. The UGMA authorizes cash, bank accounts, stocks, bonds, mutual funds, and so on as the types of investments that a custodian can hold on behalf of a minor. The UTMA broadens holdings to include real estate and other property, including limited partnership interests.

2. The second difference is that the UGMA mandates that property be transferred to the minor at the age of maturity, either 18 or 21, depending upon state law. In the UTMA states, the custodian can designate the age at

Figure 11.3

Tax Savings vs. Financial Aid Losses by Using Custodial Accts							

Initial Account Deposit $13,000
Assumed Pre-tax Interest   10.00%
Assumed Parent Tax Bracket   39.00%
Assumed Student Tax Bracket   15.00%
Financial Aid Factor for Student Savings 35.00%
Financial Aid Factor for Adult Savings   5.60%

Years	Interest	Total Taxes Student	Account Balance Student	Lost Fin. Aid Student	Account Balance Adult	Lost Fin. Aid Adult	Lost Fin. Aid Difference	Acct. Bal Difference
			$13,000	$4,550	$13,000	$728	$3,822	$0
1	$1,300	$98	$14,203	$4,971	$13,793	$772	$4,198	$410
2	$1,420	$144	$15,478	$5,417	$14,634	$820	$4,598	$844
3	$1,548	$194	$16,832	$5,891	$15,527	$870	$5,022	$1,305
4	$1,683	$247	$18,268	$6,394	$16,474	$923	$5,471	$1,794
5	$1,827	$303	$19,792	$6,927	$17,479	$979	$5,948	$2,313
6	$1,979	$362	$21,409	$7,493	$18,545	$1,039	$6,455	$2,864
7	$2,141	$425	$23,124	$8,094	$19,677	$1,102	$6,992	$3,448
8	$2,312	$492	$24,945	$8,731	$20,877	$1,169	$7,561	$4,068
9	$2,494	$563	$26,876	$9,406	$22,150	$1,240	$8,166	$4,725
10	$2,688	$639	$28,925	$10,124	$23,502	$1,316	$8,807	$5,423
11	$2,892	$719	$31,098	$10,884	$24,935	$1,396	$9,488	$6,163
12	$3,110	$803	$33,405	$11,692	$26,456	$1,482	$10,210	$6,949
13	$3,340	$893	$35,852	$12,548	$28,070	$1,572	$10,976	$7,782
14	$3,585	$989	$38,449	$13,457	$29,782	$1,668	$11,789	$8,666
15	$3,845	$1,090	$41,203	$14,421	$31,599	$1,770	$12,652	$9,604
16	$4,120	$1,197	$44,126	$15,444	$33,527	$1,877	$13,567	$10,600
17	$4,413	$1,311	$47,228	$16,530	$35,572	$1,992	$14,538	$11,656
18	$4,723	$1,432	$50,518	$17,681	$37,742	$2,114	$15,568	$12,776

which the child can access the account. This may be done, however, only at the time of account registration and cannot be changed at a later date. It is important to check the state regulations when using these accounts.

Getting Money Out of Custodial Accounts

One problem that always faces the professional advisor in college planning situations involves finding ways to remove money from custodial accounts. Technically, when a parent, grandparent or any other person places money in a custodial account, the grantor is said to have made an irrevocable gift. It is illegal to withdraw money from the account unless it is to expend it on behalf of the minor. Later, many parents find themselves eligible for financial aid but wishing they had not set up UGMA accounts since those accounts will diminish the amount of financial aid they receive.

There are ways to reduce the amount of money in custodial accounts. One way is to spend the money on behalf of the student. Many parents pay for cars, class trips, music lessons, sports fees and other expenses on behalf of their children. Instead, parents should use the children's money to pay those expenses. In that way, parents can reduce the amount of dollars in the custodial accounts. If parents feel guilty about spending their child's money, they can simply set up an account in their own name for the benefit of the student. By doing this, the parents are able to move money from custodial accounts back into the student's name. If there are large amounts of money in a custodial account, it may not be possible to spend that money on behalf of the child prior to college. We can, however, spend that money on first-year college expenses.

Financial aid is an annual event and it is recalculated every year. With money in custodial accounts, we may not be able to spend enough of it in time for the first year of college. However, we may be able to secure financial aid in succeeding years by spending the custodial account money appropriately. Before your clients start to reduce their custodial account dollars, encourage them to retain legal advice so it can be determined what is permissible in their state.

Minor's Trusts

A minor's trust is an exception to the general rule that only gifts of present interest can avoid gift tax consequences. A Section 2503(c) trust will generally qualify for this gift tax exemption, providing that a trustee has the power to use property and income from trust assets to benefit a student under the age of 21. In addition, the trust document must require that the beneficiary of the trust receive the trust property and the accumulated income from the trust at age 21.

One of the advantages of a minor's trust over custodial accounts is that a trust can control dollars until the minor reaches 21-years old as opposed to 18-years old in most states for custodial accounts. Thus, minor's trusts improve, to some extent, the control aspect which is one of our criteria for evaluating planning tools. From a financial aid standpoint, however, most financial aid officers will include minor's trusts as an asset of the student that is available to pay for college.

Thus, we have an adverse financial aid consideration. Since the trust must distribute dollars when the beneficiary reaches the age of 21, it's logical for financial aid officers to do this. From an income tax standpoint, trusts used to be quite advantageous because a large amount of income could be taxed at the 15% bracket. Recently, though, tax brackets for trusts have been increased, substantially diminishing the value of the trust as a tax planning tool. From a cost standpoint, trusts usually require an attorney to draft a trust agreement and a trustee to administer the trust annually. Tax returns must also be filed every year. Therefore, unless substantial dollars can be put into the trust, tax savings do not overshadow the cost of establishing the trust.

Although there is a place for trusts to be used in college planning, they are definitely less valuable then they have been in the past. There are two types of minors' trusts.

1.   Section 2503(c) Trust.

Under a Section 2503(c) trust, both income and principal may be spent by or on behalf of the beneficiary before age 21 or it may be accumulated. The remaining income and principal must be paid to the beneficiary upon attaining age 21 or sooner.

2.   Section 2503(b) Trust.

A Section 2503(b) trust should be considered by a donor who does not want trust corpus and unexpended income to be distributed when the beneficiary reaches age 21 or sooner. The principal can be paid to the income beneficiary at whatever dates or times are established by the donor. Alternatively, principal could be paid to someone other than the income beneficiary. However, such a trust must generally provide for a mandatory distribution of income to the beneficiary, at least annually, or more frequently. Such distributions could be deposited to a custodial account.

"In Trust For" Accounts

Another way to title college accounts is to use "in trust for" accounts. For example:

John Smith, in trust for Susan Smith

These accounts are not used very much anymore but they have a place in college planning. One reason parents like custodial accounts is because they can put a child's name on an account and designate the funds in the account for that student. An "in trust for" account can do the same thing, yet leave control of the money and official ownership in the parents' name. An "in trust for" account uses a parent's Social Security number. The parent, therefore, owns the account and has complete rights to the account. The child, or student, is named as the beneficiary of the account and will only receive funds in the event of the death of the parent. There are some disadvantages here. In the event of the death of the parent, the money will automatically go to the student. If the parent dies before or during college, the financial aid savings we hope to receive by using this type of account can be lost.

Joint Savings and Checking Accounts

Many students work during their junior and senior year of high school. The purpose of working is to accumulate some spending money. Many students open their own bank account using their own Social Security number in order to deposit their earnings. This can have a significant negative effect on financial aid since 35% of available student money is counted as available to pay for college. One way to get around this problem is to have a parent open a joint checking or savings account with the student. The parent uses his Social Security number and, therefore, he has official ownership of the account. This effectively transfers the dollars to the parent for financial aid purposes. Since the account is a joint account, however, the student has the ability to make withdrawals at any time. The student receives the benefit of having his or her own account yet the family gains the benefits of more financial aid.

The Taxpayer Relief Act of 1997

The Taxpayer Relief Act of 1997 created for parents of college bound students three vehicles that might prove useful: the ability to withdraw educational expenses from IRAs penalty free, the Roth IRA and the Education IRA.

Withdrawals From a Regular IRA for Qualified Education Expenses

Normally, parents can withdraw dollars from IRAs before age 59½ only with tax consequences and penalties. The Taxpayer Relief Act of 1997 allows parents to withdraw monies from IRAs for qualified educational expenses incurred after December 31, 1997, without paying the normal 10% penalty tax. The college term must begin after December 31, 1997, for the exception to apply. Taxes still need to be paid on the amounts withdrawn. Withdrawing funds from IRAs should be done only in emergencies. Remember, IRAs were designed primarily to save for retirement expenses. In addition to the negative affect on taxes, income generated from the IRA withdrawal will decrease financial aid eligibility. At this time it is uncertain whether or not the colleges will count IRAs as an asset available to pay for college, but the door has been opened.

The Roth IRA

Roth IRAs were designed primarily as retirement savings vehicles; however, withdrawing money from a Roth IRA to pay for college may have some advantages. The Roth IRA allows a husband and wife to contribute the lesser of $2,000 or 100% of compensation per person on a nondeductible basis. That means a husband and wife may be able to contribute a total of $4,000. High tax bracket taxpayers with incomes in excess of $95,000, but not more than $110,000 (for taxpayers filing a single return), and in excess of $150,000, but not more than $160,000 (for married taxpayers filing a joint return), will not be able to contribute the full amounts.

Monies in a Roth IRA grow on a tax deferred basis and, potentially, on a tax free basis. In general, distributions made after 5 years and age 59½ are tax free. Individuals younger than age 59½ can make penalty free withdrawals to pay college expenses on behalf of a spouse, child or grandchild. They must, however, pay tax on withdrawals that exceed total contributions.

Although it is too early to know for sure, it is highly possible that financial aid administrators will consider a Roth IRA as a parent asset. Withdrawals for college will probably not be treated as income for financial aid purposes.

Education Individual Retirement Accounts

Beginning in the year 1998, your clients will be able to set up an Education IRA to pay for certain qualified higher educational expenses. Annual contributions to Education IRAs are non-deductible and, except for rollover contributions, may not exceed $500 for each beneficiary under age 18. Education IRAs were established under the Taxpayer Relief Act of 1997 and, as with other plans established under this Act, have eligibility rules based on income. Taxpayers whose modified adjusted gross income is $95,000 or under for taxpayers filing a single return and $150,000 or under for married taxpayers filing a joint return, will be able to make the full contribution. As income increases to $110,000 for unmarried taxpayers and $160,000 for married taxpayers, contributions will be phased out.

It is important to note that no contribution is allowed to an Education IRA in any year that payments are contributed to a state tuition pre-payment program on behalf of the same student. Withdrawals from an Education IRA will not constitute income to either the parent or the student in years where qualified educational expenses are incurred. Qualified educational expenses include tuition fees and room and board. Where distributions exceed qualified educational expenses, a proportionate percentage of the earnings are includable in gross income by the beneficiary or the student. Distributions not used for qualified educational expenses will be subject to normal income taxes plus a 10% penalty. In any year that withdrawals are made from an Education IRA, the HOPE or lifetime learning credit will not be available. In the event that there are unused contributions in a plan at the conclusion of college, Education IRAs can be rolled over for the benefit of a beneficiary who is another family member.

The financial aid system will most likely consider Education IRAs as a student asset and reduce financial aid awards by 35% of the account value. Distributions will most likely be looked at as an asset reduction and, thus, have no additional effect on financial aid. While there was some initial confusion as to how many Education IRAs a beneciary could have, the general consensus currently indicates one per beneficiary. Thus, a parent and grandparent cannot both contribute unless the total contributions are $500 or less.

Planning Note

Students attending college in the next few years will get a bigger bang for their buck from the Hope Scholarship and the Lifetime Learning credits than from Roth IRAs and Education IRAs. Parents of young children may find the tax free accumulation of the Education IRA more significant and may be able to alternate Education IRA withdrawals in some years while using the Hope and Lifetime Learning credits in alternate years. Don't forget to consider financial aid effects carefully.

Business vs. Personal Accounts

Simply designating an account as a business account instead of a personal account can sometimes increase financial aid benefits. Suppose your client is a sole proprietor. He has a business savings account and a personal savings account. The financial aid formulas discount business assets; Figure 11.4 will give you an idea of just how much. However, suppose your client is ready to complete financial aid form. He has the option of considering cash as a business asset or as a personal asset. For example, a $10,000 business asset counts as a $4,000 asset for financial aid. After applying the 6% rule the actual loss of financial aid drops from $600 to $240.

Figure 11.4

Discounts of Business Assets for Financial Aid		
Amounts From	**To**	**Discount %**
$1	$85,000	40%
$85,001	$250,000	50%
$250,001	$420,000	60%
Over $420,001		100%

Using a Limited Liability Company (LLC)

Although an in-depth discussion of limited liability companies is beyond the scope of this book, they can be useful as a substitute for a UGMA. Unlike a UGMA, there is no automatic transfer of ownership at age 18 or 21. The managing partner can exert control over both income and capital distributions and may even be able to affect the taxation of the investment income stream. Some consideration of gift taxes must be made, but it appears that for control purposes, the LLC offers some interesting options.

Summary

There may be other interesting college planning investment and titling vehicles, but the above list should give you a good start. In Chapter 12 we'll look at some advanced strategies that use these tools.

12

Advanced Strategies

Introduction

In this section we are going to outline some of the more unique approaches that you, as a professional advisor, can offer your clients to make college planning easier. There are four areas we intend to discuss.

1. The first step is the process of converting a short-term planning horizon into a long-term planning horizon and how that can make a college saving strategy more efficient. Specifically, we will investigate the notion of saving for retirement, not for college. Most parents grasp the concept of putting money into a retirement plan rather than college savings but have difficulty when they are told not to withdraw money from their retirement plan when the college bills are due.

2. Second, we will address grandparent plans. Many grandparents would like to help their grandchildren attend college. However, many grandparents set up plans that don't help at all when financial aid eligibility is taken into account.

3. Third, we will examine an interesting planning option for C Corporation business owners.

4. Finally, we will look at variable life with a twist that might make variable life premiums fully or partially tax deductible. Please note this is a very aggressive approach and will not suit the great majority of your clients. Yet,

in the case of a client who is in a high tax bracket, this strategy can definitely have an impact.

Converting a Short-Term Planning Horizon to a Long-term Planning Horizon

Example 1.

The Smiths were getting ready to send their daughter to college and had saved some money in their name for that purpose. They had invested about $50,000 over several years and now that amount had grown to approximately $100,000 dollars. The purpose of that money was to send their two children, Sarah, age 17, and Robert, age 11, to college. Sarah also qualified for some need-based financial aid.

The Smiths were concerned that cashing in their investment would create a capital gain which would not only be taxable but also have a negative effect on the following year's financial aid. Since the Smiths had substantial equity in their home, they decided to use a home equity loan to pay the college bills rather than cash in their investments. As the Smiths used up their home equity dollars, they would qualify for even more financial aid because of their reduced home equity. Meanwhile, their investments, they hoped, would continue to appreciate in value.

There are several advantages to this strategy. First, total assets would decrease thus increasing financial aid eligibility for the following year. Second, the home equity loan interest should be tax deductible, thereby making it easier for the Smiths to afford their monthly payments. The Smith's plan was to liquidate their investments during the last year of college, once the financial aid was awarded, take their capital gains, pay their taxes and pay off their mortgage. The effect of capital gains on diminishing financial aid would be effectively neutralized. Remember, the parents' income (47%) counts substantially more than the parents' assets (6%).

Example 2.

Mr. and Mrs. Jones were also preparing to send their child to college. They had made some investments as well in their own name which were to be used to fund college. They did not have much equity in their home and they did not wish to liquidate their investments because of a rapidly rising stock market. Fortunately, Mr. and Mrs. Jones were able to take out a federal PLUS loan to pay their college bills. Their plan was to liquidate their investments later when they felt they would no longer appreciate as rapidly and, at that time, pay off the PLUS loan.

Example 3.

The Johnsons were developing their college savings plan but both Mr. and Mrs. Johnson were torn between maximizing their 401(k) contributions and saving for college. Both Mr. and Mrs. Johnson's employers matched a substantial amount of their 401(k) contributions but, although they wanted to take advantage of this, they could not manage saving for college and contributing to their 401(k) accounts at the same time.

The basic solution for the Johnsons was to save money for retirement and forego saving for college. Specifically, they would over-fund their retirement plan, borrow for college, attempt to pay off the college loans between the end of college and the beginning of their retirement and, to the extent they were not successful, withdraw 401(k) monies after age 59 ½.

It is important for parents and professionals to understand the relationship between college and retirement. It doesn't matter whether funds for college are in a college plan or in a retirement plan. What is important is for the parents to realize they should not withdraw money from their retirement plans before age 59 ½. There are several reasons for this.

♦ First, retirement money is accumulating on a tax deferred basis which enables the money to accumulate faster due to the principles of compound interest.

♦ Next, the money is invested for the long-term, not the short-term, so the returns should be better.

♦ Third, withdrawing money from a retirement plan usually means paying taxes and penalties.

♦ Finally, even borrowing from a retirement plan is not a good idea. Although we are, in essence, repaying ourselves, we lose the advantage of tax deferred growth. It is also very easy to trigger a premature distribution if we run into trouble causing drastic tax consequences and penalties.

In order for a retirement and college plan to work, there must be a source from which funds can be borrowed. These funds could be in the form of home equity, which can be borrowed on a tax deductible basis, or the PLUS loan Uncle Sam has so considerately made available to us.

One of the problems that often faces parents is that they start saving for college late in life and, therefore, have relatively few years to save until college begins. When we have a short planning horizon, most of us tell our clients to be cautious and invest in conservative investments. For the majority of our clients that strategy is correct. Meanwhile, how can you help a client that hasn't saved enough, has a higher than average income and is somewhat of a risk taker, deal with the college problem?

In Chapter 11 we talked about several mutual fund portfolios and how to shift from aggressive to more conservative investments as college approaches. The big problem with this method is that short-term investments, along with lower risks, usually have relatively low yields. Although this helps us accumulate some money to pay the college bills, it doesn't help us stay ahead of regular inflation let alone college inflation.

For the right client, you might try a different tact. This approach involves investing more aggressively by lengthening the time horizon before we cash in our investments. One of the things Uncle Sam has done for us is to create the PLUS loan. The PLUS loan currently allows our clients to borrow 100% of the cost of college at a reasonable interest rate. By using this tool creatively we can lengthen the time horizon for investing. That leads us into another strategy that can be useful.

Example 4.

Bill Thomas has a daughter, age 14, who is a very bright student. Bill has not saved much for college but he has substantial retirement savings and is an astute investor. He also has some discretionary income and wants to save for college. Since he started late and does not have a full market cycle over which to invest, he placed most of his money in bonds or more secure savings investments. However, Bill is very unhappy about the returns he is accumulating on these "safe" investments.

An interesting approach to this problem might be to have Bill invest more aggressively. If the investments are not performing adequately enough for Bill to sell to pay the college bills when his daughter starts college, he can use the PLUS loan to handle college cash flow. It will not be necessary, then, for him to liquidate his investments and they can continue to grow during the college years. Bill can then sell off those investments at the appropriate time and pay off the PLUS loan.

These techniques are not appropriate for every client but for the client who can understand them, the PLUS loan can give us some unique financial leverage in helping solve the college problem.

How Grandparents Can Help Pay for College

Grandparents can do a great deal to help pay for college. Before you approach the grandparents to ask them to set up a college plan for their grandchildren, you must have an idea of their objectives. Normally, there are four.

1. Grandparents want to help their grandchildren. They want to build a better relationship with them and they want to see them succeed.

2. Most grandparents want to help their children. They know their children will be under a great deal of stress while they are paying for college and they want to help if they can.

3. Third, some grandparents have a substantial amount of money and their goal is to reduce the size of their estates. They would like to make major gifts that will have an effect on their grandchildren's education while also reducing the size of their estate.

4. Finally, other grandparents are not so fortunate. Although they have less money, they would still like to help but they are concerned about their own personal needs as well as their grandchildren's. They can make smaller gifts, but they need to protect their assets for themselves.

When choosing the best plan, it is also important to address four other factors.

1. Age of the grandchildren.

2. Tax status of the parents.

3. Amount of money that is to be invested.

4. The likelihood the grandchildren will qualify for financial aid.

The two most typical grandparent plans involve either setting up a custodial account for the grandchildren or making direct gifts to them, usually during college. (Custodial accounts were discussed in Chapter 10.) Many grandparents set up custodial accounts thinking they are helping the situation only to later find out that they hurt their grandchild's chance of obtaining financial aid. Before the grandparents set up a custodial arrangement, their own children should complete a financial aid test.

There is a way grandparents can help which won't hurt the financial aid eligibility of the grandchild. The grandparents should wait until college begins but after the financial aid award has been granted before making the gifts directly to the grandchild. This plan works best when the grandparents wish to give smaller amounts of money to grandchildren already in college; it's a great way to funnel spending money to the grandchild. One of the costs of college we discussed earlier is the $2,000 to $3,000 of spending money that college kids need. A grandparent can relieve the parent of a significant burden by helping meet this need.

Grandparent Accounts

Grandparent Plan 1

Grandparent Plan 1 is a unique twist on direct gifts. It takes the direct gift approach and systematizes it into a plan. It works great for the grandparent who wants to help but can't commit a large sum of money. Many grandparents have CDs that have been put away for emergencies. They reinvest the income on those CDs and continue to roll them over on their maturity dates. Why not propose they deposit that CD money into a tax free bond unit trust? The grandparent has complete control over the funds and can redeem the fund at any time. Interest from the account, which is tax free, is gifted to the student monthly or quarterly at the whim of the grandparent. A grandparent can stop payments to the student at any time and can use the money for himself or another student. When set up correctly, this plan is tax free and will not hurt the student's ability to obtain financial aid.

One grandparent we know put $10,000 into such a plan that generated about $40 per month in revenue. Grandma and grandpa endorsed the check each month to their grandson and mailed it to him with a funny card. They included a blank postcard and asked him to write back. At last count, the grandparents have received ten postcards, one every month, without fail. The grandson obviously appreciates the money and the grandparents appreciate the attention.

Grandparent Plan 2: The Educational Needs Trust

The Educational Needs Trust is a tool grandparents should use when they wish to take money out of their estate by making irrevocable gifts to their grandchildren. If necessary, the trust can be set up for more than one grandchild. Since a formal trust is required, the amount of the gift must be fairly large to offset the cost of the trust. The trust invests its principle in loans to the grandchildren during college and those loans are repaid after college. The principal is distributed to the grandchildren after all trust beneficiaries have repaid their loans. Any taxes on investment income are paid by the trust. The Educational Needs Trust should not hurt the student's ability to receive financial aid while, at the same time, it removes the money out of the grandparents estate.

Grandparent Plan 3: Direct Tuition Payments

One option a grandparent has is to make direct payments to an educational institution on behalf of the grandchild. Amounts paid on behalf of an individual as tuition to a qualified educational organization are considered "qualified transfers" and are not considered gifts for gift tax purposes. This allows a grandparent to transfer more dollars to his grandchild than the annual gift tax exclusion allows simply by paying the tuition bill directly to the college. From a financial aid standpoint, direct payments are treated as a scholarship by college, thus reducing dollar for dollar the student's need-based financial aid eligibility.

Grandparent Plan 4: Direct Contributions to State Prepaid Tuition Plans

Contributions on behalf of a grandchild to a State Prepaid Tuition Plan can be an appealing option to a grandparent. (Prepaid Tuition Plans were explained in Chapter 11.)

Basically, a grandparent would buy tuition credits or certificates on behalf of a grandchild, the designated beneficiary, which entitles the beneficiary to a waiver or payment of a qualified higher educational expense in the future. As a general rule, a qualified state tuition program is exempt from federal income tax. Therefore, any funds contributed to the plan grow tax deferred.

Under the new tax law (the Taxpayer Relief Act of 1997), the grandparent is no longer considered the owner of the account until distributions are made. A gift is made at the time of the contribution; therefore, any funds contributed are effectively transferred from the grandparent's estate. Gifts are gifts of present interest and subject to the $10,000 annual exclusion. In addition, the grandparent can elect to spread the gift forward over five years if it exceeds $10,000. Taxes due on any investment growth will be the responsibility of the grandchild.

One concern is where the grandchild receives the funds to pay the tax. From a financial aid standpoint, the distribution will reduce financial aid eligibility on a dollar for dollar basis. Figure 12.1 illustrates how the distribution of $9,000 from a Prepaid Tuition Plan reduces financial need and, ultimately, financial aid by $9,000.

Figure 12.1

How Distributions From a Prepaid Tuition Plan Affect Financial Aid Eligibility	
College Cost	$25,000
Expected Family Contribution (EFC)	$10,000
Financial Need	$15,000
Distribution From Prepaid Tuition Plan	$9,000
Adjusted Need	$6,000

There are other possible disadvantages of a Prepaid Tuition Plan. Account values cannot be used as collateral for a loan. The contributor cannot direct the investment of contributions or earnings. Distributions not made on account of qualified higher educational expenses, death, disability or on account of scholarships are subject to plan penalties. A Prepaid Tuition Plan can be rolled over to another qualified beneficiary but gift taxes may apply.

College Planning for the Business Owner

Sometimes the way a business owner thinks through a business problem can have a significant effect on financial aid for his children's education. Here is an example.

John owns his own software company, a C Corporation. He has three children and earns a salary of $100,000 per year. When John's oldest son went to college he applied for financial aid but did not receive any assistance. John's oldest son has graduated but his daughter, his middle child, is currently a junior in college and his youngest son will start college next year. With two children in college, John is hopeful that he will qualify for at least some financial aid because he has significantly depleted his savings paying college bills for the first two children. In addition to the college expenses, John's corporation needs $50,000 in cash to fund a new project.

John has several options: One is to obtain a small business loan through the corporation; another option is to reduce his income and leave the cash in the corporation.

In order for John to pay the college expenses while also funding his company's project, we recommended the following solution.

John will borrow $50,000 using his home equity as collateral. He will also reduce his salary from $100,000 to $50,000 and keep the remaining $50,000 in his business to fund his project. John then will use the $50,000 from his home equity loan to subsidize his income for the following year. Since John has lowered his income, he will qualify for more financial aid, especially with two students in college. John will also reduce his personal income taxes although he may incur slightly higher corporate income taxes.

Figure 12.2

Business Owner C Corporation		
Activity	**Financial Aid Rule**	**Effect on EFC**
Reduce home equity but increase personal cash.	None	None
Reduce income by $50,000.	47.0%	Reduce by $23,500
Spend $50,000 of personal cash on living expenses.	6.0%	Reduce by $6,000
Increase corporate cash by $50,000 (assume corporation assets are less than $85,000)	2.4%	Increase by $1,200
Totals		Reduce by $28,300

Figure 12.2 shows how dramatic an effect shifting resources between personal assets and corporate assets can have on financial aid. S Corporations don't work as effectively as C Corporations because of flow through income. Shifting assets, however, can still be effective with small companies having few corporate assets. It also helps considerably to have a CPA who is willing to be aggressive.

The concept of borrowing from your home equity to supplement your standard of living while reducing your income can help you secure additional financial aid. Reducing a personal asset while increasing a corporate asset can also generated financial aid leverage. What about reducing the income of the owner and using the excess cash to fund a deferred compensation plan? The effect of corporate taxes needs to be considered, but a creative professional who understands college financing as well as financial planning can help his client significantly. Business owners in C Corporations can be extremely creative with college planning.

Variable Life With a Twist

In Chapter 10 we discussed the merits of variable life as a college funding product. Variable life is one of the few products that has the ability to meet all seven of the ideal features we want in a college funding product. (We outlined those features in Chapter 10.) In order to use variable life effectively, we need a fairly long planning horizon. The longer the planning horizon, the better, although ten years is an absolute minimum. Variable life is particularly valuable if the individual is in a high tax bracket. Generally, the tax free withdrawal feature from a variable life contract by using policy loans enhances the after-tax returns from the plan substantially.

In order to use variable life effectively, we need to structure the product correctly. Generally, we want to minimize the amount of life insurance in the product so we can maximize the premium dollars going into the cash values. By doing so it will reduce the target premiums and commissions. It's also important to invest fairly aggressively within this product in order to have the returns compensate for the costs inherent in the product. These costs consist primarily of the internal costs of the mutual funds and the cost of the life insurance.

In a well-constructed policy, we have found that, over a 10 to 15-year period, the cost of insurance coupled with other costs in the policy average about 3% per year. This means that if you obtain a 12% gross investment return from the funds within the policy, the client will net approximately 9%. An 11% gross return will net 8% and a 10% return will net 7%.

Although these costs seem high, we must remember that these net returns can be totally tax free if we handle the policy correctly. Figure 12.3 depicts after-tax returns for various tax brackets. The bracketed area demonstrates where variable life, even with a 3% cost, can do better than other investments. From a suitability point of view, your client should be in at least the 28% tax bracket and have high investment objectives before you suggest this approach. The higher the bracket and the better the expectations on the return, the more suitable the investment.

Figure 12.3

Equivalent After-Tax Returns						
Client's Tax Bracket	Expected Pre-Tax Return					
	6.00%	8.00%	10.00%	12.00%	14.00%	16.00%
15.00%	5.10%	6.80%	8.50%	10.20%	11.90%	13.60%
28.00%	4.32%	5.76%	7.20%	8.64%	10.08%	11.52%
31.00%	4.14%	5.52%	6.90%	8.28%	9.66%	11.04%
36.00%	3.84%	5.12%	6.40%	7.68%	8.96%	10.24%
39.60%	3.62%	4.83%	6.04%	7.25%	8.46%	9.66%

The tax favored compounding within a good performing policy can be extraordinary. In fact, sometimes we may not want to pull the cash value out of the policy to pay for college. We might want to use external loans such as the PLUS loan. This will allow us a longer planning horizon enabling us to enhance returns and amortize costs over the longer period. Remember, college is a retirement problem. It's okay to borrow for college as long as we have extra dollars for retirement. Thus, if the values in the contract are performing and we can borrow cheaper dollars elsewhere, there may be advantages to leveraging the contract. To use these techniques effectively, you need a reasonably sophisticated, high tax bracket client.

With individuals in high tax brackets, we've found variable life extremely appealing. The objection we hear from the client, however, is, "Why must I buy life insurance?" In certain cases where the client needs additional life insurance, we overcome this objection by showing the need for insurance. In other cases, we might be able to replace term insurance with the insurance in the variable life policy, thus saving the client some money. Sometimes, however, the objection to life insurance is a deal killer.

Another technique we've found to overcome this objection is to give the life insurance away to a charity and take a tax deduction. This can be accomplished in several ways. We can use split dollar insurance or we can use the concept of split ownership.

Split ownership involves splitting off a majority of the death benefit and a minimum amount of the cash value to fund premiums for the term portion of the insurance from the end of the premium paying period to maturity. This ensures that the charity will receive their portion of the benefit. A good life underwriter can manage policy values to achieve a workable result for his client. How much you enhance the returns depends upon how aggressively you allocate the premiums to the charity. Split ownership, though, should be fairly conservative tax-wise. Split dollar can be fairly aggressive depending upon how the allocations are made.

Some professionals have used an extremely aggressive technique called a Legacy Trust. The Legacy Trust attempts to receive a full tax deduction on the entire premium by donating the entire premium to charity, having the charity buy a policy on the donor, and permitting the donor to keep the rights to the cash values. Although there is interesting case law that may back this type of transaction, from a tax point of view it is extremely aggressive. Since these split owner-ship transactions can vary widely in design and can be limited by the product, these topics are best discussed with the advanced underwriting department of your life insurance carrier.

Appendix 1

Reference Books, Internet Sites and Key Telephone Numbers

Books and Other Resources on Occupations and Careers

The Occupational Outlook Handbook, 1996-1997 Edition, U. S. Department of Labor, Bureau of Labor Statistics, 1996.

Careers for the '90s: Everything You Need to Know to Find the Right Career, Research and Education Association, 1994.

The College Board Guide to Jobs and Career Planning, Second Edition, Joyce Slayton Mitchell. The College Board, 1994.

What Color Is Your Parachute, 1998, Richard Nelson Bolles. Ten Speed Press, 1997.

American College Testing (ACT) and the National Career Development Association have developed a career exploration and guidance kit called *Realizing the Dream.* Many schools around the country are using this kit to help students identify careers of interest. Ask your child's guidance counselor if *Realizing the Dreams* is being used in your child's school or district. To find our more about the kit call 319-337-1379 or write to the following address:

Heidi Hallberg
Program Coordinator
ACT
2201 North Dodge Street
P.O. Box 168
Iowa City, IA 52243-0168

How to Choose a College Major, Linda Landis Andrews. NTC Contemporary Publishing Co., 1998.

The College Board Guide to 150 Popular College Majors, College Entrance Examination Board, 1992.

The Job Vault, Vault Reports, Inc., Mariner Books, 1997.

Guide to Your Career, Alan B. Bernstein, C.S.W.P.C., and Nicholas R. Schaffzin. The Princeton Review, 1997.

Job Finder's Guide 1997, Les Krantz. World Almanac, 1996.

Career Book, Third Edition, Joyce Lain Kennedy. VGM, 1997.

Job Smarts—50 Top Careers, Bradley G. Richardson, 1997.

Discover What You're Best At, Barry and Linda Gale, 1990.

100 Best Careers for the 21st Century, Shelly Field. MacMillan, 1996.

Books About Choosing a College

The College Guide for Parents, Third Edition, Charles Shields. The College Board, 1994.

The College Handbook, 1996. The College Board, 1995.

Peterson's Guide to Four-Year Colleges, 1996, Twenty-Sixth Edition, Peterson's Guides, 1995.

Barron's Profiles of American Colleges, Twenty-First Edition, Barron's Educational Series, Inc., 1996.

Rugg's Recommendations on the Colleges, Thirteenth Edition, Rugg's Recommendations, 1996.

The Multicultural Student's Guide to the Colleges, Robert Mitchell. Noonday Press, 1996.

Barron's Top 50—An Inside Look at America's Best Colleges, Third Edition, Barron's Educational Series, 1995.

The Complete Book of Colleges, 1998 Edition, Princeton Review, 1997.

Barron's Compact Guide to Colleges, Tenth Edition, Barron's Educational Series, 1996.

Newsweek College Catalog, 1998 Edition, Kaplan Educational Centers, 1997.

The Fiske Guide to Colleges, 1998, Edward B. Fiske. Times Books, 1997.

Lovejoy's College Guide, Twenty-Fourth Edition, MacMillan, 1997.

America's 100 Best College Buys, 1997-1998, Culler, 1997.

Books About Preparing for Standardized Tests

Real SATs, The College Board, 1995.

Official Guide to the ACT Assessment, Harcourt Brace Press, 1990.

Barron's How to Prepare for the PSAT/NMSQT, Ninth Edition, Samuel Brownstein, Mitchel Weiner and Sharon Weiner Green. Barron's Educational Series, 1997.

Barron's How to Prepare for the SAT I, Nineteenth Edition, Samuel Brownstein, Mitchel Weiner and Sharon Weiner Green. Barron's Educational Series, 1887.

Barron's How to Prepare for the ACT, Tenth Edition, George Ehrenhaft, Robert Lehrman, Fred Obrecht and Allan Mundsack. Barron's Educational Series, 1995.

Preparation for the SAT, 1997 Edition, Edward Deptula (Ed.). Arco Publishers, 1996.

Cracking the SAT and PSAT, 1998, Adam Robinson and John Katzman. The Princeton Review, 1997.

Cracking the ACT, 1997-98, Geoff Martz, Kin Magloire and Theodore Silver. Princeton Review, 1996.

Word Smart: Building on Educated Vocabulary, Adam Robinson. Princeton Review, 1993.

Everything You Need to Score High on the SAT and PSAT, Fourteenth Edition 1998, Edward Deptula (Ed.). Arco Publishers, 1998.

Road Trip for the SAT, Kaplan Educational Centers, 1997.

SAT Verbal Workout, Geoff Martz. The Princeton Review, 1995.

SAT Super Course, Third Edition, Thomas H. Martinson. Arco Publishers, 1996.

Books About Financing Your Child's Education

Paying for College: A Guide for Parents, Gerald Krefetz. The College Board, 1995.

College Financial Aid, Fifth Edition, College Research Group of Concord, Massachusetts. MacMillan General Reference, 1993.

College Costs and Financial Aid Handbook, 1998, Eighteenth Edition, The College Board, 1997.

Peterson's Paying Less for College, 1996, Thirteenth Edition, Peterson's Guides, 1995.

Best Buys in College Education, Third Edition, Lucia Solorzano. Barron's Educational Series, 1994.

College Scholarships & Financial Aid, Sixth Edition, John Schwartz (Ed.). Arco Publishers, 1995.

Don't Miss Out: The Ambitious Student's Guide to Financial Aid, 1996-97, Twentieth Edition, Anna Leider and Robert Leider. Octameron Associates, 1995.

"Paying for Your Child's College Education," Marguerite Smith. *Money Magazine,* 1996.

Free Money for College, Laurie Blum. 1994.

Barron's Complete College Financing Guide, Fourth Edition, Barron's Educational Series, 1997.

You Can Afford College, 1998 Edition, KEC, 1997.

Financing College, Kristin Davis. Kiplinger, 1996.

Books About Private Sources of Financial Aid

Foundation Grants to Individuals, Ninth Edition, L. Victoria Hall (Ed.). The Foundation Center, 1995.

The A's and B's of Academic Scholarships, 1996-97, Eighteenth Edition, Deborah L. Wexler (Ed.). Octameron Associates, 1995.

The Scholarship Book, Fifth Edition, Daniel Cassidy. Prentice Hall, Inc., 1996.

The Complete Grants Sourcebook for Higher Education, Third Edition, David Bauer and David Bower. Oryx Press, 1995.

Peterson's Scholarship Almanac, 1998 Edition, Peterson's Guides, 1997.

USA Today, "Peterson's Financial Aid for College," Gannett New Media Services, 1995.

Cash for College—The Ultimate Guide to College Scholarships, Cynthia Ruiz McKee and Phillip C. McKee, Jr., 1993.

The Scholarship Book, Fifth Edition, Daniel J. Cassidy. Prentice Hall, 1996.

Scholarship—The Essential Guide, 1998 Edition, Kaplan Educational Centers, 1997.

Peterson's Winning Money for College, Fourth Edition, Alan Deutschman. Peterson's Guides, 1997.

Funding a College Education, Alice Drum and Richard Kneedler. HBS Press, 1996.

Helpful Web Sites for Applicants

Comprehensive Guides
American School Counselor Association

www.edge.net/asca/links.html

Comprehensive links to college web sites that also offer information on career choices. A resource link for all types of education K-12 through college. Also a link to counseling services and education resources.

Peterson's Education and Career Center

www.petersons.com

Comprehensive information site spanning grades K through college. Also includes information on study abroad, summer programs and special schools.

The College Board

www.collegeboard.org

Comprehensive web site discussing everything from SAT and college searches to admission and financial aid.

U.S. Department of Education

www.ed.gov

Web site to U.S. publications, programs and the latest information on education issues.

U.S. News College and Careers Center

www.usnews.com

U.S. News maintains this site with a link to the *U.S. News Magazine*. It also has an education link for information on colleges including their latest rankings.

College Search Sites

College Edge

www.collegeedge.com

A search engine where you can explore schools and careers. Information site where you can explore careers and colleges. Apply to colleges using the College Edge Web Application. It also links to other students through the Forums site.

College Net

www.collegenet.com

Information on colleges, scholarships and financial aid. There are also sites on student recruiting and 3-D campus tours.

College View

www.collegeview.com

Search engine of over 3,500 colleges. Also includes information on career choices and financial aid along with electronic application links.

College Zine

www.kaplan.com

Information web site that covers K-12 along with college, graduate school and some specialty fields. It also contains information on financial aid, international schools and standardized tests.

Online Campus

www.uophy.edu/online/

University of Phoenix web site for college courses offered over the Internet.

The Princeton Review

www.princetonreview.com

Offers all types of information on choosing the right college, how to make the most out of college visits along with links to college web pages.

U.S. Two-Year Colleges

www.sp.utoledo.edu/twoyrcol.html

Web link to two-year colleges in the U.S. Includes community, technical, junior and branches of four-year colleges along with a link to College Net and Peterson Education Center.

U.S. Universities and Community Colleges

www.utexas.edu/world/univ

Link to web sites of U.S. universities and community colleges.

Financial Aid

Education Assistance Corp.

www.eac-easci.org

Information on applying for student loans, financial aid and scholarship searches.

FAFSA on the Web

www.fafsa.ed.gov

Online application to apply for federal financial aid.

FastWEB

www.fastweb.com

Comprehensive search engine for information on scholarships and financial aid. Includes Help section and parents page.

Financial Aid Information Page

www.finaid.org

Comprehensive guide to financial aid which includes scam alerts and special interest sites.

Preparing Your Child for College

www.ed.gov/pubs/Prepare/note.html

A resource book for parents covering all areas of college planning such as financing college costs and long-range planning. It also includes information on standardized testing.

The Student Guide

www.ed.gov/prog_info/SFA

Link for instructions on completing the Free Application for Federal Student Aid (FAFSA). It is also a link for other student aid.

U.S. Department of Education

www.ed.gov

Web site to U.S. publications, programs and latest information on education issues.

Information About Opportunities in Each State

For information about state financial aid and colleges and universities in specific states, contact the agencies listed below. They can provide you with other contacts in the state for more information.

ALABAMA

Executive Director
Commission on Higher Education
100 North Union Street
Montgomery, Alabama 36104-3702
TEL: 334-242-1998
FAX: 334-242-0268

ALASKA

Executive Director
Alaska Commission of Postsecondary Education
3030 Vintage Boulevard
Juneau, Alaska 99801-7109
TEL: 907-465-2962
FAX: 907-465-5316

President
University of Alaska System
202 Butrowich Building
Fairbanks, Alaska 99775-5560
TEL: 907-474-7311
FAX: 907-474-7570

ARIZONA

Executive Director
Arizona Board of Regents
2020 North Central, Suite 230
Phoenix, Arizona 85004
TEL: 602-229-2500
FAX: 606-229-2555

ARKANSAS

Director
Department of Higher Education
114 East Capitol
Little Rock, Arkansas 72201
TEL: 501-324-9300
FAX: 501-324-9308

CALIFORNIA

Executive Director
California Postsecondary Education Commission
1303 J Street, 5th Floor
Sacramento, California 95814-2938
TEL: 916-445-1000
FAX: 916-327-4417

California Student Aid Commission
P.O. Box 510845
Sacramento, California 94245-0845
TEL: 916-445-0880
FAX: 916-327-6599

COLORADO

Executive Director
Commission on Higher Education
1300 Broadway, 2nd Floor
Denver, Colorado 80203
TEL: 303-866-4034
FAX: 303-860-9750

CONNECTICUT

Commissioner of Higher Education
Department of Higher Education
61 Woodland Street
Hartford, Connecticut 06105
TEL: 203-566-5766
FAX: 203-566-7865

DELAWARE

Executive Director
Delaware Higher Education
Commission
820 French Street, 4th Floor
Wilmington, Delaware 19801
TEL: 302-577-3240
FAX: 302-577-6765

DISTRICT OF COLUMBIA

Chief
Office of Postsecondary
Education,Research and Assistance
2100 Martin Luther King, Jr. Avenue,
S.E. #401
Washington, D.C. 20020
TEL: 202-727-3685
FAX: 202:727-2739

FLORIDA

Executive Director
Postsecondary Education Planning
Commission
Florida Education Center
Collins Building
Tallahassee, Florida 32399-0400
TEL: 904-488-7894
FAX: 904-922-5388

Office of Student Financial
Assistance
Room 255, Collins Building
Tallahassee, Florida 32399-0400
TEL: 904-488-1034
FAX: 904-488-3612

GEORGIA

Chancellor
Board of Regents
University System of Georgia
244 Washington Street, S.W.
Atlanta, Georgia 30334
TEL: 404-656-2202
FAX: 404-657-6979

Georgia Student Finance
Commission
2082 East Exchange Place
Tucker, Georgia 30084
TEL: 770-414-3200
FAX: 770-414-3163

HAWAII

President
University of Hawaii System
2444 Dole Street
Bachman Hall, Room 202
Honolulu, Hawaii 96822
TEL: 808-956-8207
FAX: 808-956-5286

Hawaii State Postsecondary
Education Commission
2444 Dole Street
Bachman Hall, Room 209
Honolulu, Hawaii 96822
TEL: 808-956-8213
FAX: 808-956-5156

IDAHO

Executive Director for Higher
Education
State Board of Education
P.O. Box 83720
Boise, Idaho 83720-0037
TEL: 208-334-2270
FAX: 208-334-2632

ILLINOIS

Executive Director
Board of Higher Education
4 West Old Capitol Plaza, Room 500
Springfield, Illinois 62701
TEL: 217-782-2551
FAX: 217-782-8548

Illinois Student Assistance
Commission
Executive Offices
500 West Monroe Street, Third Floor
Springfield, Illinois 62704
TEL: 217-782-6767
FAX: 217-524-1858

INDIANA

Commissioner for Higher Education
Commission for Higher Education
101 West Ohio Street, Suite 550
Indianapolis, Indiana 46204-1971
TEL: 317-464-4400
FAX: 317-464-4410

State Student Assistance Commission
of Indiana
150 West Market Street, Suite 500
Indianapolis, Indiana 46204
TEL: 317-232-2350
FAX: 317-232-3260

IOWA

Executive Director
State Board of Regents
Old Historical Building
East 12th and Grand Avenue
Des Moines, Iowa 50319
TEL: 515-281-3934
FAX: 515-281-6420

Iowa College Student Aid
Commission
200 Tenth Street, 4th Floor
Des Moines, Iowa 50309
TEL: 515-281-3501
FAX: 515-242-5996

KANSAS

Executive Director
Kansas Board of Regents
700 SW Harrison, Suite 1410
Topeka, Kansas 66603-3760
TEL: 913-296-3421
FAX: 913-296-0983

KENTUCKY

Executive Director
Council on Higher Education
1024 Capitol Center Drive, Suite 320
Frankfort, Kentucky 40601-8204
TEL: 502-573-1555
FAX: 502-573-1535

Kentucky Higher Education
Assistance Authority
1050 U.S. 127 South
Frankfort, Kentucky 40601
TEL: 502-564-7990
FAX: 502-564-7103

LOUISIANA

Commissioner
Board of Regents
150 Third Street, Suite 129
Baton Rouge, Louisiana 70801-1389
TEL: 504-342-4253
FAX: 504-342-9318

Office of Student Financial
Assistance
Louisiana Student Financial
Assistance Commission
P.O. Box 91202
Baton Rouge, Louisiana 70821-9202
TEL: 504-922-1011
FAX: 504- 922-1089

MAINE

Chancellor
University of Maine System
107 Maine Avenue
Bangor, Maine 04401-4380
TEL: 207-973-3205
FAX: 207-947-7556

Financial Authority of Maine
Maine Education Assistance Division
One Weston Court
State House, Station 119
Augusta, Maine 04333
TEL: 207-287-2183
FAX: 207-287-2233 or 207-628-8208

MARYLAND

Secretary of Higher Education
Maryland Higher Education
Commission

16 Francis Street
Annapolis, Maryland 21401-1781
TEL: 410-974-2971
FAX: 410-974-3513

MASSACHUSETTS

Chancellor
Higher Education Coordinating
Council
McCormark Building
1 Ashburton Place, Room 1401
Boston, Massachusetts 02108-1696
TEL: 617-727-7785
FAX: 617-727-6397

Massachusetts State Scholarship
Office
330 Stuart Street
Boston, Massachusetts 02116
TEL: 617-727-9420
FAX: 617-727-0667

MICHIGAN

Michigan Higher Education Student
Loan Authority
State Department of Education
P.O. Box 30057
Lansing, Michigan 48909
TEL: 517-373-3662
FAX: 517-335-6699

Michigan Higher Education
Assistance Authority
P.O. Box 30462
Lansing, Michigan 48909
TEL: 517-373-3394
FAX: 517-335-5984

MINNESOTA

Executive Director
Higher Education Services Offices
400 Capital Square Building
550 Cedar Street
St. Paul, Minnesota 55101
TEL: 612-296-9665
FAX: 612-297-8880

MISSISSIPPI

Commissioner
Board of Trustees of State Institutions
of Higher Learning
3825 Ridgewood Road
Jackson, Mississippi 39211-6453
TEL: 601-982-6611
FAX: 601-364-2862

MISSOURI

Commissioner of Higher Education
Coordinating Board for Higher
Education
3515 Amazonas
Jefferson City, Missouri 65109
TEL: 314-751-2361
FAX: 314-751-6635

MONTANA

Commissioner of Higher Education
Montana University System
2500 Broadway
Helena, Montana 59620-3101
TEL: 406-444-6570
FAX: 406-444-1469

NEBRASKA

Executive Director
Coordinating Commission for
Postsecondary Education

P.O. Box 95005
Lincoln, Nebraska 68509-5005
TEL: 402-471-2847
FAX: 402-471-2886

NEVADA

Chancellor
University of Nevada System
2601 Enterprise Road
Reno, Nevada 89512
TEL: 702-784-4901
FAX: 702-784-1127

Nevada Department of Education
700 East 5th Street, Capitol Complex
Carson City, Nevada 89710
TEL: 702-687-5915
FAX: 702- 687-5660

NEW HAMPSHIRE

Executive Director
New Hampshire Postsecondary
Education Commission
Two Industrial Park Drive
Concord, New Hampshire 03301-
8512
TEL: 603-271-2555
FAX: 603-271-2696

Chancellor
University System of New
Hampshire
Dunlap Center
25 Concord Road
Durham, New Hampshire 03824-
3545
TEL: 603-868-1800
FAX: 603-868-3021

NEW JERSEY

New Jersey Department of Higher
Education
Office of Student Assistance and
Information Systems
4 Quakerbridge Plaza, CN 540
Trenton, New Jersey 08625
TEL: 1-800-792-8670
TEL: 609-584-9618
FAX: 609-588-2228

NEW MEXICO

Executive Director
Commission on Higher Education
1068 Cerrillos Road
Santa Fe, New Mexico 87501-4295
TEL: 505-827-7383
FAX: 505-827-7392

NEW YORK

Deputy Commissioner for Higher and
Professional Education
Room 5B28 Cultural Education
Center
New York State Education
Department
Albany, New York 12230
TEL: 518-474-5851
FAX: 518-486-2175

The New York State Higher
Education Services Corporation
99 Washington Avenue
Albany, New York 12255
TEL: 518-473-0431
FAX: 518-474-2839

NORTH CAROLINA

Vice President for Planning
University of North Carolina
General Administration
P.O. Box 2688
Chapel Hill,
North Carolina 27515-2688
TEL: 919-962-6981
FAX: 919-962-0488

North Carolina State Education
Assistance Authority (NCSEAA)
P.O. Box 2688
Chapel Hill,
North Carolina 27515-2688
TEL: 919-549-8614
FAX: 919-549-8481

College Foundation Inc.
P.O. Box 12100
Raleigh, North Carolina 27605
TEL: 919-821-4771
FAX: 919-821-3139

NORTH DAKOTA

Chancellor
North Dakota University System
600 East Boulevard Avenue
Bismarck, North Dakota 58505
TEL: 701-328-2962
FAX: 701-328-2961

OHIO

Chancellor
Ohio Board of Regents
30 East Broad Street, 36th Floor
Columbus, Ohio 43266-0417
TEL: 614-466-0887
FAX: 614-466-5866

OKLAHOMA

Chancellor
State Regents for Higher Education
500 Education Building
State Capitol Complex
Oklahoma City, Oklahoma 73105
TEL: 405-524-9100
FAX: 405-524-9230

OREGON

Chancellor
State System of Higher Education
P.O. Box 3175
Eugene, Oregon 97403-1075
TEL: 541-346-5700
FAX: 541-346-5764

Oregon State Scholarship
Commission
1500 Valley River Drive, Suite 100
Eugene Oregon 97401
TEL: 541-687-7400
FAX: 541-687-7419

PENNSYLVANIA

Commissioner for Higher Education
State Department of Education
333 Market Street
Harrisburg, Pennsylvania 17126-0333
TEL: 717-787-5041
FAX: 717-783-0583

Pennsylvania Higher Education
Assistance Agency
1200 North 7th Street
Harrisburg, Pennsylvania 17102
TEL: 717-257-2850
FAX: 717-720-3907

PUERTO RICO

Executive Director
Council on Higher Education
Box 23400, UPR Station
San Juan, Puerto Rico 00931-3400
TEL: 809-758-3350
FAX: 809-763-8394

RHODE ISLAND

Commissioner of Higher Education
Office of Higher Education
301 Promenade Street
Providence,
Rhode Island 02908-5720
TEL: 401-277-6560
FAX: 401-277-6111

Rhode Island Higher Education
Assistance Authority
560 Jefferson Boulevard
Warwick, Rhode Island 02886
TEL: 401-736-1100
FAX: 401-732-3541

SOUTH CAROLINA

Commissioner
Commission on Higher Education
1333 Main Street, Suite 200
Columbia, South Carolina 29201
TEL: 803-737-2260
FAX: 803-737-2297

South Carolina Higher Education
Tuition Grants Commission
P.O. Box 12159
Columbia, South Carolina 29211
TEL: 803-734-1200
FAX: 803-734-1426

SOUTH DAKOTA

Executive Director
Board of Regents
207 East Capitol Avenue
Pierre, South Dakota 57501-3159
TEL: 605-773-3455
FAX: 605-773-5320

Department of Education and
CulturalAffairs
Office of the Secretary
700 Governors Drive
Pierre, South Dakota 57501-2291
TEL: 605-773-3134
FAX: 605-773-6139

TENNESSEE

Executive Director
Tennessee Higher Education
Commission
Parkway Towers, Suite 1900
404 James Robertson Parkway
Nashville, Tennessee 37243-0830
TEL: 615-741-7562
FAX: 615- 741-6230

Tennessee Student Assistance
Corporation
Parkway Towers, Suite 1950
404 James Robertson Parkway
Nashville, Tennessee 37243-0820
TEL: 615-741-1346
FAX: 615-741-6101

TEXAS

Commissioner
Texas Higher Education Coordinating
Board
P.O. Box 12788

Austin, Texas 78711
TEL: 512-483-6101
FAX: 512-483-6169

Texas Higher Education Coordinating
Board
P.O. Box 12788, Capitol Station
Austin, Texas 78711
TEL: 512-483-6340
FAX: 512-483-6420

UTAH

Commissioner of Higher Education
Utah System of Higher Education
3 Triad Center, Suite 550
Salt Lake City, Utah 84180-1205
TEL: 801-321-7101
FAX: 801-321-7199

VERMONT

Vermont Student Assistance
Corporation
P.O. Box 2000, Champlain Mill
Winooski, Vermont 05404-2601
TEL: 802-655-9602
FAX: 802-654-3765

Chancellor
Vermont State College
P.O. Box 359
Waterbury, Vermont 05676
TEL: 802-241-2520
FAX: 802-241-3369

President
University of Vermont
349 Waterman Building
Burlington, Vermont 05405
TEL: 802-656-3186
FAX: 802-656-1363

VIRGINIA

Director
State Council of Higher Education
101 North 14th Street, 9th Floor
Richmond, Virginia 23219
TEL: 804-225-2600
FAX: 804-225-2604

WASHINGTON

Executive Director
Higher Education Coordinating
Board
917 Lakeridge Way, P.O. Box 43430
Olympia, Washington 98504-3430
TEL: 360-753-7800
FAX: 360-753-7808

WEST VIRGINIA

Chancellor
State College System of West
Virginia
1018 Kanawha Boulevard, East
Charleston, West Virginia 25301
TEL: 304-558-0699
FAX: 304-558-1011

Chancellor
University of West Virginia System
1018 Kanawha Boulevard, East,
Suite 700
Charleston, West Virginia 25301
TEL: 304-558-2736
FAX: 304-558-3264

WISCONSIN

Higher Education Aids Board
P.O. Box 7885
Madison, Wisconsin 53707
TEL: 608-267-2206
FAX: 608-267-2808

President
University of Wisconsin System
1700 Van Hise Hall
1220 Linden Drive
Madison, Wisconsin 53706
TEL: 608-262-2321
FAX: 608-262-3985

WYOMING

The Community College
Commission
2020 Carey Avenue, 8th Floor
Cheyenne, Wyoming 82002
TEL: 307-777-7763
FAX: 307-777-6567

President
University of Wyoming
Box 3434
Laramie, Wyoming 82071
TEL: 307-766-4121
FAX: 307-766-2271

Appendix 2

Financial Aid Worksheet

Approximate Your Expected Family Contribution for Federal Financial Aid

The following worksheet will help you calculate the approximate Expected Family Contribution for your family for federal financial aid. Please note that many colleges use a different procedure, the Institutional Methodology, for awarding their own private funds.

⚿ Please note: Family income, for financial aid purposes, is the income from the year before the financial aid is needed. For example, 1997 income will determine 1998 financial aid, 1998 income determines 1999 financial aid, etc.

1. Parents' Income

Adjusted gross income from your
  '97 federal income tax return   _____

Subtract child support for '97.   _____

Add the total for the nontaxable income.   _____

Add back '97 deduction for IRA and
  Keogh contributions   _____

Subtract '97 federal, state and
  Social Security (FICA) taxes, if two
  working parents in the household, subtract
  employment expenses:
$2,700 or 35% of the lower salary,
  whichever is less.   _____

Subtract your Income Protection
  Allowance (Table 1),
if the result is negative enter 0 on line A; if it
  is positive, enter the amount on line A.   _____

                                              A $ _____

2. Parents' Assets

If your adjusted gross income is $50,000 or
less and you did not itemize deductions on
your federal income tax return, enter 0 on line B.
Otherwise enter the total value of your
investments, including stocks, bonds, and
real estate other than your principal home.   _____

Add sum of all cash, bank, and money
  market accounts.   _____

Subtract $40,300   _____

2. Parents' Assets (cont'd)

If the result is negative, enter 0 on line B.
If it is positive, multiply by 0.12 and enter
  the result on line.   B _____

                                            B $ _____

3. Parents' Contribution

Enter the total of line A and B.   _____

Use this number to find the parents' expected
contribution from Table II. Divide that figure
by the number of family members attending
college and enter the result on line C.   _____

                                            C $ _____

4. Student's Contribution

Enter the student's '97 Adjusted Gross Income
  as reported on his or her federal income tax
  return   _____

Subtract '97 federal, state and Social
  Security (FICA) taxes   _____

Subtract the $1,750 Income Protection Allowance.
If the result is negative, enter 0. If it is
  positive, multiply by 0.5.   _____

Add 35% of the student's investments and
  savings and enter the total on line D.   _____

                                            D $ _____

5. Total Family Contribution

Add lines C and D and enter the
  sum on line E.   E $ _____

Table I: Income Protection Allowance (IPA)
(Parents of Dependent Students/Independent Student with Dependents)

Number in College

Family Size (include Student)	1	2	3	4	5
2	$11,750	$9,740			
3	$14,630	$12,630	$10,620		
4	$18,070	$16,060	$14,060	$12,050	
5	$21,320	$19,310	$17,310	$15,300	$13,300
6	$24,940	$22,930	$20,930	$18,920	$16,920

Table II: Parents' Contribution

If line A plus line B equals:	Then the parents' contribution is:
$3,409 or less	Minus $750
$3,410 to $10,500	22% of Adjusted Available Income
$10,501 to $13,200	$2,310 plus 25% of AAI $10,500
$13,201 to $15,900	$2,985 plus 29% of AAI $13,200
$15,901 to $18,500	$3,768 plus 34% of AAI $15,900
$18,501 to $21,200	$5,732 plus 47% of AAI $21,200

Financial Aid Woorksheet

Appendix 3

Detailed Trial Financial Aid Test Printout

The following pages represent the output of a computer generated Trial Financial Aid Test. Not all software generates as much detail as the example shown in this appendix. The software used in this example is from College Money.

The first page is the client page that recaps the input data as well as generating the Expected Family Contribution (EFC) for both the Federal and Institutional Methodologies. Pages 2, 3 and 4 are counselor worksheets that track the calculations in detail. The last page calculates key numbers to help the counselor plan.

Trial Financial Aid Analysis (Ver. 98a)

Prepared for: John & Mary Sample
And Student: Joseph

Prepared by: Raymond D. Loewe, CLU, ChFC   609-596-4702
College Money
112-B Centre Boulevard
Marlton, NJ 08053

INPUT DATA VERIFICATION SUMMARY AS OF:	18-Oct-97
1	Age of older parent	44
2	Number of parents in family	2
3	No. of dependent children in the family	2
4	Number of children in college now	1
5	Father's wages	$55,000
6	Mother's wages	$60,000
7	Other taxable income	$2,500
8	Non taxable income	$0
9	Adjustments to income	$0
10	Federal income tax paid	$12,000
11	Net home equity (not used in calculation)	$135,000
12	Net equity of other real estate	$0
13	Business net value (your share)	$0
14	Parent cash	$25,000
15	Parent investments (non retirement)	$10,000
16	Student assets	$1,500
17	Student income	
	a From work	$2,500
	b From investments	$100
18	Student income tax paid	$0
	State code	NJ

FAMILY EXPECTED CONTRIBUTION SUMMARY:	Federal	Institutional
Parent Contribution Per Student	$27,287	$30,645
Student Contribution	$815	$1,716
FAMILY CONTRIBUTION THIS STUDENT:	$28,102	$32,362

This analysis provides estimated financial aid data for planning purposes only. Actual financial aid awards are determined by each college at the time of admission. *Calculations are based on the 1997-1998 Federal Methodology and the 1997-1998 Institutuional Methodology using College Money* software, copyright 1985-1997, All Rights Reserved. *College Money* is a registered trademark of Educational Planning Systems, Inc.

THIS ANALYSIS IS VALID ONLY WHEN ACCOMPANIED BY THE 1997-1998 PARENT WORKBOOK, *"A Practical Guide To Paying For College."* Contact your college planning professional or Educational Planning Systems, Inc. - 112B Centre Blvd - Marlton, NJ 08053 - (609) 596-4702

Counselor Worksheet   **Page 1**

Detailed Trial Financial Aid Test Printout

Counselor Worksheet (Ver. 98a)
Trial Financial Aid Analysis - Data Verification 18-Oct-97

Parent's name	John & Mary Sample
Student's name	Joseph
Address	123 Main Street
City, state, zip	Anytown, NJ
Home telephone	246-4081
Business telephone	236-123-5069

1	Age of older parent	44
2	Number of parents in family	2
3	Number of dependent children in the family	2
4	Number of children in college (planned)	1
5	Father's wages	$55,000
6	Mother's wages	$60,000
7	Other taxable income	$2,500
8	Nontaxable income	$0
9	Adjustments to income	$0
10	Federal income tax paid	$12,000
11	Net home equity	
	a Market value	$200,000
	b Sum of all mortgages	$65,000
12	Net equity of other real estate	
	a Market value	$0
	b Sum of all mortgages	$0
13	Business/farm net value (your share)	$0
14	Parent cash	$25,000
15	Parent investments	
	a Qualified retirement plans	$150,000
	b Other	$10,000
16	Student assets	$1,500
17	Student income	
	a From work	$2,500
	b From investments	$100
18	Student income tax paid	$0
	State code	NJ
		New Jersey

Counselor's name	Raymond D. Loewe, CLU, ChFC
Address (line 1)	College Money
Address (line 2)	112-B Centre Boulevard
Address (line 3)	Marlton, NJ 08053
Address (line 4)	
Counselor's telephone number	609-596-4702

Counselor Worksheet Page 2

Detailed Trial Financial Aid Test Printout

Counselor Worksheet
Trial Financial Aid Analysis (Ver. 98a)
(1997-98 Federal & Institutional Methodologies)

Parent's name:	John & Mary Sample
Student's name:	Joseph
Prepared on:	18-Oct-97

Parent Expected Contribution - Calculations		Federal	Institutional
Parent's income			
Father's income from work		$55,000	$55,000
Mother's income from work		$60,000	$60,000
Other taxable income		$2,500	$2,500
Non taxable income		$0	$0
Total income		$117,500	$117,500
Deductions:			
FICA tax - father		$4,208	$4,208
FICA tax - mother		$4,590	$4,590
Total FICA tax		$8,798	$8,798
Adjustments to income		$0	$0
Federal income tax paid		$12,000	$12,000
State & other taxes		$8,225	$12,925
Employment allowance		$2,700	$2,700
Income Protection Allowance		$18,070	$17,980
Total deductions		$49,793	$54,403
Available income (AI)		$67,708	$63,098
Parent's assets			
Parent cash		$25,000	$25,000
Home equity		N/A	$135,000
Market value	$200,000		
Mortgage value	$65,000		
Other real estate equity		$0	$0
Market value	$0		
Mortgage value	$0		
Parent investments (excl. ret. plans)		$10,000	$10,000
Business/Farm net worth	$0	$0	$0
Net worth		$35,000	$170,000
Asset Protection/Educ. Saving Allowance		$39,300	$38,000
Discretionary net worth (DNW)		($4,300)	$132,000
Asset conversion percentage		12.00%	12.00%
Contribution from assets (Income Supplmt)		$0	$15,840
Adjusted available income (AAI)		$67,708	$78,938
AAI taxation rate		47.00%	47.00%
Total parent's contribution	$27,287	$27,287	$30,645
Number of students in college		1	1
Parent's Contribution Per Student		**$27,287**	**$30,645**

Counselor Worksheet   **Page 3**

Detailed Trial Financial Aid Test Printout

Counselor Worksheet
Trial Financial Aid Analysis (Ver. 98a)
(1997-98 Federal & Institutional Methodologies)

Parent's name:　　John & Mary Sample
Student's name:　　Joseph
Prepared on:　　　18-Oct-97

Dependent Student Contribution:	Federal	Institutional
Student income		
Student's earned income	$2,500	$2,500
Student's other income	$100	$100
Student's total income	$2,600	$2,600
Student's deductions		
Federal income tax paid	$0	$0
FICA tax paid	$191	$191
State & other taxes	$78	$26
Income protection allowance	$1,750	$0
Total deductions	$2,019	$217
Net student income	$581	$2,383
Income assessment rate	50.00%	50.00%
Available income	$290	$1,191
Student's assets	$1,500	$1,500
Conversion rate	35.00%	35.00%
Income supplement	$525	$525
Student Contribution	**$815**	**$1,716**
TOTAL FAMILY CONTRIBUTION	**$28,102**	**$32,362**

Counselor Worksheet　　　　　　　　　　　**Page 4**

Detailed Trial Financial Aid Test Printout

Counselor Worksheet
Trial Financial Aid Analysis (Ver. 98a)
(1997-98 Federal & Institutional Methodologies)

KEY COUNSELING NUMBERS **Federal Methodology**	Totals	% From Assets	% From Income
Total Parent Expected Cont.	$27,287		
Parent Expected Cont./Student	$27,287	0.00%	100.00%
Student Expected Contribution	$815	64.39%	35.61%
Family Expected Cont. This Student	$28,102		
Parent Asset Gap	$4,300		
Student Income Gap	$0		
FINANCIAL AID PLANNING RULES OF THUMB **Federal Methodology**		% From Assets	% From Income
Parent's Marginal Contribution Percentage		5.64%	47.00%
Student's Marginal Contribution Percentage		35.00%	50.00%

KEY COUNSELING NUMBERS **Institutional Methodology**	Totals	% From Assets	% From Income
Total Parent Expected Cont.	$30,645		
Parent Expected Cont./Student	$30,645	20.07%	79.93%
Student Expected Contribution	$1,716	30.59%	69.41%
Family Expected Cont./Student	$32,362		
Parent Asset Gap	$0		
Student Income Gap	$0		
FINANCIAL AID PLANNING RULES OF THUMB **Institutional Methodology**		% From Assets	% From Income
Parent's Marginal Contribution Percentage		5.64%	47.00%
Student's Marginal Contribution Percentage		35.00%	50.00%

Counselor Worksheet **Page 5**

Detailed Trial Financial Aid Test Printout

Appendix 4

College Visit

This chart should be used as a guide as you tour each of the colleges on your list. The chart highlights areas that we have found to be important to both students and parents. The information for this chart was provided by Francine E. Block of American College Admissions Consultants.

College Name
Location: Urban, Suburban, Small Town, Rural
Overall Physical Appearance of Campus
Distance of Dorms to Main Campus area
Type of Neighborhood surrounding campus
Type of Security on campus
Type of security in dorms
Access to dorms
24-hour escort service
Library
Study carrels on all floors
Consortium Library
Hours: daily, weekend, exam
Laboratory Facilities
Gym Facilities
Places to visit
Library
Dorm
Dining Hall
Classroom Building
Student Union
Career Center
Pick up a student newspaper
Notes:

College Visit

Compare Colleges as You Begin Your Search Process

Complete the information on each college that you visit. By keeping a record of the facts about each college and your feelings about the campus and its facilities, the chart can be used as a means of comparing one college against the others.

School _____   City _____   State _____

Characteristic	Degree of Importance			Your rating of the school					Score
	Important	Somewhat Important	Not Important	Excellent	Very Good	Good	Sub Standard	Inadequate	
Size of the school: Under 1,000; 2,000; 3,000; 10,000 to 15,000 or Over 15,000	3	2	1	5	4	3	2	1	
Quality of teaching staff: Professor, Instructors, or teaching assistants	3	2	1	5	4	3	2	1	
Size of classes	3	2	1	5	4	3	2	1	
Location of university	3	2	1	5	4	3	2	1	
Required major or majors	3	2	1	5	4	3	2	1	
Quality of academic facilities	3	2	1	5	4	3	2	1	
Graduation Rate (4 years — 5 years?)	3	2	1	5	4	3	2	1	
Available special services (Learning Center, Writing Center, Tutors)	3	2	1	5	4	3	2	1	
Off-campus study options (Washington Semester, Semester at Sea, Mystic Seaport, Multi-school exchange, study abroad)	3	2	1	5	4	3	2	1	
% of students receiving financial aid	3	2	1	5	4	3	2	1	
Non-need /merit money available	3	2	1	5	4	3	2	1	
Are admissions decisions need blind	3	2	1	5	4	3	2	1	
Athletic programs available	3	2	1	5	4	3	2	1	
Good athletic facilities	3	2	1	5	4	3	2	1	
Theater Productions-Only for theater majors?	3	2	1	5	4	3	2	1	
Music Groups-open to everyone?	3	2	1	5	4	3	2	1	
Communications (TV and radio only for communications majors?)	3	2	1	5	4	3	2	1	
Diverse campus population	3	2	1	5	4	3	2	1	
Quality of social life	3	2	1	5	4	3	2	1	
Availability of religious activities	3	2	1	5	4	3	2	1	

What financial aid forms are required? _____

What is the deadline to apply for financial aid? _____

Appendix 5

Timeline of Key College Planning Activities

This appendix presents a comprehensive list of key college planning activities including financial responsibilities. It will help your clients focus on the necessary items they must accomplish and the appropriate time period in which to fulfill them.

Sophomore Year

It is not too early to think about college. Since colleges look at the curriculum a student has chosen and how well that student has performed, it is important that the student take the highest level courses available. Some schools call those courses advance placement while others call them honors classes. This selection is what determines the Weighted Grade Point Average (GPA) and, ultimately, the Class Rank.

The Preparatory Scholastic Aptitude Test (PSAT) is administered to many students in their sophomore year. It is important to take this test to get some practice as well as to know what score can be achieved. This test is also the first qualifier for the National Merit Scholarship Competition.

Junior Year

This is the most critical year as it is the most recent period that colleges will see when they receive an application. Students should plan this year wisely for their curriculum, activities and college selection.

September

Students can register for the PSAT if they did not take it during their sophomore year. Applications for the test are obtained from the high school guidance office.

The previous year's income tax returns will be the basis for the Trial Financial Aid Test. This will determine if your client is eligible for financial aid and if any changes must be made.

September of the student's junior year is also a good time to compile a list of colleges to research for possible inclusion in the application process. It is a good idea to begin with a list of about 100 schools based upon the student's academic level and demographic interests. Students can use the Internet or libraries to assist them in the college search. College fairs are another good source of information about colleges.

October to December

Take the PSAT test.

Students and parents should begin visiting campuses in their area. Suggest that they pick five different schools based upon the following criteria:

◊ The small, private college in the suburban or rural area;

◊ A medium size, private school with a fairly large campus;

◊ A large, private college with more than 7,000 students who do not go home on the weekends;

◊ An urban campus that represents what a cosmopolitan campus has to offer;

◊ The large state college with more than 10,000 students that has a large, sprawling campus.

By visiting the campuses at this time, students will see school in session and will begin to develop their requirements for what they may want out of the college experience. Likewise, students will get a first-hand look at a student's typical college day. College life is like a living room except that you cannot move the furniture around to make it more comfortable.

January

Make sure your clients are aware that their income from the current year is the information that applies for the financial aid forms so they can plan accordingly.

February

Have the student register and prepare for the SAT/ACT tests.

March

Students are encouraged to take the SAT/ACT tests. The March SAT is the only time the SAT I test is administered. Since the weather is more predictable and most seniors have completed this process, the test date is usually the most appropriate for juniors. This date will also give students time to take additional tests to raise the composite score, if necessary.

April to June

Students should visit schools that are on the top of their list. Have the students call in advance to make arrangements for a tour and an appointment with the admissions and financial aid offices. It is a good idea for students to pick up a copy of the student newspaper because it will give them a true idea of campus life.

July to August

Students can obtain information about their top college choices including applications and financial aid forms. They must be clear about what is expected and the deadlines for each phase of the process.

Senior Year

September

This is a good time to take the SAT I to improve on the score or to take the SAT II test which is required for some college programs. The SAT II test is subject to specific tests itself and is becoming the norm for the better academic schools.

Continue to visit schools and narrow down the list to ten or twelve colleges with three or four "Reach Schools", three or four "Attainable Schools" and two or three "Safe Schools" (academically).

Students will need two or three letters or recommendation from teachers or other adults. They are encouraged ask these individuals to have the letters ready by October 15 which is when the letters can be given to the guidance office. The individuals chosen to provider referrals are those who can attest to the academic and social values of the student. The more prestigious the person recommending the student, the better the outcome.

October

Students should consider overnight visits to their top college choices. This will help finalize their understanding of college life. It is also the time when students may apply for early decision or early action. It is suggested that they complete their applications and submit them before the deadline. Some colleges will waive the application fee if the student brings the application during a visit or an interview.

Some schools require the CSS/Financial Aid Profile Form administered by The College Scholarship Service. This form can be obtained from the high school guidance office. The student needs to check with the college to which he is applying to determine if this form is required.

November

November is application month and the students must not procrastinate. While the acceptance letters are usually not sent until March, a student may be accepted in December and put on the list before the letters are mailed. The financial aid package cannot be put together until the student has been accepted. This is why making sure the application is received as early as possible is crucial.

December

Students can pick up the Free Application for Federal Student Aid (FAFSA) forms from their high school guidance office.

January

Parents are encouraged to complete the FAFSA form as soon after January 1 as possible. Parents will also need to complete their income tax returns as soon as possible because the school will need a copy before the financial aid package can be finalized.

April

The anxious waiting game begins. Acceptance letters from the colleges are sent. Review all offers and do not be afraid to negotiate with a school if their offer doesn't match other schools' offers.

The student should decide which school he will attend and return the signed award letter. Letters should be sent to the other schools notifying them the student will not be attending their school so those spots can be filled by others.

May

File your student and parent loan papers with the financial aid office. Some schools will process the applications electronically but you must call them for details.

June

Forward the student's final grades to the college of his choice.

August

Attend student orientation and meet your future classmates. Most colleges arrange activities during orientation to help you become familiar with the campus.

Appendix 6
College Inflation and Future College Costs

Inflation Analysis

The inflation analysis section allows us to compare college cost inflation and the Consumer Price Index (CPI) data to establish a reasonable forecast of future college costs. It also summarizes 5, 10, 15, 20, 25 and 30-year averages to help us analyze the data.

College Cost Forecast

This section provides a 25-year forecast of college costs for five college cost categories. Base college costs are for 1997 benchmark colleges as shown in the table. These benchmark schools are representative of schools in each cost category.

The college costs that are forecasted are the sum of a tuition component and an "other" cost component. Each is forecasted separately using a different inflation rate:

- Tuition uses college inflation data.

- Other uses the CPI as a basis.

The forecast uses the following inflation data:

♦ years 1-5 average the last 5 years;

♦ years 6-10average the last 10 years; and

♦ years 11-25 average the last 25 years.

Figure 6.1

Benchmark Colleges	Cost Category	Tuition	Other	"Pizza Money"	Total
Duke University	High	$22,500	$9,500	$2,000	$34,000
St. Joseph's University	High-Med	$16,000	$9,000	$2,000	$27,000
Marist University	Medium	$12,000	$7,000	$2,000	$21,000
Rutgers University (out-of-state)	Medium-Low	$8,000	$6,000	$2,000	$16,000
Rutgers University (in-state)	Low	$6,000	$6,000	$2,000	$14,000

Chart 1

College Inflation vs. CPI

Number of Years = 30
Last Year = 1996

Year	College Inflation	CPI	Difference
Average	7.76%	5.44%	2.32%
1996	5.05%	2.95%	2.10%
1995	5.32%	3.04%	2.28%
1994	5.44%	2.56%	2.88%
1993	5.99%	2.78%	3.21%
1992	5.97%	3.16%	2.81%
1991	7.61%	4.68%	2.93%
1990	7.83%	4.81%	3.02%
1989	8.61%	4.99%	3.62%
1988	7.89%	4.16%	3.73%
1987	7.39%	3.90%	3.49%
1986	8.02%	1.61%	6.41%
1985	8.15%	3.55%	4.60%
1984	8.03%	4.14%	3.89%
1983	9.78%	2.44%	7.34%
1982	14.35%	6.48%	7.87%
1981	13.95%	10.73%	3.22%
1980	12.00%	13.22%	-1.22%
1979	9.05%	11.27%	-2.22%
1978	7.37%	7.74%	-0.37%
1977	8.10%	6.72%	1.38%
1976	9.27%	5.43%	3.84%
1975	7.20%	9.65%	-2.45%
1974	5.93%	11.53%	-5.60%
1973	3.60%	5.73%	-2.13%
1972	6.07%	3.04%	3.03%
1971	8.60%	4.37%	4.23%
1970	8.32%	5.90%	2.42%
1969	9.24%	5.45%	3.79%
1968	5.03%	4.29%	0.74%
1967	3.62%	2.87%	0.75%
0	0.00%	0.00%	0.00%
0	0.00%	0.00%	0.00%
0	0.00%	0.00%	0.00%
0	0.00%	0.00%	0.00%
0	0.00%	0.00%	0.00%

Average	College Inflation	CPI	Difference
Last 5 Years	5.55%	2.90%	2.66%
Last 10 Years	6.71%	3.70%	3.01%
Last 15 Years	7.70%	3.68%	4.01%
Last 20 Years	8.30%	5.25%	3.05%
Last 25 Years	7.92%	5.61%	2.31%
Last 30 Years	7.76%	5.44%	2.32%

College Inflation and Future College Costs

Chart 2

College Cost Projections					

Base Year 1997

	— Base Year Data —				
College Type	1	2	3	4	5
College Description	Low	Low/Med	Medium	Med/High	High
Base Year Tuition	$4,000	$8,000	$12,000	$16,000	$22,500
Base Year Other Costs	$8,000	$8,000	$9,000	$11,000	$11,500

			— College Cost Projections —				
			1	2	3	4	5
			Low	Low/Med	Medium	Med/High	High
Year	Inflation Rate Tuition	Inflation Rate Other	Total Costs	Total Costs	Total Costs	Total Costs	Total Costs
1997 Base Year Data			$12,000	$16,000	$21,000	$27,000	$34,000
1998	5.55%	2.90%	$12,666	$16,889	$22,166	$28,500	$35,888
1999	5.55%	2.90%	$13,370	$17,827	$23,397	$30,082	$37,882
2000	5.55%	2.90%	$14,113	$18,817	$24,697	$31,753	$39,986
2001	5.55%	2.90%	$14,896	$19,862	$26,069	$33,517	$42,206
2002	5.55%	2.90%	$15,724	$20,965	$27,516	$35,378	$44,550
2003	6.71%	3.70%	$16,779	$22,372	$29,363	$37,752	$47,540
2004	6.71%	3.70%	$17,905	$23,873	$31,333	$40,285	$50,730
2005	6.71%	3.70%	$19,106	$25,475	$33,436	$42,989	$54,134
2006	6.71%	3.70%	$20,388	$27,184	$35,679	$45,873	$57,766
2007	6.71%	3.70%	$21,756	$29,008	$38,073	$48,951	$61,642
2008	7.92%	5.61%	$23,479	$31,305	$41,088	$52,827	$66,524
2009	7.92%	5.61%	$25,338	$33,784	$44,342	$57,011	$71,791
2010	7.92%	5.61%	$27,345	$36,459	$47,853	$61,525	$77,476
2011	7.92%	5.61%	$29,510	$39,347	$51,642	$66,397	$83,612
2012	7.92%	5.61%	$31,847	$42,462	$55,732	$71,655	$90,233
2013	7.92%	5.61%	$34,369	$45,825	$60,145	$77,330	$97,378
2014	7.92%	5.61%	$37,090	$49,454	$64,908	$83,453	$105,089
2015	7.92%	5.61%	$40,027	$53,370	$70,048	$90,062	$113,411
2016	7.92%	5.61%	$43,197	$57,596	$75,595	$97,193	$122,392
2017	7.92%	5.61%	$46,618	$62,157	$81,581	$104,890	$132,084
2018	7.92%	5.61%	$50,309	$67,079	$88,041	$113,196	$142,543
2019	7.92%	5.61%	$54,293	$72,391	$95,013	$122,160	$153,831
2020	7.92%	5.61%	$58,593	$78,123	$102,537	$131,833	$166,012
2021	7.92%	5.61%	$63,232	$84,310	$110,657	$142,273	$179,159
2022	7.92%	5.61%	$68,240	$90,986	$119,419	$153,539	$193,346

College Inflation and Future College Costs

Appendix 7

Projected College Costs and Savings Requirements

This appendix provides a forecast of college costs for five college cost categories and calculates the approximate monthly savings required to accumulate the necessary funds at three different net after-tax investment rates: 6%, 8% and 10%.

For information about how college costs are projected, please see Appendix 6.

State College (in-state resident)

Benchmark: Rutgers

Chart 1

Projected College Costs and Savings Requirements

ASSUMPTIONS:
PLANNED SAVINGS STARTS SEPTEMBER   1997
PLANNED WITHDRAWALS START SEPTEMBER   FRESHMAN YEAR
SCHOOL CATEGORY (1=LOW, 2=Med/Low, 3=MEDIUM, 4=Med/High, 5=HIGH)   1
PROJECTED AFTER-TAX GROWTH ON SAVINGS   6.00%   8.00%   10.00%

Notes:
Assume Funding Through August of the Last Year of College
College Costs are total costs based on college budget bill plus misc. costs reported by parents.
Cost Categories - 1 Low for State schools (in-state resident), 5 High for Ivy League, 2-4 Medium range for Private

PROJECTED FRESHMEN YEAR	PROJECTED FRESHMAN COST	PROJECTED SOPHOMORE COST	PROJECTED JUNIOR COST	PROJECTED SENIOR COST	PROJECTED FOUR YEAR COST	APPROX. MO. SAVINGS REQ 6.00%	APPROX. MO. SAVINGS REQ 8.00%	APPROX. MO. SAVINGS REQ 10.00%
1997						n/a	n/a	n/a
1998	$12,666	$13,370	$14,113	$14,896	$55,045	$886	$876	$866
1999	$13,370	$14,113	$14,896	$15,724	$58,103	$756	$740	$723
2000	$14,113	$14,896	$15,724	$16,779	$61,511	$665	$644	$623
2001	$14,896	$15,724	$16,779	$17,905	$65,303	$599	$573	$548
2002	$15,724	$16,779	$17,905	$19,106	$69,513	$549	$519	$491
2003	$16,779	$17,905	$19,106	$20,388	$74,177	$510	$478	$447
2004	$17,905	$19,106	$20,388	$21,756	$79,155	$480	$444	$410
2005	$19,106	$20,388	$21,756	$23,479	$84,729	$455	$416	$380
2006	$20,388	$21,756	$23,479	$25,338	$90,961	$437	$394	$356
2007	$21,756	$23,479	$25,338	$27,345	$97,918	$422	$377	$335
2008	$23,479	$25,338	$27,345	$29,510	$105,672	$411	$363	$319
2009	$25,338	$27,345	$29,510	$31,847	$114,040	$403	$350	$304
2010	$27,345	$29,510	$31,847	$34,369	$123,070	$395	$340	$291
2011	$29,510	$31,847	$34,369	$37,090	$132,816	$389	$331	$279
2012	$31,847	$34,369	$37,090	$40,027	$143,333	$385	$322	$268
2013	$34,369	$37,090	$40,027	$43,197	$154,683	$381	$315	$259
2014	$37,090	$40,027	$43,197	$46,618	$166,932	$378	$309	$250
2015	$40,027	$43,197	$46,618	$50,309	$180,152	$376	$303	$242
2016	$43,197	$46,618	$50,309	$54,293	$194,417	$375	$298	$234
2017	$46,618	$50,309	$54,293	$58,593	$209,813	$374	$293	$227
2018	$50,309	$54,293	$58,593	$63,232	$226,428	$374	$289	$221

State College (out-of-state resident)

Benchmark: Rutgers (out-of-state)

Chart 2

Projected College Costs and Savings Requirements								

ASSUMPTIONS:
PLANNED SAVINGS STARTS SEPTEMBER   1997
PLANNED WITHDRAWALS START SEPTEMBER   FRESHMAN YEAR
SCHOOL CATEGORY (1=LOW, 2=Med/Low, 3=MEDIUM, 4=Med/High, 5=HIGH) 2
PROJECTED AFTER-TAX GROWTH ON SAVINGS   6.00%   8.00%   10.00%

Notes:
Assume Funding Through August of the Last Year of College
College Costs are total costs based on college budget bill plus misc. costs reported by parents.
Cost Categories - 1 Low for State schools (in-state resident), 5 High for Ivy League, 2-4 Medium range for Private

PROJECTED FRESHMEN YEAR	PROJECTED FRESHMAN COST	PROJECTED SOPHOMORE COST	PROJECTED JUNIOR COST	PROJECTED SENIOR COST	PROJECTED FOUR YEAR COST	APPROX. MO. SAVINGS REQ 6.00%	APPROX. MO. SAVINGS REQ 8.00%	APPROX. MO. SAVINGS REQ 10.00%
1997						n/a	n/a	n/a
1998	$16,889	$17,827	$18,817	$19,862	$73,394	$1,182	$1,168	$1,155
1999	$17,827	$18,817	$19,862	$20,965	$77,470	$1,008	$986	$965
2000	$18,817	$19,862	$20,965	$22,372	$82,015	$887	$858	$830
2001	$19,862	$20,965	$22,372	$23,873	$87,071	$798	$764	$731
2002	$20,965	$22,372	$23,873	$25,475	$92,684	$732	$692	$655
2003	$22,372	$23,873	$25,475	$27,184	$98,903	$681	$637	$595
2004	$23,873	$25,475	$27,184	$29,008	$105,540	$639	$592	$546
2005	$25,475	$27,184	$29,008	$31,305	$112,972	$607	$555	$507
2006	$27,184	$29,008	$31,305	$33,784	$121,281	$582	$526	$474
2007	$29,008	$31,305	$33,784	$36,459	$130,557	$563	$502	$447
2008	$31,305	$33,784	$36,459	$39,347	$140,895	$549	$484	$425
2009	$33,784	$36,459	$39,347	$42,462	$152,053	$537	$467	$405
2010	$36,459	$39,347	$42,462	$45,825	$164,093	$527	$453	$388
2011	$39,347	$42,462	$45,825	$49,454	$177,088	$519	$441	$372
2012	$42,462	$45,825	$49,454	$53,370	$191,111	$513	$430	$358
2013	$45,825	$49,454	$53,370	$57,596	$206,245	$508	$420	$345
2014	$49,454	$53,370	$57,596	$62,157	$222,577	$504	$411	$333
2015	$53,370	$57,596	$62,157	$67,079	$240,202	$502	$404	$322
2016	$57,596	$62,157	$67,079	$72,391	$259,223	$500	$397	$312
2017	$62,157	$67,079	$72,391	$78,123	$279,751	$499	$390	$303
2018	$67,079	$72,391	$78,123	$84,310	$301,903	$499	$385	$294

Medium Priced Private College

Benchmark: Marist

Chart 3

Projected College Costs and Savings Requirements

ASSUMPTIONS:
PLANNED SAVINGS STARTS SEPTEMBER · 1997
PLANNED WITHDRAWALS START SEPTEMBER · FRESHMAN YEAR
SCHOOL CATEGORY (1=LOW, 2=Med/Low, 3=MEDIUM, 4=Med/High, 5=HIGH) · 3
PROJECTED AFTER-TAX GROWTH ON SAVINGS · 6.00% · 8.00% · 10.00%

Notes:
Assume Funding Through August of the Last Year of College
College Costs are total costs based on college budget bill plus misc. costs reported by parents.
Cost Categories - 1 Low for State schools (in-state resident), 5 High for Ivy League, 2-4 Medium range for Private

PROJECTED FRESHMEN YEAR	PROJECTED FRESHMAN COST	PROJECTED SOPHOMORE COST	PROJECTED JUNIOR COST	PROJECTED SENIOR COST	PROJECTED FOUR YEAR COST	APPROX. MO. SAVINGS REQ 6.00%	APPROX. MO. SAVINGS REQ 8.00%	APPROX. MO. SAVINGS REQ 10.00%
1997						n/a	n/a	n/a
1998	$22,166	$23,397	$24,697	$26,069	$96,329	$1,551	$1,533	$1,516
1999	$23,397	$24,697	$26,069	$27,516	$101,680	$1,323	$1,294	$1,266
2000	$24,697	$26,069	$27,516	$29,363	$107,645	$1,164	$1,126	$1,090
2001	$26,069	$27,516	$29,363	$31,333	$114,281	$1,048	$1,003	$959
2002	$27,516	$29,363	$31,333	$33,436	$121,648	$960	$909	$859
2003	$29,363	$31,333	$33,436	$35,679	$129,810	$893	$836	$781
2004	$31,333	$33,436	$35,679	$38,073	$138,521	$839	$776	$717
2005	$33,436	$35,679	$38,073	$41,088	$148,276	$797	$729	$665
2006	$35,679	$38,073	$41,088	$44,342	$159,182	$764	$690	$622
2007	$38,073	$41,088	$44,342	$47,853	$171,356	$739	$659	$587
2008	$41,088	$44,342	$47,853	$51,642	$184,925	$720	$635	$558
2009	$44,342	$47,853	$51,642	$55,732	$199,569	$705	$613	$532
2010	$47,853	$51,642	$55,732	$60,145	$215,373	$692	$595	$509
2011	$51,642	$55,732	$60,145	$64,908	$232,428	$682	$578	$488
2012	$55,732	$60,145	$64,908	$70,048	$250,833	$673	$564	$470
2013	$60,145	$64,908	$70,048	$75,595	$270,696	$667	$551	$453
2014	$64,908	$70,048	$75,595	$81,581	$292,132	$662	$540	$437
2015	$70,048	$75,595	$81,581	$88,041	$315,265	$658	$530	$423
2016	$75,595	$81,581	$88,041	$95,013	$340,230	$656	$521	$410
2017	$81,581	$88,041	$95,013	$102,537	$367,173	$655	$513	$398
2018	$88,041	$95,013	$102,537	$110,657	$396,248	$655	$505	$386

Higher Priced Private College

Benchmark: St. Josephs, Phila.

Chart 4

Projected College Costs and Savings Requirements								

ASSUMPTIONS:
  PLANNED SAVINGS STARTS SEPTEMBER   1997
  PLANNED WITHDRAWALS START SEPTEMBER   FRESHMAN YEAR
  SCHOOL CATEGORY (1=LOW, 2=Med/Low, 3=MEDIUM, 4=Med/High, 5=HIGH)   4
  PROJECTED AFTER-TAX GROWTH ON SAVINGS   6.00%   8.00%   10.00%

Notes:
  Assume Funding Through August of the Last Year of College
  College Costs are total costs based on college budget bill plus misc. costs reported by parents.
  Cost Categories - 1 Low for State schools (in-state resident), 5 High for Ivy League, 2-4 Medium range for Private

PROJECTED FRESHMEN YEAR	PROJECTED FRESHMAN COST	PROJECTED SOPHOMORE COST	PROJECTED JUNIOR COST	PROJECTED SENIOR COST	PROJECTED FOUR YEAR COST	APPROX. MO. SAVINGS REQ 6.00%	APPROX. MO. SAVINGS REQ 8.00%	APPROX. MO. SAVINGS REQ 10.00%
1997						n/a	n/a	n/a
1998	$28,500	$30,082	$31,753	$33,517	$123,852	$1,995	$1,972	$1,949
1999	$30,082	$31,753	$33,517	$35,378	$130,731	$1,701	$1,664	$1,628
2000	$31,753	$33,517	$35,378	$37,752	$138,401	$1,496	$1,448	$1,401
2001	$33,517	$35,378	$37,752	$40,285	$146,933	$1,347	$1,289	$1,233
2002	$35,378	$37,752	$40,285	$42,989	$156,404	$1,235	$1,168	$1,105
2003	$37,752	$40,285	$42,989	$45,873	$166,899	$1,149	$1,075	$1,005
2004	$40,285	$42,989	$45,873	$48,951	$178,098	$1,079	$998	$922
2005	$42,989	$45,873	$48,951	$52,827	$190,640	$1,025	$937	$855
2006	$45,873	$48,951	$52,827	$57,011	$204,662	$983	$888	$800
2007	$48,951	$52,827	$57,011	$61,525	$220,315	$950	$848	$755
2008	$52,827	$57,011	$61,525	$66,397	$237,761	$926	$816	$717
2009	$57,011	$61,525	$66,397	$71,655	$256,589	$906	$789	$684
2010	$61,525	$66,397	$71,655	$77,330	$276,908	$890	$765	$654
2011	$66,397	$71,655	$77,330	$83,453	$298,835	$876	$744	$628
2012	$71,655	$77,330	$83,453	$90,062	$322,500	$866	$725	$604
2013	$77,330	$83,453	$90,062	$97,193	$348,038	$858	$709	$582
2014	$83,453	$90,062	$97,193	$104,890	$375,598	$851	$694	$562
2015	$90,062	$97,193	$104,890	$113,196	$405,341	$847	$681	$544
2016	$97,193	$104,890	$113,196	$122,160	$437,439	$844	$669	$527
2017	$104,890	$113,196	$122,160	$131,833	$472,079	$842	$659	$511
2018	$113,196	$122,160	$131,833	$142,273	$509,462	$842	$649	$496

Highest Priced Private College including Ivy League Schools

Benchmark: Duke

Chart 5

Projected College Costs and Savings Requirements

ASSUMPTIONS:
PLANNED SAVINGS STARTS SEPTEMBER   1997
PLANNED WITHDRAWALS START SEPTEMBER   FRESHMAN YEAR
SCHOOL CATEGORY (1=LOW, 2=Med/Low, 3=MEDIUM, 4=Med/High, 5=HIGH)   5
PROJECTED AFTER-TAX GROWTH ON SAVINGS   6.00%   8.00%   10.00%

Notes:
Assume Funding Through August of the Last Year of College
College Costs are total costs based on college budget bill plus misc. costs reported by parents.
Cost Categories - 1 Low for State schools (in-state resident), 5 High for Ivy League, 2-4 Medium range for Private

PROJECTED FRESHMEN YEAR	PROJECTED FRESHMAN COST	PROJECTED SOPHOMORE COST	PROJECTED JUNIOR COST	PROJECTED SENIOR COST	PROJECTED FOUR YEAR COST	APPROX. MO. SAVINGS REQ 6.00%	APPROX. MO. SAVINGS REQ 8.00%	APPROX. MO. SAVINGS REQ 10.00%
1997						n/a	n/a	n/a
1998	$35,888	$37,882	$39,986	$42,206	$155,962	$2,512	$2,483	$2,454
1999	$37,882	$39,986	$42,206	$44,550	$164,624	$2,142	$2,096	$2,050
2000	$39,986	$42,206	$44,550	$47,540	$174,282	$1,884	$1,824	$1,764
2001	$42,206	$44,550	$47,540	$50,730	$185,026	$1,696	$1,623	$1,553
2002	$44,550	$47,540	$50,730	$54,134	$196,954	$1,555	$1,471	$1,392
2003	$47,540	$50,730	$54,134	$57,766	$210,169	$1,446	$1,353	$1,265
2004	$50,730	$54,134	$57,766	$61,642	$224,272	$1,359	$1,257	$1,161
2005	$54,134	$57,766	$61,642	$66,524	$240,065	$1,290	$1,180	$1,077
2006	$57,766	$61,642	$66,524	$71,791	$257,723	$1,237	$1,118	$1,007
2007	$61,642	$66,524	$71,791	$77,476	$277,433	$1,197	$1,068	$950
2008	$66,524	$71,791	$77,476	$83,612	$299,403	$1,166	$1,028	$903
2009	$71,791	$77,476	$83,612	$90,233	$323,112	$1,141	$993	$861
2010	$77,476	$83,612	$90,233	$97,378	$348,699	$1,120	$963	$824
2011	$83,612	$90,233	$97,378	$105,089	$376,311	$1,104	$936	$791
2012	$90,233	$97,378	$105,089	$113,411	$406,111	$1,090	$913	$761
2013	$97,378	$105,089	$113,411	$122,392	$438,270	$1,080	$893	$733
2014	$105,089	$113,411	$122,392	$132,084	$472,975	$1,072	$874	$708
2015	$113,411	$122,392	$132,084	$142,543	$510,429	$1,066	$858	$685
2016	$122,392	$132,084	$142,543	$153,831	$550,849	$1,062	$843	$664
2017	$132,084	$142,543	$153,831	$166,012	$594,470	$1,060	$830	$644
2018	$142,543	$153,831	$166,012	$179,159	$641,545	$1,060	$818	$625

Glossary

A.A. - Refers to an Associate of Arts degree that can be earned at most two-year colleges.

A.A.S. - Refers to an Associate of Applied Science that can be earned at some two-year colleges.

Academic Year - The time period when school is in session. Normally this is September through May.

Accrual Date - The date that interest will begin to accrue on an educational loan.

ACT - This is a test published by American College Testing. It measures a student's aptitude in English, mathematics, reading and science reasoning. Many colleges in the South and Midwest require that students take this test and submit their test scores when they apply for admission. Some colleges accept this test or the SAT I. (See below for the explanation of SAT I.) Most students take the ACT or the SAT during their junior or senior year of high school.

Adjusted Available Income - In the Federal Methodology, the remaining income after taxes and the allowance for basic living expenses have been subtracted.

Asset Protection Allowance (calculated by the Federal Methodology) - The portion of the parents' assets that are not included in the calculation of the parents' contribution.

Assets (considered when determining the Expected Family Contribution) - Cash in checking and savings accounts, trusts, stocks, bonds, other securities, real estate (not including the primary residence), income-producing property, business equipment and business inventory. (Note: The Institutional Methodology does include the primary residence.)

Assistantship - A type of student employment; it usually refers to a student teaching or research position.

Associate Degree - A two-year college degree.

Award Letter - Official letter from the college financial aid office that lists all of the financial aid awarded to the student.

B.A. or B.S. - B.A. stands for Bachelor of Arts and B.S. stands for Bachelor of Science. Both degrees can be earned at four-year colleges. Some colleges only grant B.A.s and others only grant B.S.s—it depends on the kinds of courses offered at the particular college.

Bachelor's Degree - A four-year college degree.

Budget Bill - The estimated cost for attending a college or a university that includes: tuition, fees, books, supplies, room, board, personal expenses and transportation.

Bursar's Office - The university office responsible for the billing and collection of university charges.

Campus-Based Programs - U.S. Department of Education Student Aid programs administered by colleges and universities. It includes the Federal Perkins Loan and the Federal Supplemental Educational Opportunity Grant.

Central Processing System - The administrative computer system to which the student's need analysis data is electronically transmitted. The Central Processing System performs database matches and calculates the official Expected Family Contribution (EFC) and sends out the Student Aid Report (SAR).

Collateral - Property used to secure a loan but which can be seized if the borrower defaults on that loan.

Commercial Lender - A commercial bank, savings and loan association, credit union, stock savings bank, trust company or mutual savings bank.

Commuter Student - A student who lives at home while attending college.

Consolidation Loan - A loan that allows borrowers to lower their monthly payments by replacing their original loans with one loan. Consolidation loans typically have longer repayment periods and, as such, interest payments will be greater.

Cooperative Education (Co-op) - Many college programs offer paid opportunities to gain professional, full-time work experience while enrolled in college. These programs are often designed to provide substantial dollars to pay college expense.

Cosigner - The individual who assumes responsibility for a loan if the borrower defaults on the repayment.

Cost of Attendance - See ***Budget Bill.***

Custodial Parent - In cases where a student's parents are divorced or separated, the custodial parent is the parent with whom the student lives the most during the previous twelve months.

Default - Failure to repay or otherwise meet the terms and conditions of a loan. For student and parent loans, default typically occurs after six months of delinquent payments. Penalties include a bad credit rating, loss of future financial aid eligibility, withheld tax refunds, garnished wages and the loss of monthly payment options.

Default Rate - The default rate is the percentage of students who took out federal student loans to help pay their expenses but did not repay the loan properly.

Deferment - The period during which the repayment of the loan is suspended because the borrower meets certain eligibility requirements such as being enrolled in college at least half of the time.

Delinquency - Failure to make a scheduled loan payment.

Dependency Status - A student's dependency status determines the degree to which the student has access to parental financial resources. For federal financial aid, an independent student is at least 24-years old as of January 1, is married, is a graduate or professional student, has a legal dependent other than a spouse, is a U.S. Armed Forces veteran or is an orphan or ward of the court.

Direct Loans - A new federal program whereby the school becomes the lending agency and directly manages the loan funds with the federal government providing the loan funds. Most large colleges and universities are direct lenders, but not all schools currently participate in the program.

Disbursement - The process by which financial aid funds are made available to students for use in meeting educational and related living expenses. Funds may be disbursed directly to the student or applied to the student's account.

Early Action - Allows students to apply early to a college and receive earlier notification of acceptance.

Early Admission - An early admission program allows exemplary high school juniors to skip their senior year and enroll directly in college.

Early Decision - An early decision program has earlier deadlines and earlier notification dates than the regular admissions process. Students who apply to an early decision program commit to attending the school if admitted which means the students must accept the offer of admission before they see their financial aid package.

Education IRA or Education Savings Accounts - These were created under the Taxpayer Relief Act of 1997. Basically, they allow a family to contribute up to $500 per beneficiary under the age of eighteen. Dollars saved in an Education IRA are not tax deductible but accumulate tax free. Withdrawals from Education IRAs will not be subject to income tax even on investment gains. Eligibility for Education IRAs are subject to certain income limitations and all funds in an Educational IRA must be used before the student reaches age 30.

Enrollment Status - Indicates full or part-time student status. Typically, students must be enrolled at least half of the time, and in some cases full time, to qualify for financial aid.

Expected Family Contribution (EFC) - The dollar amount that a family is expected to pay toward a student's educational costs. The EFC is based upon family earnings, assets, the number of students attending college and family size.

Federal Direct Student Loan Program (FDSLP) - This is a loan provided by the U.S. government directly to the students and their parents through their schools. This loan is available when the school is the direct lender.

Federal Methodology - The need analysis formula used to determine a family's Expected Family Contribution. The Federal Methodology considers family size, the number of family members attending college, taxable and nontaxable income and assets.

Federal Processor - The Federal Processor is the organization that processes the information submitted on the Free Application for Federal Student Aid (FAFSA) form that is used to compute eligibility for federal student aid.

Federal Stafford Loan - A federally guaranteed, low-interest loan for students. There are two types of Federal Stafford Loans: subsidized (need-based) and unsubsidized (non need-based). Both types allow deferment of the repayment until a student leaves school.

Federal Supplemental Educational Opportunity Grants (FSEOG) - These are federal grants for students with exceptional financial need (as determined by the college). Approximately 5% of undergraduates are recipients of FSEOG.

Federal Work Study - Federally sponsored Work-Study (FWS) Program provides undergraduate and graduate students with part-time employment during the school year. The federal government pays some of the student's salary which helps departments and businesses pay for and, ultimately, hire students. Eligibility is based upon financial need.

Fees - These are charges that cover costs not associated with the student's course load such as the price of some athletic activities, clubs and special events.

Financial Aid Administrator - A university employee responsible for preparing and communicating information about student loans, grants, scholarships and employment programs, and for advising, awarding, reporting, counseling and supervising student financial aid office functions.

Financial Aid Package - The total amount of financial aid a student receives including grants, loans and federal work-study programs. Unsubsidized Federal

Stafford Loans and Parent Loans for Undergraduate Students (PLUS) loans are not considered part of the package.

Financial Need - The difference between the student's educational costs and the Expected Family Contribution.

Fixed Interest Loans - A loan in which the interest rate stays the same for the life of the loan.

Forbearance - The approved temporary suspension of loan payments due to a financial hardship; however, interest continues to accrue.

Free Application for Federal Student Aid (FAFSA) - The application students must first complete to apply for virtually all forms of financial aid. The application is available at high schools and colleges or by calling 1-800-4-FEDAID, and on the Internet by following the links at http://www.fafsa.ed.gov.

General Education Development (GED) Diploma - The certificate students receive if they have passed a high school equivalency test. Students who do not have a high school diploma but who have a GED will still qualify for federal student aid.

Gift Aid - Grants and scholarships that do not need to be repaid.

Grace Period - The period after a student either graduates or leaves school and before loan payments must begin, typically six to nine months.

Grant - Financial aid that does not have to be repaid and which is typically based on financial need.

Guarantee Fee - A percentage of the loan that is paid to the guarantor to insure the loan against default. The fee is usually 1% of the loan amount.

Guarantor - A state agency or private, nonprofit organization that administers a student loan insurance program.

Home Equity - The current market value of the home minus the mortgage's unpaid principal. (Based upon market value).

Hope Scholarship - Created under the Taxpayer Relief Act of 1997, Hope Scholarship credits allow a $1,000 tuition credit for qualified tuition expenses on the first $1,000 of educational expenses during the first two years of a post-secondary school degree program. There is also a credit of 50% of the next $1,000 of expenses. Hope Scholarship credits can only be used by families with incomes below certain limits. It cannot be used in conjunction with withdrawals from Educational IRAs or prepaid tuition programs.

Income Contingent Repayment - The size of the monthly payments depends upon the income earned by the borrower. As the borrower's income increases, so do the payments.

Institutional Methodology - A formula some schools use to determine financial need for allocating their own institutional financial aid funds.

Internships - Part-time and full-time opportunities in order to gain professional work experience while attending college. Some interns are paid while others gain college credits.

"Kiddie Tax" - An increased tax rate imposed on investment earnings for children under age 14. The first $600 of investment earnings are not taxed. The second $600 of investment earnings are taxed at the child's tax rate, normally 15%. Interest earnings above $1,200 are taxed at the parents' highest tax rate. The "Kiddie Tax" is a disincentive to use a child's Social Security number on savings accounts or to use Custodial Accounts or Uniform Gift to Minors Act Accounts.

"Kiddie Tax Credit" - Sometimes called the Child Tax Credit, it is for families who have children under age 19. Subject to certain income limits, families qualifying for the tax credit will receive a credit of $500 per year after 1998 and $400 per year for 1998 for each dependant child under age 17. This is a great source of funds for parents who wish to save money for college.

Lender - A bank, credit union or other financial institution that provides funds to the student or parent for an educational loan.

Lifetime Learning Credit - A tax credit of 20% of the first $5,000 of qualified educational expenses at eligible educational institutions for students who are enrolled at least part-time in a degree or certification program. Credit is subject to certain exclusions and limitations are based on income and the use of other educational savings programs.

Merit-based Financial Aid - Financial aid based upon academic, artistic, athletic or other merit-oriented criteria (not financial need).

Need - The difference between a student's total cost of attendance at a specific institution and the student's total available resources, including financial aid.

Need-based Financial Aid - This kind of financial aid is given to students who are determined to be in financial need of assistance based upon their income and assets and their families' income and assets, as well as other factors.

Needs Analysis - The process used by a college to evaluate an applicant's financial resources and determine how much the student or family can pay toward the cost of the education.

Need-Blind Admissions - A process by which the school decides whether or not to offer admission to a student without considering the student's financial situation. Most schools use a need-blind admissions process.

Need-Sensitive Admissions - The method by which the school takes the student's financial situation into account for some admissions decisions. Some schools use need-sensitive admissions for borderline students.

Open Admission - This term means that a college admits most or all students who apply to the school. At some colleges it means that anyone who has a high school diploma or a GED can enroll. At other schools it means that anyone over age 18 can enroll. Open admissions, therefore, can mean slightly different things at different schools.

Packaging - A financial aid administrator's attempt at combining various types of student aid (grants, loans, scholarships and employment) in an effort to meet a student's financial need.

Parents' Contribution - A quantitative estimate of the parents' ability to contribute to post-secondary educational expenses.

Pell Grant - A federal grant program for undergraduate students who demonstrate financial need and have not yet completed their baccalaureate degree.

Perkins Loan - A low interest federal loan (5%) for students with exceptional financial need as determined by the college.

PLUS Loans - These federal loans allow parents to borrow money for their children's college education.

PLUS Loans (Parent Loans for Undergraduate Students) - Federal loans available to parents of dependent undergraduate students to help finance their child's education. Parents may borrow up to the difference between the education costs and the financial aid received from a bank or other lending institution.

Post-secondary - This term means "after high school" and refers to all programs for high school graduates including programs at two and four-year colleges, vocational and technical schools.

Prepaid Tuition Plan - A college savings plan guaranteed to rise in value at the same rate as the college tuition. Several states and institutions offer such programs.

Principal - The amount borrowed or owed on a loan.

Professional Judgement - For need-based federal aid programs, financial aid administrators can adjust the Expected Family Contribution (EFC), the cost of attendance (COA), or change the dependency status (with documentation) when extenuating circumstances exist. An example is if a parent becomes unemployed, disabled or dies.

Promissory Note - A legally binding contract a student signs before receiving loan funds that details the terms of the loan and obligates the borrower to repay the loan.

Proprietary - This is a term used to describe post-secondary schools that are private and are legally permitted to make a profit. Most proprietary schools offer technical and vocational courses.

PSAT/NMSQT - This stands for the Preliminary Scholastic Assessment Test/ National Merit Scholarship Qualifying Test, a practice test the helps students prepare for the Scholastic Assessment Test (SAT I). The PSAT is usually administered to tenth or eleventh grade students. Although, colleges do not see a student's PSAT/NMSQT score, a student who does very well on this test and who meets many other academic performance criteria may qualify for the National Merit Scholarship Program.

ROTC - Reserve Officer Training Corps. This is a scholarship program wherein the military covers the cost of tuition, fees and textbooks and also provides a monthly allowance. Scholarship recipients participate in summer training while in college and fulfill a service commitment after college.

Roth IRA - Created under the Taxpayer Relief Act of 1997, it allows families within certain income limits to invest up to $2,000 on a nondeductible basis. Investment earnings on Roth IRAs accumulate tax free and when withdrawn, income earned is not taxed. Roth IRAs can be used for educational expenses and are not subject to early withdrawal penalties when used as such.

SAT I - This stands for the Scholastic Assessment Test which measures a student's mathematical and verbal reasoning abilities. Many colleges in the East and West require that students take the SAT I and submit their test scores when they apply for admission. Some colleges accept this test or the ACT. (See above for an explanation of the ACT.) Most students take the SAT I or the ACT during their junior or senior year of high school.

SAT II Subject Test - SAT II Subject Tests are offered in many areas of study including English, mathematics, many sciences, history and foreign languages. Some colleges require students to take one or more SAT II Tests when they apply for admission.

Satisfactory Academic Progress - A school's policy concerning the minimum number of courses that must be completed each semester, the maximum time frame and the minimum Grade Point Average (GPA) required in order to receive financial aid.

Scholarship - A form of financial assistance that does not require repayment or employment and which is usually offered to students who show potential for distinction, or who possess certain characteristics important to the scholarship provider such as religious beliefs, hobbies, ethnicity, etc.

Secondary Market - An organization that buys loans from lenders which provides the lender with the capital to issue new loans.

Servicer - An organization that is paid by a lender to administer it's student loan portfolio.

Simplified Needs Test - An alternate method of calculating the Expected Family Contribution for families with adjusted gross incomes less than $50,000, who have filed or are eligible to file IRS Form 1040A or IRS Form 1040EZ, or who are not required to file a federal income tax return.

Stafford Loans - These are student loans offered by the federal government. There are two types of Stafford Loans, one need-based and the other non-need-based. Under the Stafford Loan programs, students can borrow money to attend school and the federal government will guarantee the loan in case of default. Under the Stafford Loan programs, the combined loan limits are $2,625 for the first year, $3,500 for the second year and $5,500 for the third or additional years. An undergraduate student cannot borrow more than a total of $23,000.

State Student Incentive Grants (SSIG) - States receive matching funds from the federal government to help fund this program for state residents.

Student Aid Report (SAR) - The official notification sent to students after submitting the FAFSA form. Students may be required to submit this document to the college's financial aid office.

Student Contribution - A quantitative estimate of the student's ability to contribute to post-secondary education expenses, typically 35% of his or her savings and ½ summer earnings above $1,750.

Subsidized Loan - A loan on which student borrowers do not have to pay interest until after their grace period expires.

Supplemental Education Opportunity Grant (SEOG) - A federal grant program for undergraduate students with exceptional need. SEOG grants up to $4,000 are awarded by the school's financial aid office.

Title IV Programs - Federal student aid programs authorized under Title IV of the Higher Education Act of 1965, as amended. This includes Federal Pell Grants, Federal Supplemental Educational Opportunity Grants, Federal Work-Study Programs, Federal Perkins Loans, Federal Stafford Loans, Federal PLUS Loans, Direct Loans, Direct PLUS Loans and State Student Incentive Grants.

Transcript - This is a list of all the courses a student has taken along with the grades the student earned in each course. A college will often require that a student submit his or her high school transcript when applying for admission to the college.

Trial Financial Aid Test - A dry run of the financial aid formulas to help a student and his family determine their eligibility for need-based financial aid for planning purposes in advance.

Unsubsidized Loans - A loan on which student borrowers must pay all of the interest while they are enrolled in school.

Verification – The review process in which the financial aid officer requests documentation from a financial aid applicant to verify the accuracy of the application.

William D. Ford Federal Direct Loans - Under this new program, students may obtain federal loans directly from the college or university with the funds provided by the U.S. Department of Education instead of a bank or other lender.

Work-Study Programs - These programs are offered by many colleges. They allow students to work part-time during the school year as part of their financial aid package. The jobs are usually on campus and the money earned is used to pay for tuition or other college charges.

INDEX

Need Additional Copies?

Use these handy postage-paid forms to order additional copies of *A Professional's Guide to College Planning* by Raymond D. Loewe. Or call **1-800-543-0874** and ask for **Operator BB** or Fax order card to **1-800-874-1916.**

Single copy.................$32.00	50 copies, ea..................$23.90	250 copies, ea...............$21.00
10 copies, ea. 26.95	100 copies, ea..................22.50	500 copies, ea.................19.45
25 copies, ea. 25.50		

PAYMENT INFORMATION

*Add shipping & handling charges to all orders as indicated. If your order exceeds total amount listed in chart, call 1-800-543-0874 for shipping & handling charge. Any order of 10 or more or $250.00 and over will be billed for shipping by actual weight, plus a handling fee. Unconditional 30 day guarantee.

Shipping & Handling (Additional)	
Order Total	S&H
$20.00 - $39.99	$6.00
40.00 - 59.99	7.00
60.00 - 79.99	9.00
80.00 - 109.99	10.00
110.00 - 149.99	12.00
150.00 - 199.99	13.00
200.00 - 249.99	15.50

Sales Tax (Additional)
Sales tax is required for residents of the following states: CA, DC, FL, GA, IL, NJ, NY, OH, PA.

NATIONAL UNDERWRITER®
The Last Word For Over 100 Years

2-BB

The National Underwriter Co. / Customer Service Dept #2-BB
505 Gest Street / Cincinnati, OH 45203-1716

Please send me_____copies of *A Professional's Guide to College Planning* (#126)

❑ Check enclosed*   Charge my: ❑ VISA ❑ MC ❑ AmEx   ❑ Bill me

Card # _____ Exp. date _____

Signature _____

Name _____ Title _____

Company _____

Street Address _____

City _____ State _____ Zip_____

Business Phone (_____) _____ Fax (_____) _____

*Make check payable to The National Underwriter Company. Please include the appropriate shipping & handling charges and any applicable sales tax. Offer expires 12/31/98.

NATIONAL UNDERWRITER®
The Last Word For Over 100 Years

2-BB

The National Underwriter Co. / Customer Service Dept #2-BB
505 Gest Street / Cincinnati, OH 45203-1716

Please send me_____copies of *A Professional's Guide to College Planning* (#126)

❑ Check enclosed*   Charge my: ❑ VISA ❑ MC ❑ AmEx   ❑ Bill me

Card Number _____ Exp. date _____

Signature _____

Name _____ Title _____

Company _____

Street Address _____

City _____ State _____ Zip_____

Business Phone (_____) _____ Fax (_____) _____

*Make check payable to The National Underwriter Company. Please include the appropriate shipping & handling charges and any applicable sales tax. Offer expires 12/31/98.

BUSINESS REPLY MAIL
FIRST CLASS MAIL PERMIT NO 68 CINCINNATI, OH

POSTAGE WILL BE PAID BY ADDRESSEE

NO POSTAGE
NECESSARY
IF MAILED
IN THE
UNITED STATES

The National Underwriter Co.
Customer Service Dept. #2-BB
505 Gest Street
Cincinnati, OH 45203-9928